STOLEN LIVES

Trafficking & Slavery on the Streets of Britain

LOUISE HULLAND

SANDSTONE PRESS

First published in Great Britain by
Sandstone Press Ltd
Willow House
Stoneyfield Business Park
Inverness
IV2 7PA
Scotland

www.sandstonepress.com

Sandstone Press is committed to a sustainable future. This book
is made from Forest Stewardship Council ® certified paper.

ISBN TPB: 978-1-913207-18-2
ISBNe: 978-1-913207-19-9

Cover design by Mark Ecob
Typeset by Biblichor Ltd, Edinburgh
Printed and bound by CPI Group (UK) Ltd, Croydon, CR0 4YY

For E & L
'Boja me Gisht'

'You may choose to look the other way, but you can never say again that you did not know'

William Wilberforce

FOREWORD

With *Stolen Lives*, Louise Hulland has become a powerful voice for the dispossessed and enslaved, those for whom freedom is their lost past, or a longed-for future.

If all your knowledge of human trafficking and modern slavery is from news reports, as is the case for most of us, then this book is full of shocks. Three things struck me most forcibly. First, the majority of victims in Britain today are not trafficked from other countries, but British citizens. Second, they are not hidden away in locked rooms: they're in plain sight, in nail bars, hotels and car washes, on construction sites and farms. Third, this is a multibillion-pound industry; it's big business.

The British citizens who are enslaved are most often recruited from the streets. Homeless people, often with learning difficulties or mental health problems, frequently addicted to alcohol or drugs, are easy prey for determined criminals. They have no protective family network and no defences. They live in shadows and can disappear all too easily. The other British people who are particularly vulnerable are teenagers, especially those who are, or have been, in care. They are targeted for what is now known as County Lines drug smuggling. In other words, these are people about whom nobody cares enough to notice they are missing, or in serious trouble.

Most people are aware of how people from other countries are brought in on lorries and containers, sometimes with horrific outcomes, as in the case of the bodies of thirty-nine Vietnamese people found in a sealed container in Essex in October 2019, whose deaths in that confined space we don't want to imagine. Less known about are the lives they are likely to live in the UK, if they survive the journey. *Stolen Lives* carries reports from those working on the front line, trying to identify and support victims, and it's clear from their experience that 'rescuing' survivors is not straightforward. People who have been enslaved, often for years, are terrified of moving from the situation they're in, which is at least familiar, to another, which they fear might be just as bad. They are also terrified of those who have imprisoned and controlled them.

Bernie Gravett, formerly a Metropolitan Police Superintendent, now an expert in this complex subject, tells Louise Hulland, in no uncertain terms: 'Trafficking is a business. It's all about making money. *All* about making money.' Perpetrators are interested primarily in profit, but they don't have the qualms or the moral compass that most of us have, to hold them back from exploiting other people simply to make money. These are not impressive people, however dangerous to their victims. Louise, in court to see a group of people on trial for multiple trafficking offences, is taken aback by how puny and pathetic they look when she sees them in the dock.

What makes this book riveting are the individual stories of courageous men and women who have escaped and the testimony of the selfless and tireless people from charities and from the statutory authorities who support survivors. The linking thread in *Stolen Lives* is the story of 'Elena', a young woman trafficked from Albania and kept prisoner in a brothel in Belgium, who escaped to the UK, then had to find a way to stay here. Her voice is heard clearly and movingly, but this is a traumatic and nail-biting account.

For ten years, Louise Hulland has explored this difficult subject, becoming familiar with (and to) all the major organisations working in the field. She also puts the subject in its political and global context, describing the progress made in tackling this appalling crime, and the long road that must still be travelled. When she tells us what must change, in the law and in government policy, she is worth listening to.

Sandstone Press is proud to publish this important and wide-ranging study of trafficking and slavery in Britain today. It will open your eyes, and it will also let you see what we all, as individuals, can do to promote that change.

Moira Forsyth
Publishing Director, Sandstone Press

CONTENTS

INTRODUCTION

Imagine completing your degree, going on holiday with your boyfriend, then finding yourself imprisoned in a brothel.

Imagine meeting a friendly benefactor at your local church, who offers you a new life in the UK but who on arrival takes your papers, refuses to pay you and threatens your family if you complain.

Imagine befriending a kindly neighbour as a child, who then passes you around groups of men, inflicting on you repeated sexual and physical abuse.

Imagine your money, your passport, your phone, your family, your friends and your freedom snatched away from you, and every last shred of dignity sapped by violent, manipulative criminals working you to the bone, limiting your food intake and making you sleep eight to a room.

These things are happening all around us.

Whoever you are, reading this, I can make a few basic assumptions about your life. You freely decided to buy the book, with your own hard-earned money. You're maybe at home with a cup of tea or a glass of wine – either of which you selected and poured yourself. You chose the brand, decided when and how you wanted to enjoy it, grabbing ten minutes on your own before you have to do the washing-up or check the kids' homework. You might be reading this on the bus or train, commuting to or from work – perhaps in a career that makes your heart sing, perhaps in a job that drives you to distraction but pays the bills.

1

No matter what brought you to this book, to this moment, I'm guessing most of the decisions you made in the run-up to purchasing it and sitting down to read it were made by *you*, with no coercion or control, no psychological bullying or threats, and no fear of reprisal. No one is controlling your cash flow, your ability to go to a shop or get online, no one is restricting your daily movements, or what you eat or drink, or how you travel.

That is exactly how your life should be.

Yet in the twenty-first century there are victims of modern slavery hidden in our communities, in the shadows and in plain sight, for whom this kind of control is all they have come to know.

It's their daily routine. It's a waking nightmare. It's their life.

If you'd told me ten years ago that I would write a book exposing the scale of slavery in Britain today, I would not have believed you. This may be a country with many flaws and faults, but slavery isn't the kind of thing that goes on here, is it? That's for 'other countries'. The dodgy ones. Full of corruption and, you know, 'foreigners'. The sort of place where Organised Crime Groups (OCGs) hold the real power, and where life is cheap, if not worthless. It doesn't happen here.

It does.

LIES, DAMN LIES AND STATISTICS

The statistics around trafficking and slavery can often be difficult to navigate, because of the intrinsically manipulative, secretive and deceptive nature of the crime. Victims are controlled through fear and abuse, so they are too scared to come forward for fear of reprisal for them or their loved ones. Once rescued, victims may not even recognise themselves as victims at all. There are sources, however, which can give us some idea of the scale of slavery within the UK.

Back in 2013, the Home Office estimated between 10,000 and 13,000 people were held in slavery in the UK, but this number was widely debunked at the time, with the National Crime Agency

(NCA) saying it was 'the tip of the iceberg' and the then Anti-Slavery Commissioner Kevin Hyland claiming the figure was 'far too modest'.

Statistics from the Global Slavery Index (GSI) paint a far more shocking picture. According to their figures released on 19th July 2018, there were a staggering 136,000 people living in modern slavery in the UK 'on any given day in 2016'.

In March 2019, the NCA released their Modern Slavery and Human Trafficking statistics in the UK for the year 2018. These are based on the number of potential victims in 'the system', i.e. people who have been identified as possible victims and who are in the care of the National Referral Mechanism (NRM), the system which identifies victims of trafficking.

Just under 7,000 potential victims were referred into the NRM in 2018. That's a 36% rise on 2017, when the number of referrals was just over 5,000. In 2016 it was 3,804.

For the second year running, it was *British citizens* making up the largest number of victims (1,625), followed by Albanians (947) and Vietnamese (702). The number of British citizens reported was almost double the number in 2017.

These numbers reflect only the number of people referred into the NRM in 2018, and do not show the total number of people *confirmed* as victims. They include only the potential victims known to the authorities, the victims who have been found, or who have sought help. The real number of victims is unknown, and will be far higher.

As awareness of the issue grows, and as the public and authorities get better at identifying trafficking and modern slavery, more victims will be found, and the statistics will therefore rise. Victims who may previously have been treated as perpetrators (for example if they were forced to work in cannabis farms or sell drugs) *should* now be treated as victims, and their inclusion therefore adds to the rise in victims identified.

However tentative, the figures surrounding slavery in the UK make for grim reading. But when we look at the rest of the world, the numbers are devastating. The International Labour Organization (ILO) estimates that in 2016, 40.3 million people were in modern slavery, including 24.9 million in forced labour and 15.4 million in forced marriage. This means there are 5.4 victims of modern slavery for every 1,000 people in the world. One in four victims of modern slavery are children.

Numbers can only tell us so much. While it is important to have an understanding of the scale of modern slavery in the UK, *nobody* should be living without their freedom.

ACTION IN THE UK

Britain claims to be a global leader in the fight against trafficking and modern slavery. In the run-up to the inception of the Modern Slavery Act in 2015 (which is thought of as a ground-breaking, though imperfect, piece of legislation), the then Home Secretary Theresa May stressed her commitment to stamping out modern slavery, hoping for the UK's strategy to be an example to the world.

Though the Act was an important step in the right direction, in practice the fight against modern slavery is set against an ever-changing landscape. It must adapt to the constantly evolving tactics and strategies of the perpetrators and have the safety of the deeply complex needs of the survivors at its heart. It has been argued, by those on the front-line fight against the crime, that the Modern Slavery Act didn't go as far as it could have in managing that balance. The convictions attached to the legislation are depressingly low, and not enough is being done to protect these most vulnerable of victims.

However, the Act was only one part of the Government's initiative. There are multiple aspects to the Government's Anti-Slavery strategy, and there is now a complex system which survivors are expected to navigate. Failings in both areas are having a negative impact on the outcomes for survivors. From the length of time vulnerable victims are left waiting for decisions on their futures to the rights afforded to them while they are living in limbo, the Government's policy appears to be in stark contrast to the Government's actions. One of the fundamental criticisms which has come up time and time again is the fact that decisions on the fate of survivors are being made, for the most part, by the arm of Government also tasked with keeping immigration figures low and enforcing Theresa May's controversial 'hostile environment'.[1]

At the time of writing, the entire system is still in a state of flux. The Modern Slavery Act has been reviewed, but the NRM is going through a series of changes, a Victim Support Bill is working its way through Parliament, and the Home Office is making changes to the way victims are identified.

All of this has been happening in the shadow of Brexit. For more than three years Parliament and Government were paralysed by their attempts to leave the EU, and there has been widespread criticism that all other important business of the country ground to a halt during that time. Political upheaval sees changes to the residents of both Number 10 and the Home Office. Added to that, nobody working in the fight against slavery can know how leaving the EU will affect their endeavours in the future.

I have immersed myself in the world of anti-slavery work in order to establish the scale of modern slavery around the nation and what's being done about it. I have gathered the views of police officers, policy makers, lawyers and charities all working towards stamping out this horrendous crime; explored the 'business' of trafficking to find out why it's such a lucrative model for organised gangs; scrutinised the legislation and systems currently in place; examined the territory vulnerable survivors have to navigate once they've regained their liberty, and of course gauged the impact of the Government's hostile environment policy. From the moment of identification to the legal ramifications of applying for asylum, I have followed step by step what a survivor goes

---

1   See Chapter 2.

through in the UK once they are set free of their captors, and looked also at the emotional impact such a trauma has on the victim, and how they begin to put their lives back together after their ordeal.

Most importantly, I have listened to the survivors themselves, the men and women who have had years of their lives ripped away from them, who have lost their dignity, their possessions, their sense of self and often their entire network of loved ones.

The story of 'Elena'[2] has accompanied me every step of the way.

Throughout these pages, you will read how her life changed from being a university student in Albania, three short years ago, to finding herself as a trafficking survivor in England fighting to stay in the safety of the UK. Her story is told through a combination of notes I made during our time together, recorded interviews, and the formal statement about her case given to the Home Office.

When speaking to survivors of trafficking, no matter how empowered they feel to tell their story, reliving their experiences time and time again is deeply traumatic. Elena wanted to tell her story, but I wanted to ensure we did so in a way that protected her mental health as well as her identity. From our first meeting where her English was limited, and we relied on a friend to interpret for us, to meetings with her lawyer where we had an exceptional interpreter and finally to our more recent interviews, the language barrier has gradually broken down, the trust she has in me has grown and the distance from her experiences has widened. Therefore over time, it has been easier to establish the full extent of Elena's experience. It is important to bear this in mind, as her tone changes depending on whether she's speaking to me or an interpreter.

Elena's story is significant in itself, but also because it highlights the pathway of every survivor – from the moment the coercion

---

2   Elena's name and the names of all survivors and perpetrators have been changed to protect identities.

and deception began to the daily struggle to be believed by decision makers in the Home Office.

To have witnessed the last eighteen months of her life has been emotionally draining. To have lived the last three years of her life, unimaginable.

1

ELENA'S STORY: MEETING ELENA (2017)

My child is 2 years now. I want to do something, to work, but I am not allowed to work. I just take £70 in week for us . . . is hard, somebody should understand this . . . I am just 24 years old and alone here . . . my life is very hard . . . please, I know it's not your fault . . . but I am tired.

A text from 'Elena' on 24th May 2018

Walking into a busy Caffè Nero in London, on a damp, cold November day in 2017, I'm greeted by three young women. Sarah, who works for a local charity, jumps up from her chair and greets me warmly, as I apologise profusely for keeping them waiting (I'd been sitting in the wrong coffee shop). I'm then introduced to an attractive, confident, dark-haired woman in her thirties with a friendly smile, who tells me her name is Kristina and that she's here to translate for her friend.

Holding herself back from these cheery and slightly nervous greetings is the woman I'm there to meet: Elena. She's tiny, with long, dark blonde hair tied back. Her pretty face can't hide her exhaustion, and despite a brave smile, she seems haunted.

The baby she's jiggling in her arms smiles and reaches out to me, and I reach for a cuddle without hesitating. As I bounce the child on my waist and pull ridiculous faces by way of a 'hello', Elena turns to Kristina in surprise, but I sense her nerves at meeting a journalist have receded a little.

It's not just Elena who's nervous. I'm quite anxious too, despite the fact I've interviewed countless vulnerable people about the most horrific experiences of their lives. Indeed, most of my career has been spent talking to contributors who have experienced a trauma or life event that most of us couldn't possibly imagine. When someone has experienced an assault, a crime, a life-changing experience or diagnosis, it takes tremendous courage to recount it to a complete stranger, never mind the British public, and it's a responsibility I've always taken seriously.

From what I knew about Elena's short life so far, I was even more wary than usual about making her relive her trauma, pressing too hard, saying the wrong thing or triggering an emotion which could set her recovery back. I knew she wanted to tell her story, and I knew the charity responsible for her welfare had given it the go-ahead, but I had to judge for myself how vulnerable she was and – considering my experience of working with trafficking survivors was at that point zero – I wasn't entirely sure how to establish that.

An email from Sarah two weeks earlier had first drawn my attention to Elena's story. Sarah and I had met several times about the work she does with a small, community-based anti-trafficking charity with which I'd been interested in volunteering. When the email arrived in my inbox, I'd assumed it was to do with an upcoming training session. Little did I know it was a message that would change my life.

Hi Louise, hope you're well. There has been an interesting development! While I was meeting with a charity which supports trafficking survivors last week, an Albanian lady who was trafficked into the UK and is now living in temporary accommodation said she would be willing to tell her story. And she'd like me to lead on it. I wanted to run this by you and ask if you might be interested in getting involved.

After I'd spoken to Sarah, and the charity responsible for Elena's immediate care, we arranged to meet informally near where she lived, so that she could get to know me in the comfort of her own surroundings, and to see if I was a journalist she felt she could talk to. Sarah had given me a short overview of Elena's background, so I had a basic understanding of what had brought her to London, but I wasn't at all prepared for the story which unfolded.

Over hot chocolate, the noise of the rain battering outside, the hubbub of the busy London coffee shop and the wriggles and cries of her baby, Elena and I tried to communicate as best we could – with her good but un-confident English, and my non-existent Albanian.

I wanted to check that Kristina, her friend and translator for the day, was aware of Elena's background, and whether Elena was comfortable sharing such intimate details of her life with her friend, two relative strangers and the danger of prying ears. But Elena was ready, and over the next hour or so, with the help of Kristina, I began to build a picture of what had happened to the young woman sitting before me.

In the summer of 2015, Elena was a university student in Albania. She had left her small, traditional village to experience a more metropolitan existence, and at the age of twenty-one had been enjoying the freedom of student life after growing up in a staunchly traditional Albanian village.

'The village we lived in was very conservative and narrow-minded. My father was very strict. We had to stay indoors most of the time and we were restricted in the type of clothes we wore, our clothing had to be conservative and not revealing or provocative. This was what was expected of us, particularly girls.'

University had been a very different experience for Elena, living in dorms and making friends with other women from more liberal areas of Albania. Like most young people at university, spending time in the company of new, different kinds of people opened her eyes to other ways of life.

But there was still a clash with the culture she'd been brought up in. When Elena had asked for a mobile phone just before she left for university, her father's immediate response was to find out if she wanted the phone so that she could speak to boys. Though her parents were happy she was studying at university, they were worried about Elena living alone, and warned her often that she shouldn't go out too much, and that she should focus on her education.

One night, months before she finished her course, she met a young man at a local bar. Marco took her number and they started speaking on the phone, then dating once or twice a week. He was Albanian, and though he had made Belgium his home, he returned to Albania a couple of times a month. When they were apart, Marco called Elena regularly. He was her first boyfriend, and Elena thought he was the man for her.

'Because of the way I was brought up, I always thought the first person I met and had a relationship with would be the person I married. This was the way I was thinking when I began my relationship with him – that he was who I would marry.'

Marco, however, appeared in no rush to meet her family. He told her he was worried that if he agreed to be introduced to her parents, her father would want to make the relationship more formal, and he wasn't ready for that.

After finishing university, Elena moved back to the family home in the small village, and told her family she was in a relationship. Her father insisted that if this man was serious about her, then he would have no problem coming to meet him.

'I was taught to respect my parents' conservative values. For example, they believed that any husband I ended up with should be someone chosen for me by my family members. This is what they expected of me. At that time since I was living in a more open-minded way, I thought that perhaps Marco was right and it was my father who was in the wrong. I know now that my father was right to think that about Marco.'

Knowing her parents were set against her relationship, she carried on her love affair with Marco in secret, conducting all contact with him over the phone.

'My father said to me that if I chose to stay with Marco then he would disown me, and my mother stood by my father's decision.'

After almost five months together, Marco appeared to have come round to the idea of moving forward with their relationship, and suggested to Elena that she join him on a trip to Belgium in order to meet his family. Elena of course agreed, believing that marriage was the obvious next step for them.

Elena didn't have a passport, so she told her father she needed to apply for one in order to be able to travel for her studies. Her plan was to spend up to three months in Belgium and to return to Albania to study for a master's degree. Marco appeared to support this idea, telling her he could get her a temporary job in Belgium to help her save for the next step in her education. Because their plans were quite fluid, Elena didn't think anything of the fact that she didn't have a return ticket for the trip. It made sense, because they hadn't committed to when exactly they would return. Besides, she was twenty-one, excited about visiting Europe, seeing more of the world, and experiencing a different culture. Most importantly she was keen to meet Marco's family – her future family.

Before they set off on their adventure, there was one more hurdle to overcome: Elena's parents. When Elena informed her family of her trip and her intentions to travel abroad with a man they didn't know and who was not her husband, they were furious. Travelling as an unmarried couple is unacceptable in Albanian culture.

'I explained to my family that I loved him and intended to go with him. They tried hard to convince me not to, but I had made up my mind.'

Her parents made it clear that they wanted nothing to do with Elena should she go on the trip, and if she ever returned they would simply disown her.

'I had changed so much I could no longer relate to the village mentality in which I had been brought up. At the time I believed there was nothing wrong with what I was doing. I was just excited by everything that was happening.'

Elena assumed that despite her parents' protests, they would accept her again when she returned to Albania in a few months' time as an engaged woman.

Elena was never to return to Albania. That was the last time she would see her parents, her siblings, her friends or her country.

2

THE SCALE OF THE ISSUE

'Slavery did not end with abolition in the 19th century. Instead, it changed its forms and continues to harm people in every country in the world' – AntiSlavery.org

When we hear the word 'slavery' we tend to think of chains and physical restraints. Pictures from history books of a time we thought long since gone. One human owning another. Yet in modern Britain, slavery exists in many different forms, under our very eyes, and the victims are often in plain sight. From the men who wash our cars for £6 to the women painting our nails; from the teenagers caught up in drug gangs to our neighbour's live-in cleaner, the phenomenon of modern slavery is all around us.

In the Government's Annual Report into Modern Slavery released in 2018, the then Home Secretary Sajid Javid put the financial cost to the UK at 'as much as £4.3 billion in 2016/17'. It's impossible to put a price on the human cost.

The Government defines modern slavery as 'the recruitment, movement, harbouring or receiving of children, women or men through the use of force, coercion, abuse of vulnerability, deception or other means for the purpose of exploitation'.

According to Bristol-based charity Unseen, someone is in slavery if they are:

- forced to work through mental or physical threat;
- owned or controlled by an 'employer', usually through mental or physical abuse or the threat of abuse;

- dehumanised, treated as a commodity or bought and sold as 'property';
- physically constrained or have restrictions placed on his/her freedom.

The Modern Slavery Act defines the crime as 'holding a person in a position of slavery, servitude, forced or compulsory labour, or facilitating their travel with the intention of exploiting them soon after'.

There are several categories of exploitation linked to modern slavery, into which most of the crimes fall:

- sexual exploitation
- forced labour
- domestic servitude
- organ harvesting
- child exploitation

HUMAN TRAFFICKING

Bernie Gravett, former Metropolitan Police Superintendent and current Anti-Trafficking consultant, distilled a variety of complicated legislation into one pithy statement for me: 'Human Trafficking is basically moving somebody from A to B for the purpose of exploitation or the intention to exploit'. He added, 'If it's a child that is all you need to prove. However, if the victim is an adult you also have to prove that their recruitment or cooperation was achieved through the use of deception, lies, fraud, other forms of coercion of the use of threats and/or force.'

The more formal definition is from the UN Convention against Transnational Organized Crime, more widely known as the 'Palermo Protocol':

The recruitment, transportation, transfer, harbouring or receipt of persons, by means of the threat or use of force or other forms of coercion, of abduction, of fraud, of deception, of the abuse of power or of a position of vulnerability or of the giving or receiving of payments or benefits to achieve the consent of a person having control over another person, for the purpose of exploitation.

There are some important nuances within this definition. It is possible to be a victim of trafficking even if consent has been given to be moved – because you may have given your consent through fear for your life or the lives of others (coercion), or you may be deceived as to the purpose of your employment or trip (fraud).

PEOPLE SMUGGLING

Legally, people smuggling is a crime against the state, while people trafficking is a crime against the person. Practically, the difference comes down to consent. Bernie once again helped with a clear definition:

Trafficking of adults is when a person is tricked or deceived. They may think they are being smuggled for work but are in fact exploited when they enter the country. Trafficked victims enter either with legal documents or illegally. Smuggling is always illegal. It is when a person pays another to transport them illegally from one country to another. The service ends when they are dropped off. Trafficking can take place inside a country and takes place every day in the UK.

Examples of cases in the UK can be found across the whole country.

Bath

When thinking of Bath, I'm more likely to picture bonneted young ladies in a BBC Jane Austen adaptation, than Thu Huong Nguyen, the forty-eight-year-old woman convicted of trafficking young women into the city to work in nail bars for no pay. She was found guilty in November 2017 of 'conspiring to arrange or facilitate the movement of people for labour exploitation and conspiring to require others to perform forced or compulsory labour', following a trial at Stafford Crown Court. Two of her accomplices were also found guilty.

The crimes were exposed after a complex police investigation involving the National Crime Agency and *five* police forces. The Bath Chronicle at the time reported that investigations began after a 'multi-agency welfare visit' to Nail Bar Deluxe in Bath city centre in February 2016. Two young women, aged seventeen and eighteen, were deemed to be victims of modern slavery when they were found working inside.

After being taken into protective custody and then into care, the girls went missing. (This isn't unusual for victims of modern slavery – especially in the Vietnamese community.) Following further police investigations, the girls were traced to *another* nail bar – Gorgeous Nails in Burton-on-Trent – which triggered a joint investigation with Staffordshire Police. This investigation uncovered criminal activity at this second nail bar too. Not only were the two original victims found, two more, aged sixteen and seventeen, were identified. Links were then made to similar operations in Bath, Cheltenham, Burton-on-Trent, Gloucester and Derbyshire.

In a statement, DI Charlotte Tucker, of Avon and Somerset Police, reported:

Through analysis and intelligence work we were able to connect all the defendants to each other. Evidence found at their properties also supported our case, including calendars, identity documents and data from mobile phones. The victims, who are all Vietnamese, have had traumatic childhoods and were treated by traffickers as commodities – forced to live and work in unsuitable conditions, with little or no pay, and enduring both physical and verbal abuse. Traffickers don't recognise national or international boundaries and are hiding their victims in plain sight. We all need to recognise how these criminal networks operate and understand the signs potential victims can display.

Thu Huong Nguyen was sentenced to five years in prison, with the judge calling the defendants 'devious and manipulative', treating the victims as commodities and exploiting them for 'pure economic greed'.

Blackburn

In Lancashire, a series of operations from the police force uncovered a Romanian gang trafficking women to Blackburn to work in enforced prostitution.

Officers carried out a raid on Accrington Road, Blackburn, in May 2016 as part of an ongoing investigation. Inside the modest house, two women in their twenties were found, suspected of being trafficked to the UK from Romania. While the usual safeguarding procedures were carried out in order to protect the women, they 'refused to make any complaints against the men, and did not identify themselves as being victims'.

Despite this, brothers Ionut and Cristian Stan, and a third man Cristian Vasile, were arrested on suspicion of human trafficking for sexual exploitation and later charged.

Operation Proteus officers, part of the team working to identify both the victims and perpetrators of trafficking and slavery in Lancashire, discovered that the Stan brothers had trafficked the women from Romania. Once at the address in Blackburn they arranged for the women to be sexually exploited as prostitutes. The third man, Vasile, was established as the ringleader, setting up websites to advertise the women's services, and arrange payments.

In March 2017, the three men pleaded guilty at Preston Crown Court and were jailed for a total of ten years. Ionut Stan was sentenced to two years four months in prison, Cristian Stan to three years two months, and Cristian Vasile to five years after also pleading guilty to keeping a brothel used for prostitution, and causing prostitution for gain.

Newport

In Wales, in October 2014, David Daniel Doran was jailed for forcing Darrell Simester to work unpaid at a farm near Newport. Darrell is one of the few survivors who has openly spoken of his ordeal, and in an interview with the BBC he explained how he was made to work for up to sixteen hours a day at a farm in Peterstone near Newport. His living conditions make for harrowing reading. He was forced to sleep in a rat-infested shed, then a caravan, with a 'horse trough to wash in and no soap or toothbrush'.

David Daniel Doran was jailed for four and a half years after pleading guilty to forcing Mr Simester to perform forced or compulsory labour.

RESPONDING TO SLAVERY IN THE UK

Despite the many criticisms which can be made of the current British system, the UK is at the front and centre of the global response to modern slavery. The Modern Slavery Act of 2015 put modern slavery on the map in terms of publicity and policy, but law enforcement was tackling the crime long before Theresa May vowed to end this 'evil in our midst'.

In 2004 the country was horrified to hear of the deaths of twenty-three Chinese cockle-pickers in Morecambe Bay. After the tragedy, the Labour Government set up the Gangmasters Licensing Authority (then GLA, now Gangmasters and Labour Abuse Authority or GLAA), with the aim of preventing any further exploitation of workers. Its role is to 'protect vulnerable and exploited workers' and has a remit to 'investigate reports of illegal activity such as human trafficking and forced labour'. Its licensing scheme regulates businesses providing workers to agriculture, horticulture, shellfish gathering and 'any associated processing and packaging'.

In 2006 the UK Human Trafficking Centre was set up, which was the precursor to today's NCA's Modern Slavery Human Trafficking Unit (MSHTU). In 2009, the UK established the National Referral Mechanism, or NRM. This sounds dry and impersonal, but it's fundamental to the care of victims. It is the framework used to identify victims of trafficking and slavery: once they're identified and in the NRM, it's how they receive the most appropriate support. That, at any rate, is the intention.

The NRM was in action in the UK long before the Modern Slavery Act came into being, and it's not without its critics. A number of reforms are slowly being implemented, but one of the key criticisms aimed at the British response to modern slavery is the haphazard and un-strategic way the Government cares for victims. The NRM is a way to identify victims and put them in the system, but from then on, it leaves a lot to be desired.

In March 2013, the Centre for Social Justice (CSJ) unveiled the findings of a two-year report on the extent of modern slavery in the UK called 'It Happens Here', revealing 'a hidden world of appalling exploitation of some of society's weakest and most vulnerable'. The CSJ called on the Government 'to take a much more direct and aspirational lead on fighting this crime'. Recommendations included creating the role of Anti-Slavery Commissioner in order to bring a level of consistency to the response, rather than having it remain under the control of the ever-changeable Immigration Minister. It also highlighted the fundamental problem of victims of modern slavery and trafficking being treated first as illegal immigrants. This is an argument still being fought seven years on.

However, everything changed in terms of public perception and Government policy after 2013, when the then Home Secretary, Theresa May, announced the launch of the Modern Slavery Bill. She had taken heed of the CSJ report from earlier in the year, and stated the current legislation should be revised, emphasising the need for tougher legislation on modern slavery in order to tackle the 'shockingly low' prosecution rates.

Mrs May said that 'tackling this abhorrent crime is a personal priority for me', and that modern slavery 'is all around us, hidden in plain sight. It is walking our streets, supplying shops and supermarkets, working in fields, factories or nail bars, trapped in brothels or cowering behind the curtains in an ordinary street'.

THE 2015 MODERN SLAVERY ACT

The Modern Slavery Bill became an Act of Parliament in England and Wales in 2015, and was lauded as a ground-breaking piece of legislation around Europe, if not the world. It has gone on to inspire similar legislation globally.

Not all voices were supportive of the text, with many victim-focused charities left deeply concerned by the lack of clear guidance on how to care for survivors. The charity Anti-Slavery International, in an article by Klara Skrivankova, said it left them with 'mixed feelings', remarking that 'on the one hand it is a big step in the right direction with many good clauses, but on the other hand there are still deficiencies that leave us – and the victims of modern slavery – wholly unsatisfied'.

Until the enshrinement of the Modern Slavery Act, while it was still illegal to hold someone 'in slavery', the police and judiciary had to use other legislation in order to charge someone with such crimes, because there was no purpose-made legislation. They relied on other laws such as the Sexual Offences Act, the Police and Criminal Evidence Act, and the Coroners and Justice Act 2009. The Modern Slavery Act was set to change all that by consolidating legislation, meaning the police no longer had to search for the most appropriate way to charge a perpetrator. The legislation was finally bespoke and in one place.

The maximum sentencing for traffickers was increased from fourteen years to life imprisonment, and the perpetrators could be forced to pay compensation to their victims, with the authorities permitted to seize their assets.

The Act also contained anti-trafficking measures, including Slavery and Trafficking Prevention Orders and Slavery and Trafficking Risk Orders, which can be made by a court in essence to prevent those convicted from working with children and young women, and restricting their ability to visit certain areas or own a company. The orders can be handed down if a court is satisfied the defendant *may* commit a slavery or human trafficking offence, even if they've not been convicted.

In May 2019, the BBC reported that Salvatore Lopresti of Lopresti Ice Cream in Bristol was made the subject of such a Risk Order. Because he had dementia, he was ruled unfit to stand trial on assault and modern slavery charges but was accused of exploiting staff.

Picking up on the suggestion by the CSJ report of 2013, and earlier calls for some form of monitoring role (e.g. in the Anti-Trafficking Monitoring Group's report 'The Wrong Kind of Victim') the Modern Slavery Act created the role of the UK's first Independent Anti-Slavery Commissioner (IASC). Former Metropolitan Police Detective Kevin Hyland OBE was the first to hold this post. He eventually resigned in 2018 citing concerns over how 'independent' he could actually be.

Sara Thornton became the second Commissioner on 1st May 2019.

The arrival of the Modern Slavery Act also meant businesses and commercial organisations (with a turnover of more than £36 million) must, by law, publish a slavery and human trafficking statement each year, outlining what steps have been taken to ensure modern slavery is not happening in their business or supply chains. This was seen as a significant innovation, and many anti-slavery charities welcomed its inclusion.

The TISC (Transparency in Supply Chains) Report (June 2019) states that there are 16,835 UK registered companies which are required to comply. Four years after the MSA (Modern Slavery Act) came into being, over 4,500 have yet to comply. More than a quarter of companies legally obligated to publish the Modern Slavery statement have not done so – without any sanction being imposed.

It was hoped and expected by those working on behalf of survivors that the MSA would put the care of those who had suffered most at the heart of the legislation.

That has not happened.

Sections 49 and 50 relate to the 'Protection of Victims' – stating they require 'guidance to be issued to public authorities and other persons as considered appropriate by the Secretary of State in relation to identifying and supporting victims'.

The guidance mentioned was supposed to cover 'arrangements for the provision of assistance and support to persons who there are reasonable grounds to believe may be victims of slavery or human trafficking'.

At the time of writing, this guidance for English and Welsh law has still not been written. The people for whom these protections matter the most are pretty much a blank page in the statute books[1].

Scotland and Northern Ireland

The Modern Slavery Act of 2015 relates to England and Wales, while Scotland and Northern Ireland have created their own legislation: the Human Trafficking and Exploitation (Criminal Justice and Support for Victims) Act (Northern Ireland), and the Human Trafficking and Exploitation (Scotland) Act.

In October 2016, the Anti-Trafficking Monitoring Group (ATMG) launched a report, 'Class Acts', which compared the three pieces of legislation, and provides a fascinating (and digestible!) look at how each nation has approached its legislation.

---

1 The Victim Support Guidance in Section 49 of The Modern Slavery Act 2015 has now been published, but Section 50 has yet to be completed.

The Act in England and Wales is the most criticised in relation to care of victims: 'Adult victims of modern slavery identified in England and Wales now have significantly fewer statutory support entitlements than in Scotland and Northern Ireland'. The report goes on to specify:

The Modern Slavery Act is significantly weaker than the respective Acts in Scotland and Northern Ireland regarding support for adult victims. The Scotland and Northern Ireland Acts include all of the four key elements of the Trafficking Convention and Directive, and in some regards go beyond the minimum international standards.

Both Acts place a legal duty on Ministers to provide support and assistance to victims, and explicitly state the minimum types of support that should be provided (the list is non-exhaustive), which reflect the support standards set out in the Convention and Directive. The Northern Ireland Act goes further still by stating that support can continue to be provided to persons who are conclusively determined *not* to be victims, if continued support is deemed necessary, and to eligible victims even if they leave Northern Ireland.

The report goes on:

The Modern Slavery Act [of England and Wales] does not explicitly place a duty on the State to provide support and assistance to victims, nor set out victims' support entitlements. Rather, the arrangements for identifying and supporting victims are to be set out in guidance to be issued by the Secretary of State, which may be revised from 'time to time'. The Secretary of State may also make regulations in this regard. Therefore, unlike those in Scotland and Northern Ireland, victims in England and Wales cannot look to the Modern Slavery Act to claim their rights to support.

THE HOSTILE ENVIRONMENT

'The aim is to create, here in Britain, a really hostile environment for illegal immigrants.' Theresa May, Home Secretary 2012

Theresa May's 'hostile environment' for illegal immigrants provides a deeply ironic counterpoint to the Government's impressive rhetoric in its response to modern slavery. In 2012, when questioned about the Conservative Government's response to its immigration targets, Theresa May declared that her intention was to bring a zero tolerance approach to illegal immigrants in the UK.

Now the Government prefers to call this the 'compliant environment policy', but it essentially amounted to the introduction of a range of policies aimed at reducing the number of people living in Britain with no immigration status which allows them to remain. The Home Office brought in measures aiming 'to restrict illegal immigrants renting property in the UK, driving, having bank accounts and accessing benefits and free healthcare' (House of Lords' Impact of 'Hostile Environment' Policy Debate on 14th June 2018). For example, landlords were required to check the immigration status of potential tenants under the Right to Rent scheme. The same was to be required of the NHS, but the Government eventually backed down over this policy in 2018.

Few will forget the so-called 'Go Home' vans which circulated various boroughs in London in the summer of 2013, in the hope that illegal immigrants would leave the country voluntarily if they thought the alternative was arrest and deportation.

While the aim of the 'hostile environment' may have been to clamp down on those immigrants who were in the UK illegally, the tentacles of the policies stretched further into the workings of the Home Office, and infamously have impacted on the lives of those *with* the right to live in the UK – the Windrush scandal being the prime example. Since the onset of Brexit, the atmosphere in Britain for 'others' has deteriorated even further, with EU citizens facing greatly increased bureaucracy. The Liberal

Democrats' Home Affairs spokesman Ed Davey told *The Guardian* in 2017, 'The Conservatives seem hellbent on creating a hostile environment for anyone not from the UK. These scare tactics should be beneath any civilised government.'

WHERE DOES THIS LEAVE US TODAY?

When I began researching modern slavery for the purposes of this book, Theresa May was Prime Minister and Sajid Javid Home Secretary. In 2020 Boris Johnson is in Number 10, and Priti Patel occupies the Home Office. The priorities and passion projects of those in power inevitably change, but two things have remained consistent. The Conservative Party remains in power, and the Home Office continues to oversee the country's response to modern slavery.

The Home Office declined to be interviewed. A request for an interview with the Modern Slavery Unit went unanswered, and a bid for an interview with the Minister for Crime, Safeguarding, and Vulnerability, Victoria Atkins, brought me a written response, the main points of which are set out here:

This Government is grateful for your engagement and it is reassuring to hear you, like many parliamentarians and other interested parties, are so passionate about the fight against modern slavery. We are committed to tackling the heinous crime of modern slavery and ensuring that victims are provided with the support they need to begin rebuilding their lives. Not only is this a personal priority for the Prime Minister, who chairs the Modern Slavery Taskforce, but it is also a priority for the Minister for Crime, Safeguarding, and Vulnerability.

The Modern Slavery Act is a landmark piece of legislation and establishes the UK's commitment as a world leader in tackling modern slavery. The Act gives law enforcement agencies the tools to tackle modern slavery and ensure perpetrators can receive suitably severe punishments for these appalling crimes, including maximum life sentences. The Act also provides enhanced support and protection for victims, with Section 49 and Section 50 allowing the National Referral Mechanism (NRM) – our system for identifying and supporting victims – to be put on statutory footing via statutory guidance and regulations.

In 2017, the Government commissioned an independent review of this Act . . . The Government welcomes the findings of the Review, which has now published its final interim report . . .

Internationally, the UK is leading the fight against modern slavery. In 2017, the Prime Minister launched a global Call to Action to End Forced Labour, Modern Slavery and Human Trafficking, to outline practical actions to meet UN Sustainable Development Goal 8.7 to eradicate modern slavery by 2030. It now has 88 country endorsements and significant steps have been taken to step up global efforts against modern slavery. In addition, we are strengthening cooperation with countries from where victims are regularly trafficked to the UK, and we are pushing for change on a global scale by working with other countries and multilateral organisations such as the Commonwealth and UN. Our international approach is supported by a £200 million UK aid investment and an international network of advisers in our Embassies, including experts from the National Crime Agency and Crown Prosecution Service.

Protecting victims from the heinous crime of modern day slavery is a top priority for this Government and the UK is leading efforts to drive modern slavery from global supply chains. The UK is the first country in the world to require businesses to report on how they are preventing modern slavery in their supply chains, and at the G20, the Prime Minister announced that the UK will now become the first country to publish a Modern Slavery statement for central Government. This is a significant step forward.

Finally, the Government is committed to ensuring victims receive the support they need to begin rebuilding their lives. Far-reaching reforms to the NRM . . . involve radical changes to the system . . . [which] include for example, the establishment of the Single Competent Authority, which launched on 29 April 2019. This new single, expert unit will make all NRM decisions, improving the decision-making process. The recent launch of this new unit marks a significant milestone on our NRM reform journey.

. . . We are confident the newly appointed IASC, Sara Thornton, will strengthen the UK's response to modern slavery. This Government is as determined as ever to eradicate modern slavery and ensure that victims have the support they need to begin to rebuild their lives.

There have been many criticisms of the Government's strategy, or perceived lack of, and as Elena's story unfolds, it reveals the stark difference between the passionate rhetoric of the Home Office and the impact of its actual policies.[2]

---

2   **Modern Slavery Act Review:** In July 2018, the Home Office announced it was to review the Modern Slavery Act – with Frank Field MP, Maria Miller MP and Baroness Butler-Sloss at the helm. The aim was to 'strengthen the UK's ongoing response and accelerate progress from Government and businesses in eradicating modern slavery'. In the statement from the Home Office in 2018, it was stated the panel's scope of work included 'developing an understanding on the nature of modern slavery offences, the provisions around legal access and compensation to victims and improving the support given to child victims as well as looking at what more can be done to strengthen Section 54' (the section of the Act relating to supply chains).

3

THE BUSINESS OF TRAFFICKING

'Trafficking is a business. It's all about making money. All about making money.'

Bernie Gravett, Anti-Trafficking Expert

For most of us, the idea of making money from another's suffering is abhorrent. To consciously entrap a fellow human into slavery and exploitation in order to make a profit should be an inherently alien concept to all of us in the twenty-first century. Yet human trafficking is a multibillion-dollar business which, according to the International Labour Organization (ILO), is a crime generating $150 billion a year. For traffickers, the financial gain far outweighs human life.

In 2010, when I was investigating the potential rise in sex traffickers targeting East London in the run-up to the 2012 Olympic Games, I was introduced to the work of Bernie Gravett.

A former Metropolitan Police Superintendent, Bernie spent thirty-one years in the force, primarily investigating organised crime across London. He is considered a global expert in human trafficking, slavery and exploitation. His journey from Met officer to international trafficking expert has been an unexpected one.

We tend to associate human trafficking with sexual exploitation, and in recent years perhaps enforced criminality in cannabis farms, or enforced labour in nail bars and car washes. But in 2003, as a Chief Inspector, Bernie's introduction into fighting human trafficking began by policing low-level street crime on Oxford Street. Pickpockets, thieves, street gamblers and beggars were on his radar when he began heading up the policing of Westminster, and before long he started examining the connection between these crimes and links to human trafficking gangs.

It may seem like quite a leap, but traffickers, as Bernie told me nearly a decade ago, utilise their human assets in any way they can to make money. Whether it's women in brothels, children begging on the high street or tricksters engaging tourists in gambling cons, every victim has a use and a revenue stream. What starts off as a job offer or some form of coercion in, for example, Romania, can end up as unsophisticated criminal activity on the British high street, depending on the gang's business model.

During his analysis of street crime in W1, Bernie was also alerted to the disproportionate prevalence of foreign national children becoming suspects of crime within London, and he began investigating the crime of child trafficking within the capital. By 2006, his investigations showed a link between crimes committed by children, and organised criminal groups from Romania, in particular the Roma community. In one piece of research he discovered that over sixty per cent of Romanian children arrested in London, when interviewed, were attended by an appropriate adult who was not a family member. Further investigations uncovered that many of these 'appropriate adults' were suspected of trafficking.

From then on, Bernie ran key investigations into exploitation and trafficking, and over the last ten years has become a leading expert on the investigation of human trafficking. He has since advised the Home Office and the Foreign & Commonwealth Office on organised crime, child trafficking and Romanian Organised Crime, and developed and facilitated delivery of training for law enforcement officers in the UK and around the world, including in Azerbaijan, Bosnia, Moldova, Turkey, Albania, Pakistan and Switzerland. He also gives expert witness evidence before UK criminal courts where victims of human trafficking are being prosecuted for crimes that they were forced or coerced to commit, and also in Immigration Tribunals where victims face deportation from the UK.

So when it comes to understanding how the business of human trafficking works, there's no one better to give me an insight into both the thinking and the activities of these highly organised and ruthless criminals.

Going through notebook after notebook from 2010, documenting all my calls and meetings with Bernie, I was struck with how, over time, more and more countries were added to the scribbles in my books, and how more and more sophisticated the methods of the Organised Crime Groups (OCGs) had become. Bernie agreed to a fresh interview for this book, but due to his work demands and travel schedule, we had to speak several times – over email and in person where possible.

The day we met for the first interview, Bernie had had a meeting at the Home Office, so we arranged the interview spot in a coffee bar nearby. As he entered, I was reminded of how much, to me, Bernie is the epitome of a police officer. Even though he was dressed in smart jeans and a shirt, he still carried himself with the authority of a man who had spent thirty years wearing a Met uniform. I always remember him being taller than he actually was; three decades as a London police officer gives a man a physical presence which seems to stay with you for life.

At a first meeting, you'd be forgiven for thinking he was cynical and world-weary – he doesn't smile much when talking about his work (which is hardly surprising) and you get the impression he doesn't suffer fools gladly. But the more time you spend with him a warm, compassionate and softer side emerges, and his sense of humour is revealed by a twinkle in his eye – hidden, I suspect, after so long on the policing front line. I imagine those who know him in his personal life wouldn't recognise him in the workplace, and vice versa.

As we began our meeting at a less than private table in the coffee shop, I could only imagine what our neighbours would think if they overheard us. Bernie began without preamble.

'Trafficking is a business. It's all about making money. *All* about making money. There are slightly different methodologies within different gangs, different nationalities.'

When I asked him how long trafficking had been an issue in the UK, he replied bluntly, 'Forever'.

Why had it only been in the headlines these last few years?

'Everyone thought that slavery ended with William Wilberforce. Wrong. It has never gone away. Economics has changed trafficking. Slavery was about getting a low or unpaid workforce. Modern slavery and human trafficking is about making money. As consumerism and wealth has grown so has greed. The business of supply and demand has increased. People want drugs, they want domestic workers, they want low-cost or no-cost labour. However, they want to use others to gain wealth for themselves.

'The modern drive [against it] started with the publishing of the Palermo Protocol in 2000, when all governments were supplied with the definition and told to make laws against it. Prior to the Modern Slavery Act we had five different laws on trafficking. That was crazy and complicated.

'The Modern Slavery Act was created to simplify the law and increase the punishment to life in prison as a deterrent to the crime. Previously the maximum punishment for human trafficking was fourteen years, with the average sentence being a couple of years. No one ever got the maximum. It also created a non-punishment (defence) Section 45 stating that a victim of trafficking should not be punished for crimes they are compelled to undertake.

'More training has led to more victims being discovered, leading to more media reports, leading to more knowledge and awareness, in turn leading to more victims being identified.'

While the Government has been grappling with Brexit, the nation has been grappling with its relationship with immigration.

Or, perhaps more specifically, its relationship with 'others'. Foreign nationals in the UK who have arrived here as victims of trafficking are, of course, first and foremost victims. But for some, namely those who resent globalisation, or who question the worth of immigrants within the UK, the experience of the victim is secondary to the fact that they are not from the UK. Looking at the comments section below trafficking articles, including those I've written myself, can often indicate not only an inherent misunderstanding of the issue, but a bundling up of any crime being committed by 'a foreigner' as purely a failure of border control, with Britain being seen as a soft touch.

Given this backdrop, I was keen to know from Bernie if the UK is specifically targeted by crime gangs, and if the country is at increased risk from international traffickers as opposed to indigenous culprits.

'No. Every country is affected by human trafficking.'

He went on to explain that countries can be described in one of three ways: the 'Source Country' (where the victim comes from or started from); the 'Transit Country' (a country a victim passes through where they are not exploited but may stop in during their journey); the 'Destination Country' (where the victims end up and where they are exploited).

'The UK is primarily a destination country. Traffickers tell potential victims that conditions are better, that the pay is better and that life is better. That there are lots of work opportunities.'

I brought up the perception many have that this is a crime committed by foreign nationals against other foreign nationals, and asked him if that was correct.

'No! There is a common idea that a trafficker is a man in a leather jacket draped in gold. Wrong. Traffickers are the recruiters in a victim's home location, the drivers, the people who house victims on their journey, and the people who exploit them at the destination. This also includes the big guys behind the operation who never meet the victims. Traffickers come from all countries, and recruitment could happen anywhere from Hackney to Vietnam.

35

'Albanians are at the centre of prostitution and drugs – have been for donkey's years. 80% of UK cocaine is managed and imported by Albanian gangs. They are also top in prostitution, and have now moved into cannabis farms.

'Romanian gangs work everything from children begging to credit card fraud and sexual exploitation. In Romania it's actually quite sophisticated, in that even within the country, and I think this is probably the case in other countries, the different types of criminality are divvied up by different gangs, by the leadership, the hierarchy.

'Credit card crime comes from Bacau. Child trafficking for begging and stealing from Tandarei. Pickpockets come from Arad county, in Timisoara, labour exploitation Craiova – all divvied up at a very high level, to avoid inter-gang conflict. You lot can go and earn money doing this, you lot can do that.'

I asked how active British gangs were. Did they have a presence in the trafficking business? In response, Bernie delved into the issue of County Lines.

'Trafficking is about exploiting people by using them to make you money or to take a risk that you don't want to take personally. Human trafficking is the recruitment of vulnerable people, moving them and then exploiting them. You don't have to move people personally, movement can be *sending* someone from A to B.

'As we have gained a better understanding of the crime and its principles, we have discovered that some people we previously saw as criminals are actually being exploited and made to commit crime. This has been going on for years. Take drug mules. In the past someone might have been paid £1,000 to take drugs from country A to country B. They are taking the risk, not the drug trafficker. If that person is caught and sent to prison the gang recruits another and perhaps they don't get caught. In the past we would have seen the carrier as a drug trafficker. But what if they were made to do it through threats or fear, or were tricked into doing it? That would make them a victim of trafficking.

'There's a lot of publicity now about County Lines human trafficking. This is where London street gangs target vulnerable children in their area. They attack them or offer protection. They groom and recruit them. The traffickers are the "Elders" and their victims are the "Youngers". Police see them as wannabe gangsters. However, we have to look at how they were recruited and what happens to them. In the first instance, they are given small tasks such as holding drugs and weapons. Then they are tasked to go to Cambridge, Eastbourne, Portsmouth or any other town across the country with drugs and sell them. Then bring the money back. If they don't sell the drugs they are punished. If they lose the drugs through robbery or being cheated by buyers, they are punished and owe the gang for the drugs. They're then in debt. The challenge for police is to identify if they are a mini gangster or if they have been trafficked.'

I asked Bernie what kind of profits the trafficking gangs would make.

'An approximate guess would be $150 billion worldwide. But it is only a guess, as are all human trafficking statistics. So, take a sexual exploitation victim in a standard off-street brothel with maybe fifteen clients per day. Intercourse costs £50 minimum per client, and she's working six days a week. That's an income of £4,500 per girl per week. If she keeps thirty per cent, then the profit per victim is £3,000 per week. If you have fifty girls working for you that's £150,000 per week.'

He went on to tell me about one of his earlier cases, and the money involved for the perpetrators.

'In Operation Golf children were earning EUR 40,000 every two to three months from begging and stealing. For example, a boy steals ten iPhones or high-end Samsungs per day, six days a week. Each new phone is £600 – so a value of £36,000 a week. Even if it's sold on for only £200, income is £12,000 per kid per week. If a child steals six handbags per day that could include credit cards, driver's licence, phone, cash, store cards, house keys and addresses.'

*

In 2005, when Bernie was still in the Met and had identified the link between organised street crime on Oxford Street and human trafficking, he began a criminal investigation named Operation Golf.

The investigation uncovered children from Tandarei, in Romania, being trafficked to the UK, among other countries, and forced to commit crimes in every EU country from Austria to Norway. They were being sold between gangs for up to £20,000 each, and they could generate up to €40,000 every two to three months on the streets of Europe's capitals. Once in the UK, they were assigned to teams by the trafficking kingpins, to target tourists, mainly in the crowded places of central London (Oxford Street, Marble Arch, Buckingham Palace and Hyde Park Corner). They could make hundreds of pounds a day, with all the cash going back to the traffickers.

Though it wasn't formally a human trafficking investigation, Bernie partnered with the Immigration Service and NGO Every Child Protected Against Trafficking UK (ECPAT), and through working with Europol, intelligence gathering and operational activity indicated that children were potentially being trafficked into the UK.

'Case studies showed that some children had eleven alias names, with a range of dates of birth, and when caught were collected from police stations around the country by different "appropriate adults". The presenting of forged documents, that were certainly provided by organised groups, was common.'

In early 2007, Bernie was asked by the Foreign & Commonwealth Office to travel to Romania, where he became aware of a Romanian criminal investigation named Operation Europa.

'This investigation had identified four organised criminal networks operating out of the town of Tandarei in South East Romania. They suspected the Organised Crime Networks of human trafficking, and between 2005 and 2006 the investigation uncovered the details of 1,087 children taken from Romania into Hungary. The Romanian investigation suspected that the children were being trafficked across Europe and forced to beg and steal, but they could not gain sufficient information from other law enforcement agencies to prove the "exploitation" element of the offence of human trafficking.'

Bernie took a list of all the children and, once back in the UK, he and his team ran criminal record checks, and checks with other agencies, on the names on the 'Europa' list.

'Two hundred of the children from Tandarei had been convicted of criminal offences in the UK in 2005 and 2006. More importantly, many of the children were offending in London, particularly in Westminster. Many of the children had been encountered in Operation Golf. This was the first true indication that some of the children on the Europa list were being used to commit crime in London and the UK.'

Bernie's investigation went on to identify over 181 victims of trafficking, and achieved the first UK convictions of child trafficking for forced labour in the form of begging and selling *The Big Issue* illegally as a result of force by traffickers.

Between 2008 and 2010, 120 members of the Romanian gangs were convicted of crimes ranging from human trafficking, child cruelty and neglect to fraud, money laundering and other crimes. These included Speranta and Gheorghe Mihai. They were a Roma couple from Tandarei.

Back in Romania, evidence gained through Bernie's operation proved the exploitation of 181 children from Tandarei, and by 2010, a team of 400 Romanian officers and 26 Metropolitan Police officers teamed up to close the case. During the operation, recovered proceeds of crimes included cash (UK bank notes, US dollars, Euros and Romanian currency) and firearms including AK47 assault rifles, handguns and shotguns. The Romanian team subsequently charged 26 gang members with trafficking 181 children to the UK, being members of an organised criminal network, money laundering and possession of firearms.

However, in February 2019, the case in Romania was dropped. It had dragged on through the courts for nearly a decade, postponed countless times and the subject of legal toing and froing. Then, in what turned out to be the final hearing, the charges against the gang were changed from 'trafficking in human beings and transnational organised crime' to 'money laundering'. The state prosecutors are now engaged in an appeal against what Bernie calls 'this momentous failure of justice'. He was 'gutted' at the news of the reduced conviction.

Another lucrative operation for traffickers, mainly in Vietnam, but now being explored by Albanians, is cannabis farms.

Bernie talked me through a typical operation.

'A three-bed house, converted. One gardener, getting no pay. In proper conditions cannabis grows to harvest maturity in eight to twelve weeks. Value per crop is £250,000. Four crops per year is £1 million per house.

'In order to set up a cannabis farm in the UK you need to acquire premises (a three-bedroom-house in Cambridgeshire, Essex, Nottingham, London – wherever). You would rent the premises, probably, very few cannabis farms are acquired in any other way. Then you have to equip it with about £10,000 worth of electrical equipment –hydroponic beds, lighting, fan systems to take heat out, foil covering on the windows to keep the heat in. You have to run the rooms at different temperatures, because in order to promote the growth along a proper lifespan for the plants, you have to have different temperatures and different humidities at different stages of growth in order to get the best crop.

'So you have one room for seedlings, one for medium plants and one for mature plants – and they will be grown in a cycle. So the equipment will be temperature control, fans getting rid of the hot air, because there has to be fresh air.

'On average, in a three-bed house, the growth cycle of the cannabis plant is eight to twelve weeks depending on how good you are. You will only grow the female flowering plant, of the cannabis genus. All the male ones are not productive, so they get chucked in the bin. That needs scientific knowledge. Some-one's then got to buy the seedlings and plant them. And then someone – "the gardener" – almost certainly a victim of trafficking, is put in there simply to keep the water filled. On an eight-to-twelve-week cycle, if you've got three rooms, with an average of five, six or seven hundred plants, that's £250,000 every eight to twelve weeks. So even if you're pretty crap, and your crop takes twelve weeks, so it's four crops a year, that's still a million quid per three-bedroom house.

'The guy in there looking after the plants hasn't got the electrical capability to set this up, doesn't have the finance behind him, so someone else did that. He gets paid nothing. He'll have a phone, with three phone numbers in it, to ring in case there's a problem, for example the power goes out, or someone's taken an interest in the property. The "gardener" is already in debt. The majority are young boys, a few older men. When the police raid a cannabis farm, they'll find this one little lad in there, who has only the clothes he's wearing. He's sleeping on the floor in a corridor or in a spare bit of space, maybe in the loft, and he has no money.

'What's important to note is there are no drying facilities there. The drugs are not prepared there for the market, so this shows it's just one part of a much bigger operation. He's looking after the growing/cultivation stage. At some point the mature plants will be harvested, then the other plants will be moved from room to room. All the medium plants will be moved to the mature plant room, the seedlings will have grown a bit and go into the medium room, and then there'll be a new crop, so it's a constant cycle.

'The reason they do this instead of putting seedlings in all three rooms, letting them grow and then harvesting them, is that you'd have one harvest every eight weeks. This way you can harvest every two or three weeks. So they're providing a constant supply to the market.

'The drying and bagging facilities are somewhere else altogether and the cops never look for them. That's the frustrating thing. They've arrested "the gardener" for cultivating cannabis – eighteen months to three years imprisonment, job done, headlines in the local paper. Then the fella gets deported. He still owes the gang $20,000, the levy Vietnamese trafficking gangs demand from their victims for the "costs" of trafficking them. So his future is simply to be re-trafficked back to the UK or to some other country.

'One of the tricks the gangs are doing now is (and I've had three cases so far) is this. On his arrival at the cannabis farm they give the gardener £100, so if he's been in the farm for three months, and the police come and kick the door in they say, "Oh, he's being paid, he's got £100 so he can't be a victim of trafficking". And, yes, he's still got that £100 – because he can't go out and spend it. However, if he was in regular employment working twelve-hour days, seven days a week, even on the living wage he should be paid over £900 per month. If he has been in the "farm" for three months, his £100 equals about £1 per day!

'Recruitment is local, at village level in Vietnam. Although it's a communist country and you'd think education would be great, only primary school education is free. Any education if you're over eleven years old, has to be paid for.[1]

'Only forty per cent of kids go on to what we would call second-ary school. What do the other kids do? They work on farms. Or they go and work effectively as child labour. The traffickers know this, so they'll approach the families and say, "We'll take your kid and you'll get money sent back to you". It's a classic con.

'The route for Vietnamese victims is first to Russia. I've had a victim who's walked across Ukraine with a group of others under armed guard, walked all the way from Russia across Ukraine, before being put on a lorry and taken across Europe. No borders so no checks. They're in the back of a lorry, then they get to Calais.

'To explain why the Vietnamese gardeners go to Russia first, you have to look at geopolitics and cultural history. There are

---

1   A 2013 report from Al Jazeera stated that although primary school itself was free for students, the costs of textbooks and uniforms, for example, meant the poorest and most vulnerable children were excluded from even free education.

communist links between Vietnam and Russia from the Vietnam war. Why do they go from Russia to either Poland or the Czech Republic? If they go across Ukraine it's a porous border, so they then get on a truck on the other side of the Ukraine or they're taken into the Czech Republic where they're put on a truck. The Czech Republic is in the EU, so there are existing clandestine means to get them here.

'If you look at the jungle in Calais, you've got the camp which is controlled by Iraqis and Kurds, and 40km north you've got Vietnam City which is another camp. It's in the woods, and it's just shacks. The victims are put there, probably there for up to three months, while the Vietnamese gangs negotiate with the Iraqis and the Kurds to get them on lorries to come from Calais into the UK. Quite often the victims I'm dealing with are found by the French police in the backs of lorries and just thrown out. Never treated as victims. Just thrown out. So the gangs take them back to Vietnam City, then try again later. Eventually they do get to the UK on a lorry.

'They are now in debt. The cost of that journey is 20,000 dollars. In Vietnam, if you carry a debt you have to pay it. They know where you come from. They know your family. It's not uncommon, for the initial 5,000-dollar payment to get to Russia, for families to take out a legal mortgage, or a mortgage from moneylenders, to pay for that first leg of the trip. Because the gang wants the money up front. However, when you get to the UK, you've still got to pay off the rest of that debt – about 15,000 dollars. So you do it by working it off, or they threaten your family back home.

'The debt can actually be sold from gang to gang. So victims can be passed from one gang to another, because they've become their property. They might also have been forced to work in a factory or a farm in Russia while waiting to continue their journey. I've known victims who've worked on farms in Russia for three months, before they were moved on to the next stage of their journey. I've known a couple of victims who, if they can't get on a lorry at Calais, they're told to steal from the lorries to pay their way. So a lot of the theft in the waiting areas, in the truck stops overnight, in and around Calais, is being conducted by migrants. That's enforced criminality. The gangs instruct them that this is how they can pay their way. They're just doing as they're told.'

One of the other areas of concern for many British consumers is the risk of supporting modern slavery and trafficking by using the omnipresent and always cheap Vietnamese nail bars. I've spent the last decade either avoiding them, or doing my own 'surveillance' before committing to a manicure, but it turns out there was a whole other element of organised crime involved that I wasn't even aware of.

'Nail bars that are run by Vietnamese are more than likely a front for money laundering of cannabis proceeds. It is not illegal to run a cash business but it's dodgy on all levels in terms of accounting. No record of what comes in, what goes out, wages etc. So where do you get rid of £250,000 every quarter? How do you legitimise that? Vietnamese-controlled nail bars are cash-only businesses. They don't take credit or debit cards. They rarely issue you with a receipt. Twenty pounds for your nails, over the counter, you think you've got a good deal. If say, thirty women go to that nail bar during the day, they'll put a hundred clients through the books.'

This was news to me, so I asked him if it could possibly be fair to say this of every cheap nail bar in the UK. His answer was firm. 'Vietnamese? Yes, most likely.'

Without question?

'I can't say without question but what I can say is that we've got victims recovered from cannabis farms who've been discovered three months later in nail bars. Bearing in mind they will be working with one network, it's a reasonable assumption that the guys who are running the cannabis farm are also running the nail bar.'

At this point I was dubious about Bernie's claims. I went into great detail about the effort I put in to establishing that my local Vietnamese-run nail bar simply did not conform to what I'd come to believe were criminal enterprises. The women were chatty and they left the premises at the end of the day separately rather than being driven home together in a van (I know this because I loitered outside at closing time for a few nights to put my mind at ease). Besides, the nail industry in Vietnam is a well-known and established career path for young women. It's not unusual for women in their twenties to train in nail bar schools then leave the country in search of new opportunities.

Bernie turned police investigator on me. 'Ok then. Where does the money go?'

'I don't know.'

'How much are they paid?'

'I don't know, point taken. But I've been focusing on them as victims of trafficking and slavery. Could it be they have their freedom, as you and I would understand it, but they are working for a dodgy operation?'

Bernie sighed, clearly wondering if anything he'd taught me over the last nine years had gone in.

'Let's forget the money laundering because you're asking if they're victims or not. Say you live in a village in Vietnam. Your education is moderate, in terms of qualifications. Your opportunities are negligible. Put yourself in their position. Is this better, even if it's not right, is this better than they had in Vietnam in terms of opportunity and living standards? So with the nail bars, you may be getting £4 an hour – that's probably the weekly wage in Vietnam if you get a crap job. And you're living with your mum, your dad, your grandparents. You can't watch TV, you can't have all the shiny things. Are you really going to complain?

'How do these people suddenly decide they're going to come to the UK to paint nails? Who pays for their trip? Who gets their visa? Which visa are they actually on? You only have to google nail bars and find the number of illegal immigrants lifted from them to decide if they're legitimate business or illegal.

'In the raids in Operation Golf, we found one three-bedroom house in Slough with thirty-one people in it, with entire families of two adults, five children and two other trafficked children, *in each bedroom*. Babies sleeping in the sink. Girls sleeping in the bath. But they were not complaining. They've been told that this is what you've got to put up with. Because you owe your masters 20,000 dollars.

'Most victims don't see themselves as victims.'

As the coffees were topped up, Bernie explained how gangs recruited their victims, and how anyone could fall victim to their tactics.

'Gangs recruit by a variety of methods, false promises, lending money etc. There are 40 million people in slavery around the world. It all comes down to *control mechanisms*. A control mechanism is a way to keep your victim happy or compliant.

'Generally, in an Albanian, Romanian or Lithuanian controlled brothel the girls will keep half of the takings from every punter. On average that's £50 for full sex. The girl keeps £25. It's a *control mechanism*. In her mind she's getting paid well, even though she's being raped. She was forced into this, so it is rape. From her £25, she has to pay "the maid", she has to pay for condoms, oil, advertising, so she may end up with £15 for every trick. The "house", i.e. the gang, keeps £25 for every trick.

'So if she services ten men a day, and that's a pretty quiet day, for even five days a week, just do the maths. She could be keeping £500 a week, maybe more if she's servicing more clients. What would she be earning in Albania, China, Vietnam, Romania, Nigeria, Eretria, Estonia, Lithuania, Poland, Bulgaria, Turkey or Romania? Most likely little or nothing. By the way, these are the countries most represented in the UK data of victims of sexual exploitation discovered in the UK in 2018. Victims reported into the UK National Referral Mechanism in 2018 came from 129 countries.

'In many cases the door is not locked. She could run away, but she doesn't. To understand why we have to go back to control mechanisms. The control mechanism there is: "You run away, we'll get you". Perhaps you haven't got your passport or your documents, so "The cops will take you and deport you, or put you in prison". It could be "We know where your mum and dad live". Even if she never willingly wanted to have sex with all these strangers and hates it, she has never run away. She hasn't run into the arms of the police. Very few people "self-present". The ones who do that are in the lowest state because the gang they've been with is probably nasty. They've got a supply of new victims so they can treat their girls worse.

'Traffickers are quite clever. The threat of force is not uncommon, but the *use* of force is quite uncommon, because they don't want girls seeing clients with bruises on their faces or body. If they're having sex then usually they've got few clothes on. The traffickers use *psychological* control mechanisms.

'The majority of victims don't run away, otherwise we would have 10,000 victims a year on the books, 20,000 victims. There were nearly 7,000 victims going into the NRM last year. We also have to take into account the adults who did *not* want to be referred but have nevertheless been recovered. We don't even know what that number is. Those on the NRM are only the ones we know about.

'What about the ones we haven't found yet? How many victims of trafficking in the UK are there today? If 7,000 are known about, how many do you think are not known about? On average we know one in ten. So that's 70,000 possible victims of trafficking in this country at any one time. Who *aren't* running into our arms. Sitting in a nail bar. Working in a cannabis farm. Because they know no different.'

4

ELENA'S STORY: ALBANIA TO BELGIUM (2015)

After our initial off-the-record meeting in November, Elena agreed to meet with me again so that I could record a more formal interview with her about her experiences. In January 2018, we met in the same coffee shop, this time with Elena's caseworker from the charity which supported her, and a professional interpreter.

Listening to the recording now is an odd experience. Elena and I were practically strangers, her English was basic and my questioning was very hesitant. I'm struck now by how much her English has improved, but how little her security in the UK has.

I couldn't have foreseen then what a huge part Elena and her child would play in my life.

While it was hard to imagine, looking at the timid and cautious young woman in front of me, it was clear from what she said that in the autumn of 2015 Elena had the confidence and spirit of most new graduates.

Despite her parents' objections, Elena left Albania with Marco, convinced that this trip would be the beginning of their journey to marriage. Though she had never left her home country, didn't have a passport and had never been on a plane, she trusted Marco implicitly and happily followed his instructions as they travelled to Belgium. But the plans Marco had put in place for their special trip together appeared to unravel from the moment they landed.

Elena was expecting them to travel to his family home, in order to meet and stay with Marco's parents. It wasn't long before Elena realised this was not going to happen as soon as she had expected.

'After we arrived he said to me we would be staying in a hotel because his family had gone on holiday. I thought this was strange because he had repeatedly said that I was going to meet his family, and I wondered why they were not there.'

Marco assured Elena it wasn't a problem, they'd stay in a hotel together, and she would finally be introduced to his family the following week. When pressed on the details of this period, like so many survivors of trafficking, Elena was vague. She didn't know the name of the city or town he took her to, and certainly not the hotel.

While this may seem strange and probably naïve to many hearing Elena's account, it's not unusual for survivors of trafficking to be unable to recount what we would see as basic facts around travel arrangements or experiences. Over the last couple of years, Elena has been asked to tell her story time and time again to the authorities, decision makers tasked with ruling if she was a victim of trafficking or not. The Home Office officials examine every part of a victim's testimony, and question them about every detail of their experience. One of the key problems with this strategy, however, is that often the majority of victims are so traumatised it can take years for facts and details to be recalled and then disclosed.

In addition to this, victims like Elena who had no control over their travel arrangements simply didn't realise the gravity of the journey they had embarked on. Elena trusted Marco to get her from Albania to Belgium, and had no idea at the time how vital it would be for her to be able to identify basic points in her journey.

'It was my first time going abroad and I felt completely overwhelmed. I was entirely reliant on Marco and he didn't explain anything to me. All I knew was that I was in Belgium, because he told me.'

For the next week, somewhere in Belgium, Elena was alone in a hotel with Marco. As the days went on, she repeatedly asked him why he didn't know his family had gone away, and if there was a reason their plans had changed. No answers were forthcoming, and Elena stopped asking him as he became more and more agitated and angry.

During this time, she did manage to make contact with her sister.

'My last telephone call was with my youngest sister, because the others didn't want to talk to me. I talk to my little sister that I am in Belgium and I am fine.'

Clearly Elena knew at this point that something was wrong, or was about to go wrong, as her instinct warned her not to tell her sister the truth.

'I started to have a little bit of doubt in my mind, I didn't want to make my sister angry or be sad for my situation.'

Still Marco had not taken Elena to the family home, but around a week later, he told her they were going to meet some of his friends. Thinking it was a simple afternoon engagement, she left her belongings at the hotel, taking only her handbag. Marco's friend Philippe collected them, and they drove for around forty minutes to what appeared to be the outskirts of the city. They arrived at a house, a big house, Elena recalled, and once inside she was introduced to three other women.

The first thing Elena told me about the initial meeting with Marco's friends was that the women made her feel uncomfortable and self-conscious about her clothes.

'I couldn't get used to being with the girls around me. Their way of [dressing] was something that you had to think about. I was simply in my trainers, a top and blue jeans. At the very beginning, when they saw me, they said, "Look at her, what is this way of dressing? You're so young, you should be more glamorous".'

The women told Elena they would give her some new clothes to wear, and she simply thought they were trying to be kind, sensing her discomfort at the difference in their styles. Elena felt uncomfortable and out of her depth in this group, but Marco made matters worse when, despite initiating the visit, he told Elena he was going out for a coffee with someone, and would come back and collect her later. He encouraged her to spend time with the girls, and left.

Elena was there alone for about an hour, feeling increasingly distressed. She recalled, 'I wasn't feeling comfortable, so I called him on the phone and said, "Please come and pick me up from here. Take me away from here".'

Eventually, true to his word, Marco did come back to the house. But he didn't take Elena away.

'He came back in the late afternoon and he said to me, "I'm not going to be here again to pick you up. You have to stay here, and you'll see what will happen later".'

Frightened and confused, Elena found herself alone in a strange house, in a strange country, deserted by the man she trusted and with no idea what was about to happen to her.

It's at this point the conversation became harder to listen to. Elena's distress was visible and I could see her physical demeanour change as she relived that first evening.

'Later on the same night I was in my room. Somebody came in. Somebody that I didn't know, and you can imagine what happened in that room. There it was. It was the first time that I was with a client.'

Elena began to cry, and I apologised for making her talk about this betrayal, and this abuse. I felt that, despite her willingness to open up to me, I was somehow prying or, from the safe, middle-class comfort of my job, intruding on her grief like a voyeur.

It was impossible not to put myself in her shoes and wonder what the hell I would have done should the same fate have befallen me. I still wondered where, as she talked to me, she found the strength to cast her mind back to that dark time, and relive the horror.

In this ordinary café in London, on a miserable day in January, we were surrounded by bored mums, gossiping pensioners and moaning commuters, no doubt feeling worn down by their day-to-day existence, but oblivious to the unimaginable suffering of the young woman weeping nearby.

'It's a long time now, it's gone away. I've tried to wipe it out, but sometimes it comes back.'

For over a year, this was all I knew about Elena's first hours in the anonymous brothel in Belgium. It wasn't something we would chat about as small talk, and it wasn't until the summer of 2018, in the presence of a lawyer and interpreter, that I could fully grasp what had happened.

I learned more about what happened after Marco abandoned Elena in the house. When he told her he wasn't coming back, his tone towards her had changed completely. Now he was threatening her, and telling her she had to stop calling him because there was a reason he didn't want to speak with her. He did return to the house that night, but by then, Elena was too scared to speak to him.

Instead she was facing a new horror.

'That night something happened to me but I don't ever want to think about it. The girls came and gave me clothes to wear, and seeing what was happening around me it was at that stage I realised what it was I was going to be required to do.'

It was at midnight that her first client walked through the door.

She tried to refuse to have sex with him but she said, 'It was impossible. He was violent with me because I was resisting him. He slapped me, then he raped me.'

He was Elena's only client that night. Her level of distress meant she was deemed to be in no state to work.

It was at that point she realised that no matter how much she screamed or cried, nobody was going to help her.

*

53

Elena was in the house for around ten months.

It was a four-bedroom property with a basic, functional kitchen. Her bedroom had a small window which could open a little – but had bars on the outside.

During her time in the brothel, she was allowed out of her room, but not out of the house. There was a man who guarded the front door, to whom she never spoke, and a woman who guarded the girls' bedrooms.

'I would wake up, have coffee and breakfast, and I just wanted to sleep, but I would have a shower. I kept a diary, writing things in a journal.'

The other women tried to be friendly, but Elena retreated into herself.

'We had coffee. They would come to eat, have their food in the kitchen. They were Albanians, they would invite me. But I didn't like to be part of their company. It was clear they were there willingly. Sometimes they would pick me up and take me when there was a party in other houses. They would organise these parties and take us, and we would work there. Whether I liked it or not I had to go to these places. They were not far. Ten minutes.'

In the early days she would see two or three clients a day, and with enormous bravery, she told the men she was there against her will, that she didn't want to be there and she hadn't chosen this life. Hearing this didn't appear to affect their libido. Often they were violent, slapping her, hitting her and pulling her hair.

'I was brought up in another way of tradition and culture, and I'd only heard about this on television. I didn't imagine it would happen to me. But I was feeling very bad, I was crying, I didn't have a phone.'

In an attempt to make herself a less attractive prospect to punters, she would try to look as unappealing as possible.

'I was depressed. I was ill. There were not many people coming to me because I was crying all the time and I wasn't taking care of myself, so that I could feel . . . so that the punters didn't like me. I was trying to do anything so that when they saw me they would say, "I don't want to stay with this woman".'

But the business of selling sex continued for her captors. The women were tasked with bringing Elena food, and appeared to be managing the house. They received male visitors during the day, but according to Elena's interpretation these were social visits, and all the clients appeared in the evening.

'Philippe [who had picked up Marco and her from the hotel] was the boss. He came occasionally, but he didn't come to the house very often. One of the girls was in charge. I don't know if the others were trafficked or not, I can't say that. At that time it looked like they were there willingly. They seemed happy to me, the money they got they said they would never need to go back to Albania.'

When I asked Elena how much money she was making, her answer was simple.

'The girls in charge would get the money. I didn't get any money from this.'

In early 2016, after a few months being held captive in the brothel, and with no word from Marco, Elena's life was to change once more.

She discovered she was pregnant.

'After five months of staying there, I realised I was pregnant in January or February. I suspected I was pregnant. My periods stopped coming. I was sick. I felt like fainting.'

She tried to hide the pregnancy for as long as she could, but as soon as she started showing, it was impossible. Elena told the other women with whom she now found herself sharing her life, and they told her they were going to call Marco.

He came to the house, the first time she had seen him since he had abandoned her there last October.

He arrived at the house and simply told her he was taking her to the doctor. Elena shared with me all the details about that week: the meeting with the doctor; the fact she was in her second trimester by the time she saw a medical professional; the rage expressed by Marco, and the resulting threats made by her traffickers.

They are all deeply distressing. To reveal the extent of the cruelty Elena's captors threatened her with during this stage of her pregnancy would illustrate graphically the tactics and fear employed by such gangs to control their victims. I am conscious though of Elena's child, and the need to be circumspect in print about what happened to its mother.

Inevitably, the pregnancy affected her physical health and therefore her ability to work and earn money for the gang, so she was at least given a temporary reprieve from the daily rapes and assaults. But when Marco made it clear she would be expected to return to work after the birth, Elena knew that she had to do whatever she could to protect her unborn child and its future.

'I said to myself, I don't have any idea what it means to be a mum, but I will do anything to protect my child. At that time I was in a cloud, I didn't know what was happening, or what I was going to do. My aim was that I have to do something to get out of this situation. The only thing that I could keep in my mind was to get out of this place.'

Then fate intervened.

'When I was seven months [pregnant], completely by chance – I left.'

One summer evening later in the year, the other women in the brothel were in high spirits. It was the birthday of one of the more senior sex workers, and the girls were planning a birthday party for her.

'There had been some other parties during the time I was there, but it seemed they were making a bigger deal about this party.'

Utterly distracted by the impending gathering as they put up balloons and decorations, a weak and seemingly defeated Elena was far from their minds.

'Normally there was a man guarding the main door, but on that particular day he wasn't there. I don't know why not, but I presume it was because he was also helping with the party. There was also a girl who used to watch my door, but as there were no clients and she was busy with the party, she was also not watching that particular day. I think it didn't cross their minds that I would try to run away.'

After ten months in the brothel, being forced to have sex against her will, falling into what appeared to be a deep depression, and then at seven months pregnant unable to work, it was hardly a surprise that no one in the house bothered to give Elena a second thought. Broken and alone, this petite, vulnerable woman was hardly going to give them any trouble.

They underestimated her determination to get her unborn baby to safety.

'I saw the front door was open, and no one had been there for a few minutes. I grabbed my bag which I always had ready just in case. I took the opportunity and ran out of the house. It was getting dark. It was the first time I had been out on my own – and it was an area without people, and I was scared, breathless. The gods, I think, gave me strength. When I realised I was not being followed I slowed down. It was difficult for me to go quickly because I was pregnant. I rested for a few minutes to get my breath back and then I walked for an hour and a half, I think.'

At this point Elena had no idea where she was. She described coming to a main road, but not a place where cars could stop and help her. She admitted she was close to giving up, but then realised she was by now next to some sort of lorry park. Sensing a potential opportunity, Elena entered the park and spotted a man having a cigarette break while boxes were being loaded into the back of his vehicle. She took a chance and asked him for help.

Speaking a combination of Albanian, French and English, in a desperate attempt to be understood somehow, she managed to make the driver realise she needed to get away, begging him to take her wherever his lorry was going – it didn't matter where. Distressed, crying and heavily pregnant, Elena somehow managed to make herself understood by the man, who realised the extent of her predicament and told her to get in the lorry.

When I was asking Elena about this, I was confused as to how, after everything she'd been through at the hands of men – those she had trusted and those who were complete strangers – she could possibly have trusted this man to take her to safety?

The look she gave me then hammered home once more the difference between her experiences and mine.

'It was getting dark and I was on my own. I simply wanted to get away from the area, I didn't want to see them any more. They would have found me after I escaped and would have done something wrong to me. So for that moment I wasn't thinking about trusting that person, it was my good luck that he helped me.'

To the best of her recollection, Elena was in the back of the lorry for around six hours.

'I was scared. But also relieved to think I may have got away. I didn't see anything, I didn't know where I was going. It was darkness around me, and I slept. I didn't think about what may happen to me. At the end of the journey he opened the doors and told me to get out quickly. He told me I was in London. He told me I was fortunate he helped me. He told me, "There are no cameras here. I can't do anything any more, ask for help from the people here. Please carry on going as I don't want any problems, I might get in trouble".'

Elena left the lorry knowing only that she was in London. To this day she doesn't know where she was exactly, just that she was far from home.

'From what I have heard on the TV about London, I knew I was far away. I was so far away.'

At this point, Elena broke down sobbing and there was a long, uncomfortable and desperate pause on the recording. It's awful to listen to again.

'I was thinking of my family. And the baby in my tummy.'

By now, despite the fact that it must have been way past midnight, Elena managed to find someone on the streets of London who would listen to her.

'Then I ask for help. I ask a black lady for help. She said there is a place called Home Office. I will take you there.'

'It was around 2am when I got there, so I waited outside until it opened.'

5

FIRST ON THE SCENE

In an unremarkable sixties building in the Elephant and Castle, London, lives The Salvation Army.[1]

Most of us associate the Sally Army with jolly brass bands performing Christmas carols in our town centres. Until I became immersed in the world of anti-slavery work, that was my impression too.

What goes on behind the doors of the Elephant and Castle building is a world away from festive cheer. It is here that the operation to restore the lives of modern slavery victims begins. In 2011, The Salvation Army was awarded the Government contract for England and Wales to provide specialist support to all adult victims of modern slavery. This means that as soon as any potential victim of modern slavery (in England or Wales) is identified, it's The Salvation Army that gets the call to help them.

In Scotland, women who have been trafficked for the purposes of sexual exploitation are supported by TARA (Trafficking Awareness Raising Alliance) while Migrant Help provide care and assistance for male victims of sexual exploitation, and

---

1 The day I spent with The Salvation Army was during a period where countless reforms into the NRM were being introduced, when several cases regarding the care and financial support of victims were being fought in court, and before the conclusions of the Modern Slavery Review were released.

victims of wider modern slavery crimes. Migrant Help also support victims in Northern Ireland, alongside Belfast & Lisburn's Women's Aid.

In England and Wales the Army manages and co-ordinates all first contact with a victim, and ensures they get to safety, though some of the support services offered, once in safety, are sub-contracted. For example, in Wales, the charity Bawso works closely with The Salvation Army and can assist with the care of vulnerable people who have been trafficked, or can pick up the support if it's deemed that a victim from elsewhere needs to be moved into the area for safety.

Since I had worked with The Salvation Army on previous projects, I was hopeful they'd agree to speak to me for this book, because it's their First Responder volunteers who day in, day out, are working directly with victims.

On a rainy, blustery day in May 2019, I headed to The Salvation Army's London HQ to meet Kathy Betteridge, their Director of Anti-Trafficking and Modern Slavery, and Norree Webb, the Army's First Responder Co-ordinator.

Kathy is petite with short blonde-grey hair. She's hugely passionate, yet clearly and very calmly spoken – and I suspect quite a dynamo. Norree is one of those women you want near you in an emergency. Warm, calm, and seemingly unflappable, she is the sort of person who makes you feel everything is going to be all right. I got the impression she had tried to retire (she was a teacher) but found it an uncomfortable waste of her time, which could be better spent helping the vulnerable.

When we sat down to start the interview I was keen to know how The Salvation Army became involved in the fight against human trafficking. Kathy explained.

'We've been active in this area since way back in 1885 when our founder's son, Bramwell Booth, with a journalist and an ex-brothel owner who'd become a Christian, wanted to highlight the issue of young girls being sold for prostitution and slavery. We've always been involved in helping the vulnerable, those that are marginalised and those that are abused in some way by society. We've always tried to be a voice for them, because of our whole mission, and values, and ethos, and everything about who we are as a Church and a charity.'

1885 is not 2019, so how were we even talking about slavery on the streets of Britain today?

'After William Wilberforce everyone thought that it had been abolished but there is probably more slavery now than there was then. The estimate in the UK is between 10 and 13,000 but they think it's a lot larger than that – maybe 40,000 is still an under-estimation but it's a more likely figure.

'Since the Modern Slavery Act in 2015, these crimes have been better highlighted. Prior to that there was work going on. We as The Salvation Army have had the contract since 2011. We had a safe house for twelve years before then. We were one of the organisations putting our own money into providing support, on a much more limited basis, even prior to the contract or the Modern Slavery Act.'

The National Referral Mechanism, or NRM, is the system in which victims of trafficking and slavery are identified and helped. It's based on a system created by the Council of Europe Convention on Action against Trafficking in Human Beings, ratified by the UK in 2008, for launch in 2009. NRM, and the UK's implementation of it, is not without its critics or its flaws, and in 2017 the process was reviewed, with some of the changes made after that finally trickling their way through to the front line now.

Various agencies have the authority to refer victims into the NRM: Local Authorities, the UK Visas and Immigration Authority, the Police, the National Crime Agency, The GLAA, Barnardo's and the NSPCC, and a variety of victim-facing charities such as Kalayaan and Medaille Trust. The Salvation Army itself is also a First Responder.

Kathy was clearly well versed in explaining the NRM and how it affected survivors.

'We are called because someone needs to be rescued, or they have been rescued by the police, and they're in maybe a police station or some other building of safety. We have a team of over 400 volunteers. We will contact one or two of those volunteers who will pick up that person and drive them to one of our safe house accommodations. So they have a place of safety to go to.

'The person will then be required to tell their story, and we capture that story through our First Responders. This can take quite some time, because they're likely to be agitated and anxious, but our volunteers are able to calm them and help them tell their story.'

Norree is one of these First Responders, and I imagine she would be a welcome sight for the victims she meets in their hour of need. She explained how she was first informed a new victim had been rescued and that she and her team were needed.

'The office in Birmingham will receive a referral. They will try and do those over the phone, if they can, as it gets people into the system more quickly. That email will be sent to me, because I co-ordinate all the trained First Responders. I will then send an email round the database of First Responders with very brief details as to roughly where the victim is – the Manchester area, or the Rotherham area, and whether it's a male or female, whether or not they need an interpreter. Then I wait for a response from someone to tell me they can do it. Some people are retired, but some people work and have to fit this in.

'Officially, a face-to-face interview should be done within forty-eight hours of arriving in the referral office. However, there are times when that can't happen – if someone is in prison, or detention, or hospital. Or if they're too traumatised to be interviewed over the telephone. In a prison you've got to wait to book a legal visit and that can take a long time – two or three weeks to get a legal slot. If you need an interpreter you've got to wait for them to find one, and for some languages that can be quite difficult. Vietnamese is a nightmare. Albanian is quite difficult as are some of the African languages where there are different dialects.

Although we are officially required to do this within forty-eight hours, we keep a log which tracks each referral, and as long as I give a reason why the interview has not happened within that time the Home Office can't fine us.'

One of Norree's comments unnerved me. Why on earth would a victim be in a prison or detention centre?

'Lots of victims are criminalised by their traffickers. For instance, young Vietnamese boys are brought over and locked into a house full of cannabis. They're told to water the plants. When the police raid, the person in the property growing the plants is the young victim. The bosses are nowhere to be seen, and won't be. The victims have been locked in with food delivered two or three times a week. They're usually just in underpants and a T-shirt, so they can't escape. Doors are locked. But when the police raid, they're the ones growing the plants so they're the ones arrested.

'One of the problems we have is very often when they're first arrested, a duty solicitor is called in and unfortunately, particularly with the Vietnamese boys, he or she says, "Oh, plead guilty, you'll get home quicker". However, if they've picked up another solicitor in the meantime, then I would contact that solicitor and when the case goes to court they're able to say the National Referral Mechanism is in process. So nothing can happen at that point. Very often judges will adjourn the case until a decision is made about their trafficking situation.

'Sometimes the solicitors will apply for bail, and they may come out and go to a safe house, if the judge agrees. Unfortunately, some Vietnamese clients do go missing, so it's a little difficult. I do have lists of solicitors who will take cases on, some I know quite well now. I will ring one of them and say, "Can you help this person?", as it's obviously Legal Aid. We try and get them a solicitor who will fight their case, which they need in order for a court case to be fair.'

'What about victims in detention centres?' I asked naïvely.

'Sometimes we're not aware of their case, so they've possibly been to court, or been to an immigration interview probably, and been put in detention from the immigration interview. We do get calls from detention centres where a chaplain or a support worker within that centre may have picked up that there's something not quite right, and they believe the person may be a victim.'

'So,' I asked, 'you're relying on someone having enough knowledge to make a call – otherwise the victim will just get deported?'

'Exactly. Exactly.'

Often it's not just a case of a single victim being discovered. The Salvation Army is also on hand for police raids, when a force will go into a property and potentially rescue numerous victims in one go. The police contact the project office, say they're doing a raid, and ask Kathy if the Army has reception centres available.

The reception centres provide an immediate safe haven for multiple victims to be treated with care and begin their journey to freedom. It's not only the Army that can provide this. The Red Cross run reception centres which can also be used to provide a safe environment for victims to be taken to in the immediate aftermath of a raid.

In terms of notice, Kathy said, 'We may get a few days, may get a week, or it could be an emergency.'

This can be hard if there's not much notice, and Kathy's team have to find emergency accommodation, for example, for fifteen men in a matter of hours.

I was curious to know how Norree prepared to interview a complete stranger, a traumatised victim of a horrific crime, when they might be only hours out of an unthinkable situation.

'It's about building trust with the person, so that they understand I'm there to help them. Some of them can be very suspicious. They've lost trust. They don't trust the people who have been holding them. They've lost trust with humanity completely. So for somebody to come along whom they don't know . . . "Who are you? Why should I talk to you?" I tell them I'm there to help, but I don't make the decisions. How you are physically matters too, smiling, your approach when you're actually in the room with them.

'To understand what's happened to them now, I need to find out where they've come from. I always take them back to birth and build their story. It's a problem at the moment as the Home Office require the background to be much briefer and bullet pointed, which I find more difficult. I feel what has happened to them up until the point they have been recruited is vital in understanding why they've ended up where they are.

'Let me give you an example. A young girl from Sierra Leone had been orphaned. Someone came along and said she was her aunt, took her to Nigeria to look after her at the age of nine. By thirteen she was being used as a prostitute by the "aunt". She was regularly having to have abortions, which were done by the local doctor, without any real medical care, shall we say. Let's put it that way.

'One of the clients said to her one day, "I can get you to England. I can get you to England where you can get an education and get away from all of this." They managed to arrange that, as they do, with false documents. They got her here, and she was straight into a brothel. She managed to escape, and eventually got herself some work in a care home. Then the owners discovered her papers were not valid, and got Immigration in. So of course she was put in prison for having false documents.

'But until you know that background, you don't realise *why* she's here on false documents. So that's why that background is so important: she's been *brought* here on false documents.'

After establishing the background of the victim, Norree explained, that was the last contact she would have with them.

'I do remember lots of my cases but I can't hold on to them emotionally. I remember them, and when I'm doing training I use lots of examples, with details of cases I know. But emotionally I can't hang on to them. I've interviewed over 150 people. I can't hold on to all those cases. It doesn't mean that I don't care, or I don't think about them. I have to pass it on, as I just can't cope otherwise.'

67

After Norree or one of her team have carried out their interviews, the information on the victim is then passed to the Home Office.

Until 29th April 2019, potential victims were divided at this point. British victims and those from the EEA were processed by the National Crime Agency, so decisions on their future were decided by criminal investigators. Those from non-EEA countries had their cases processed by the UK Visa and Immigration Authority, so decisions on their future were decided by those with a focus on the immigration status of the victim. It was a much-criticised distinction.

Since then, changes have come into force which mean all decisions are now decided by a team within the Home Office. In theory, all victims should be examined on the merits of their cases and not their country of origin but, in the shadow of the Windrush scandal and of course the hostile environment, many working directly with survivors of trafficking are far from hopeful that this will lead to better outcomes for such a vulnerable group of people.

There are two phases, as Kathy explained, to the decision-making process.

'Using the information we have captured, there are indicators that will help them decide whether a person is a confirmed victim of trafficking and modern slavery. Before that happens, they will get what's called a *Reasonable Grounds* decision. Just by the very nature of the fact they have been rescued and there are *some* signs, they will get confirmation that there is *probably* evidence that, yes, this person is *potentially* a victim. That's when the support starts. While they wait for their final confirmation they will be in our service, getting that support for as long as that decision takes to be made. Then they get a letter to confirm whether they are deemed a victim of trafficking and/or modern slavery. This is the *Conclusive Grounds* decision.'

While a victim is waiting for the Conclusive Grounds decision, they are cared for by either The Salvation Army itself, or by one of its sub-contractors. This will be done via outreach, if they have somewhere safe to go, or in a safe house.

For obvious reasons the team wouldn't commit to the number of safe houses they currently have, but I was told there are 'a lot' with 'more every month or so', which is impressive and deeply depressing at the same time. To realise that there is a growing need for such specialist accommodation is sobering.

The safe houses are all very different, in order to cater for the wide variety of victims and their specific needs. On one end of the scale are the safe houses for men with high risk and high needs, so these would more than likely have round-the-clock staffing. At the other end of the scale is more low-key accommodation with five or six women where there would be constant support but at the end of the phone, because they have been assessed as not needing the same level of intensive support. Their support workers would attend during the day.

As the team explained, everything is funded through the Government contract, but in the case of The Salvation Army, and other organisations working with victims, staff tend to supplement the offerings with their own voluntary donations, wanting to do the very best they can for residents and making the safe houses as good as they can be.

What victims of trafficking and slavery are entitled to during their recovery is based on the ECAT (European Convention Against Trafficking) entitlement.

Kathy explained that anyone going through the NRM is entitled to specific support.

'Either safe house accommodation or outreach. As long as it's agreed that they are in a safe place then they will have outreach, so that means a support worker who meets them regularly and assesses their needs, and works with them in the same way they would in a safe house, but they're out in the community as opposed to in our accommodation. They get medical treatment, legal support, counselling and translation if they need it. If they have children, and some do come into the service as mothers with a child because they've had a child as a result of their exploitation, their child is then entitled to education in the UK system.'

As the issue of modern slavery has grown in the public conscious-ness since 2015, I wondered if the types of cases The Salvation Army was seeing were changing. Was there a 'typical' case? Norree answered immediately.

'With Romanian and Albanian girls it's sexual exploitation. Vietnamese boys involved in cannabis growing is very common – *very* common. I almost know before they've told me. There are two main ways these boys are caught by traffickers. They encourage them to gamble, so they build up such a big debt that they can't pay it back. Or they say to their parents, "I can get your child to the UK for an education, and they can work and send you money. But the fee is so-and-so".

'They usually take them by plane to Russia, then across land in various ways. Sometimes they'll have them working along the way, in warehouses. They'll come across the continent in a lorry, but when I ask them to describe where they were every time they got out of the lorry, they say, "I was in a forest". Every single time. I still can't work out where this forest is!

'They're given a phone to make a call, and a car will come and pick them up. Then they're taken to a house, and locked in. That pattern happens with nearly every Vietnamese person who's involved in cannabis growing. Most of them are obviously trau-matised and frightened. There's a lack of trust, they don't know who I am or whose side I'm on. Albanian girls wouldn't trust a male or the police in their own country at all.'

For some, agreeing to be helped is not an easy decision. Cultural differences, years of manipulation and fears for their future mean that some victims, when rescued, refuse help.

'The traffickers will also have convinced them that you don't trust the police, or you don't trust authority, and we're sometimes seen as that. But as we talk with them, they may change their minds. Sometimes it's because the police encourage them to, then they meet us, and then they will go through the process. But there are those who choose not to. They may just not trust authority or they may be frightened that they will then be deported straight away. They don't want that to happen.'

I wondered whether victims were more likely to trust The Salvation Army than 'the authorities', as it's a faith organisation.

'That is the case with certain cultures. For Nigerian woman particularly, you do find they trust us as a faith organisation. We also have feedback from victims saying that when they are rescued, it's the first time somebody has smiled at them, or shown them any kind of care. So the way we treat victims, because obviously there is a different approach, does seem to give people that element of trust – so I would say probably yes. Others may think differently but I would say yes, it does.'

I asked Kathy more about victims hidden in the UK, and if they tended to be targeted in certain countries for specific exploitation here.

'The figures from our last report suggest that the most common source country for women is Albania and that tends to be sexual exploitation. For men, it's Vietnam – more around workforce exploitation. That could be cannabis growing, or agriculture or the fishing industry. Nigeria, that's women again, then China, Poland and Romania. Sexual exploitation used to be the highest form of exploitation, but there's evidence to show it's now actually the labour force that is the highest.

'The number of British victims has doubled over this last year. Criminals target the vulnerable, so we've advised our Salvation Army Homelessness Service to be aware of this. Someone in our homelessness service, who may have left for whatever reason, maybe an addiction, could now be on the streets. They could then be targeted for forced criminality or labour "opportunity". They may be supplied with drugs to keep them trapped: they stay with the criminal as their drug addiction is being fed. That's a common route for some of our British victims.'

*

71

When it comes to trafficking and exploitation, nail bars and car washes tend to be foremost in the mind of the media and the public. But are there any other areas we should be aware of? Kathy offered some advice.

'The hospitality industry. Hotels may sub-contract their services, and within that supply chain there may be people who are victims of trafficking or slavery in particular. It's a question of looking out for the signs when you're in a hotel. If you feel confident, you can ask the hotel. Are they aware of the Modern Slavery Act? Do they have a Modern Slavery statement? Who are they sourcing as sub-contractors?

'Don't assume anything. In one case, a hotel was paying the sub-contractors but the sub-contractors weren't passing the money on to the people doing the work. So it was going into their bank accounts, but the bank accounts were being controlled by the sub-contractors.'

The construction industry is also somewhere where historically people have been exploited, often in respectable, blue-chip companies but through an intermediary. For example, workers would be employed by an agency who would in turn sub-contract, but each time a new agency became involved, the background of staff would become murkier, leading, in some cases, to traffickers bringing victims onto the staff of a well-known and reputable company, without that company being aware.

One example that sprang to mind for Kathy and her team was the case of a woman they worked with who was a cleaner in a sixth-form college. She was in full view of countless members of staff and students, no doubt considered a 'normal' member of the school's staff. Not one of them knew she was being controlled away from the school and wasn't receiving the money she was earning as their cleaner.

A significant source of information for those trying to rescue victims is the inspection by health and safety inspectors of food establishments. By the very nature of their role as someone who attends kitchens regularly and over time, they can spot changes in workers if they get more malnourished and unkempt – an important signal someone may be in the control of others, as is appearing cowed, and not wanting to make conversation.

One thing that was still on my mind as we talked was the mental state of the victims when they arrived in the care of The Salvation Army, and how on earth the team began to gain the trust of such traumatised people and help them on the road to recovery. They had fallen prey to the actions of unscrupulous traffickers, suffered physical and emotional abuse at their hands – and were now expected to once again follow the lead of strangers asking them to get in a car and be taken somewhere out of their control. How did the First Responders ensure that a vulnerable victim felt safe in their care?

'Some victims don't even know they're in the UK,' Kathy replied. 'They don't know where they are, they just know they're not in their own country. At the point of rescue, they're traumatised but also relieved to be out of the situation they've been in. So when they're introduced to one of our drivers – just from the way they're spoken to – they know they can trust us. It's all about how they're dealt with. They're treated with care: the driver will stop off and get food for them for instance. It's not a question of driving them somewhere and dumping them. It's a question of caring for them during the journey, and making sure there's a support worker ready to meet them. The very fact they're being cared for is different to the treatment they've had.'

Then I was told something devastating. Female victims, on arrival at a safe house, sometimes assume it's simply another brothel. There is a woman on the door ready to greet them, it's full of bedrooms, and why would she trust anyone again anyway? They search the house to ensure there are exits for escape, and check the wardrobe to make sure it's not full of sexually explicit clothing. Then, when they realise the only thing waiting for them is a welcome pack, there is a moment of realisation that they're safe.

However, as Kathy pointed out, 'Just because they're in a safe house doesn't mean that's it. It's just the beginning of the road to recovery.'

6

SURVIVOR'S STORY: MR M

It's rare for survivors of trafficking and slavery to want to speak about their experiences – for understandable reasons. Imagine having to talk about the darkest time in your life, over and over and over again – especially knowing that your entire future relies on the right people believing your account.

Some victims are so traumatised they have shut many details out of their minds in an effort to survive, and for others they may have so many other emotions wrapped up with the memories, like guilt and fear, it can take years for their entire experience to be disclosed. So when I received confirmation that a survivor was not only willing to meet me, but was adamant he wanted to tell his story, I was surprised but pleased.

To protect his identity, I won't disclose the precise location, but Mr M has built a new life in a town by the coast. On the blustery day I arrange to meet him I'm blown around as I walk past couples eating ice cream, through streets full of the smell of fish and chips. Faced with this postcard of absolute British normality, I can't help but wonder how many people like Mr M are living within our towns and cities, trying to put their lives back together, the horror of their previous existence utterly unfathomable to their neighbours.

The place Mr M had asked to meet me was down a back street which I doubt I could find again if I tried. Maybe that's why it was chosen. I couldn't work out if it was a soup kitchen, a drop-in centre or perhaps a community centre. It was full of groups of men laughing and joking, their worn faces and clothes telling another story.

When I finally found Mr M, he was sitting in a quiet room with a younger man, his friend, who was there to interpret for us. Both were dark-haired and darker-skinned, the younger friend in his early thirties and I'd guess a hit with the local ladies. Mr M was older, probably mid to late forties, with a kind but exhausted face. He appeared at ease and delighted to meet me. I could see no outward sign of trauma or distress, unlike Elena. He seemed to be almost grateful to be in the situation he was in now – grateful I'd come to talk to him, grateful for his new life, grateful for the support he'd had, and the community he'd found within his local church.

When we settled down to talk I was a little concerned about the language barrier. He is Slovakian with basic English, and I was worried some of the nuances would get lost in translation. I hoped his friend would step in if I got stuck.

The first thing I was keen to establish was how he was now, if he felt he was on the road to recovery.

'Yes, I'm fine, thank you. I'm happy because I'm home.' He was beaming as he spoke, and laughed with contentment. 'I like it here, I start new life! Jesus give me new life here and new family. I'm happy here. Here this country is not dangerous. Because my country is dangerous, very dangerous.'

I asked him how he met the man who'd brought him to the UK.

'This man, he live in my country, in my city. I meet him at church. Before this I had no money because I came out of prison. I had no money, no anything. He asks me if I need job. "You looking for job?" Yes, I tell him, and he gives me . . .'

Mr M was struggling for the right word, and his friend intervened. I can't tell now, from the recording, if he said 'help' or 'hope', but either version is chilling.

'I was very happy because he tells me it's good money, good job, not a hard job. I was happy!'

76

It sounded as if the man who targeted Mr M already lived in the UK and had established work contacts here, as Mr M knew the UK was to be his destination.

'Job was very important to me, because I have family, children. No money, no good life. And he promised me job. Job and new life, very important.'

At this point my questions seemed to become slightly confusing for Mr M, until his friend pointed out I have a Manchester accent, which is why it was harder for him to understand me. His guess was forty miles out but I was impressed that this young lad had a better grip on regional accents than most people I meet in London.

'In the beginning I was promised I'm living with him and his family. And after he promise me my family will come here. And then new everything, new life for me.'

It sounded as if he was deliberately given somewhere nice to stay in order to convince him moving his family here was a good option.

'The first time [beginning] was very good. He knows about my family, my family knows I'm here, and with him, is good. I'm happy, good job. No problem.'

We got onto the subject of the 'job' he came to do. At first he was put to work in a car wash, but then it was a stream of different factories – mainly processing meat and rice. Then he became a driver.

'He had too many people. I had driving licence. It was very important for him. I pick up him, his people, to airport and back. For him it's very dangerous, everywhere here there is cameras. For the first time he's happy with me.'

I asked if he got paid for this work. He heaved a deep sigh.

'Yes. But. First time I come here, he tell me, "You debt [owe] me money because I buy for you transport, I give you food, money for your family, passport and everything". First time he give me £20 for week. That's it. After it's same situation. One week he give me just £5. No good! For the first month I did not work. First time, first month I speak every day with him, "I need here my family. Please help me". For one month.'

At some point after this Mr M's family did arrive. 'My family in my country – no money, no eat, children are small. I am happy because here good job, good life.'

I tried to establish at what point, once his family had joined him, Mr M realised things were not getting any better. Mr M said it was a complicated situation. Then he spoke directly to his friend, who translated his words back to me.

'After, comes my family, and after, changed *every situation*. My documents, taken off [here he snatched his hand away to demonstrate his papers disappearing] and after everything changed. Maybe two months is good, then it changed.'

Mr M stressed that it was very important to his trafficker from the beginning that he had a family. That he knew what he was doing. He appeared to be caring, in order to win over the support of Mr M's wife, and the manipulation started subtly and carefully. It sounded as if the trafficker was pleasant in the early days in order to get more money from Mr M, and to lure his family into the deception.

Looking back, Mr M suspected the trafficker planned to bring the family to the UK purely to claim benefits. Before he lived here, he didn't know what benefits were so wasn't aware that it was a ploy used to trick families. The trafficker even implied that bringing Mr M's family here was an inconvenience to him.

His friend translated: 'The most important thing about the whole situation is that the trafficker wanted to get me into a place where I was really, really happy that my family was here, even though it wasn't difficult to bring them in.'

After this exchange of complex information, Mr M's friend put his head in his hands and sighed. I apologised for how complicated the interpretation had become, and asked if he needed a break.

'No, it's not about that. It's the story. How people could have . . .' He fell silent, dropping back in his seat. Then he and Mr M began speaking again, and the younger man told me it was really important for Mr M that I told his story to others. He wanted to make it clear to the public how trafficking gangs work, and how victims are treated.

'These people work in dark shadows,' he said. 'They have amazing methods to manipulate people.'

I broached the subject of abuse with Mr M, asking him if he was beaten or physically hurt.

'Not me, but they did to different people. I see it every day. But to him I was very important. He knew me. I was for him very important. I am driver. Every day, every day physical. But I was different to them. These people were alcoholic, homeless.'

Mr M told me the name of the town he was living in at the time. It was an ordinary town, and this reminded me once more that this isn't just a problem for big cities. Despite the difficulties with translation, the picture of Mr M's life under the trafficker was becoming clearer. I was trying to get an indication from him of how large the operation was.

'There were four houses. All the people on the job. I'm living with him. Other people living in different place. One house here, one house there. All people – human trafficking.'

'How many people in total?' I asked.

'Too much, too much. Maybe forty-five. One month, January, forty-five. In March, sixty.'

I assumed that at this point the operation was growing month on month, but as Mr M went on talking, I began to wonder if the trafficker brought victims in, got what he needed from them, then sent them back.

'Every week I transport . . . change. Airport and back – new people. Every time change. One week, first job is mobile phone, credit card, benefits – he go home. No need for you. Every time change, new people, new people, new people.'

I felt I had to ask him how he felt knowing that he was transporting people to this new life, knowing what awaited them. While Mr M was a victim too, he struck me as the sort of man who would have struggled with this role. His answer was very clear. He

was comforted by the fact that these people would be here tempo-
rarily and would get to go home, but also he feared for his family.
Although I didn't want to ask him this, I felt I needed to hear
directly from him why, with access to a car, he didn't leave.

He may have had a car, but the trafficker had the family's passports, and someone in the gang was always at home with his wife
and kids, watching them. They also made sure that at least one
child was always in the house – ensuring the rest couldn't leave.

I couldn't imagine how Mr M remained so composed, so I
asked him about his feelings towards the trafficker.

'It was hell on earth. All I could think about in my mind, in my
sleep, was my children. This situation was not about me. Every
night I think of the children. I know what he [the trafficker] was.
My job was a dangerous job. I am not happy for two years. It's very
hard. The situation finish[ed being] about me. The situation is
about my children.'

We then turned to how he made his escape. It began with
devastating news from home. He heard his father had died.

'Something inside me happened. My feelings were different. I
stopped doing anything for that person. My father to me was
everything. Everything.'

The trafficker, seeing that Mr M was now resisting his threats,
realised he would not be manipulated any more and bought the
family tickets to Slovakia for the funeral – but on one condition:
Mr M had to return to the UK afterwards. His family returned
to Slovakia with him, but after the funeral, Mr M agreed only to
return to the UK if his family could stay in their home country. He
might be travelling back into his life of slavery, but he had at least
released his family.

We took a break from the conversation at this point. I was
struggling to keep my emotions in check, and Mr M's friend
needed a moment to compose himself, telling me he was shocked,
as it was the first time he'd heard this part of the story.

When Mr M began speaking again, he explained that he wanted
to come back to the UK as he was aware of all the other men still

living there and under the control of the trafficker. He knew he had the potential to help them because of his position within the trafficker's organisation.

'I was here three more months without my family. I was praying as I didn't want to see the break-up [of my family]. I believe God listened to my prayer.'

In a karmic twist of fate, not long after Mr M returned to the UK without his family, there was then a death in the trafficker's family. He left the UK to attend the funeral in Slovakia, and put Mr M in charge of the operation while he was away. During that time, Mr M was able to break into the trafficker's room, and steal back his own documents. He then went to the four houses where he knew the other trafficking victims were and told them he would come back to get them. He didn't know at the time how he would do that, but he promised.

Months earlier, Mr M had been in contact with a friend from Slovakia, via Facebook. When Mr M described what had happened to him, the friend, who was aware of the work of The Salvation Army, knew what Mr M was describing was human trafficking. This friend now offered to get his contact, a Salvation Army officer called Kathryn, to call Mr M. Kathryn did call, and told Mr M they were there to help. He didn't know anything about the people who were offering to help him, but admitted, 'They were my only hope.'

'She asked me, "How are you?" It was very important to me. I was under stress. I was not thinking. Imagine. Someone calls you and asks you if you're all right. So I say, yes, now I am ok. This moment give me power. I say yes, this moment, now I go. My family is home, they're ok, but these people here, not ok.'

After that first call from The Salvation Army, and the subsequent acceptance of help from Mr M, the police were called. The houses were raided, with the other victims rescued. The Salvation Army arranged to meet Mr M in a safe location which he could get to quickly and safely – a supermarket on the outskirts of town. He took the car and drove, where he was met by two Salvation Army

First Responders, and taken to a safe house. 'Then I speak with police.'

He spent a few days in the town, but was then moved to a different city, then the safe house on the other side of the country.

Mr M described his first meeting with the First Responder, giving his 'testimony', as he called it.

'I sit with the lady. The translator. After fifteen minutes it's too much. I cry. I'm crying. I don't know why! This story, not just for me but for every people, is very hard. Because this is true. This is my life. Seven years, very hard, my life.'

Mr M was in the care of The Salvation Army for around seven months. He told me that the lady who reached out to him initially called him every day, and every day asked him, "Are you ok?". This clearly meant the world to him, a simple phrase most of us use daily without thinking of its impact on those we're asking.

Mr M began to talk about his first day of pure freedom, with no police and no Salvation Army support. He started speaking passionately about the new life he intended to start that day. Jubilantly he left the safe house, and travelled back to a city nearer to where he'd been living for so long – but not back to the same town. But by the end of the day he found himself face to face with one of his traffickers.

He had gone to a meet-up with other people from Slovakia, and one of the gang was also there. 'Same day!' he yelled. 'Same day! No!'

Mr M ran out of the building and called his Salvation Army support worker. He was helped to move immediately to an entirely different location. This was where he had been for several years, and he seemed to have reached contentment.

'Now I know this is good. Jesus gives me this. I want to tell people. I want to help people. This story will maybe help situation in England, and everywhere. Every day God spoke with me. "Wait. Wait. One day". Every day I see my child crying, and God say, "Wait, wait, I give you time". Now I believe Jesus is alive. He helped me.'

I asked Mr M if he was afraid his trafficker would ever track him down.

'No,' he replied. 'Now, no.'

Years after his ordeal, Mr M was settled in a new relationship with more children, and the children he last saw in Slovakia had been reunited with him. He had a job and a future, and was still being informally supported by The Salvation Army.

'I feel here, this is my home. It's a new life and I know it will be ok.'

7

SLAVERY ON OUR STREETS

It's not often I'm invited to the House of Commons. Certainly not through the politically tempestuous spring of 2019, as the Brexit debacle raged on, the world's media was camped outside in College Green, and Westminster was awash with protestors waving either UKIP or EU flags.

It was thanks to the kind invitation of Wales's Anti-Slavery Co-ordinator Stephen Chapman that I was walking through security ready to attend the Modern Slavery Helpline Annual Assessment. Key figures in the fight against slavery – from police officers to MPs, heads of NGOs to academics – had come to listen to the findings of twelve months in the life of the Modern Slavery Helpline, run by the charity Unseen.

A terrace in Parliament might be a gloriously traditional location for sandwiches and cakes and debate, but the topic we were there to discuss was a world away. The Modern Slavery Helpline has been answering calls from concerned members of the public, activists, health and legal professionals, even the police, as well as from slavery victims themselves, since October 2016. Today, I was about to find out what the data collected by the Modern Slavery Helpline could tell us about slavery in the UK for the year 2018.

It makes for tough reading.

The report states that during 2018 the Helpline received over 7405 calls and contacts from across the UK, as well as 38 other countries. These contacts reported modern slavery instances across

England, Scotland, North Ireland and Wales, and in 57 countries outside of the UK. The number of modern slavery cases raised was 1,849, and 2,281 referrals were sent to law enforcement, support services or some form of safeguarding team. Around 46% of potential victims were male, 21% female, 33% unknown and 0.04% transgender. A staggering 94 different nationalities were recorded (of potential victims).

Labour exploitation was the most prevalent form of slavery reported to the Helpline, with 990 cases reported, making up 54% of slavery cases. The top five sectors for labour exploitation were car washes, beauty/spa, construction, hospitality then agriculture and farming. In 47% of these cases a bogus job ad was used as a recruitment tactic. In sexual exploitation, 89% of potential victims were female, and the top race/ethnicity was Asian then White Caucasian. The top three methods of control were sexual abuse, isolation and physical abuse.

Looking at the picture for criminal exploitation, 77% of potential victims relating to the handling of drugs were male, with drugs and begging the top two most common forms. 9% of victims were reported to be minors. The most common age bracket for *all* potential victims was 18–24. The five most common nationalities were people from Romania, Vietnam, England, Poland and Bulgaria.

The statistics on Domestic Servitude were enlightening. While it is one of the most secretive forms of slavery, it is the area in which a greater proportion of victims themselves call the Helpline – 17% of domestic servitude cases versus 11% for the other types of exploitation. Data also showed emerging trends from 2018, such as an increase in recorded cases relating to churches or religious sites as areas for potential recruitment of potential victims, plus a (cautious) increase in cases around working in waste and recycling sites.

The data also reveals information on the 2,171 potential exploiters. Seventy different nationalities were reported, with over 1,000 exploiters being defined as the employer of the victim; 157 had a familial link, and 108 exploiters were the 'intimate partner' of a victim – most notably in sexual exploitation.

A year earlier, in 2018, the Gangmasters and Labour Abuse Authority had produced a report exploring the nature and scale of labour exploitation around the UK, and identifying the UK as 'one of the main destinations of trafficked workers in Europe'. It also broke down regional trends throughout the UK.

In Northern Ireland, for example, GLAA intelligence showed that potential victims are most frequently recorded as working in the Poultry and Eggs sector. In Scotland, the nationalities identified as potential victims of labour exploitation were most frequently Vietnamese (47%), followed by Chinese and Sudanese. Where the GLAA intelligence for Scotland showed that potential victims were most frequently recorded as working in agriculture, in Wales potential victims were most frequently recorded as working in the shellfish-gathering sector.

In 2019, the homelessness charity The Passage released its Modern Slavery Handbook, designed to highlight how trafficking and slavery presents itself in the homeless community. Its work in the area has been well known, especially since in 2017 it published a report, commissioned by the then Anti-Slavery Commissioner Kevin Hyland OBE, on the links between the vulnerable homeless community and the traffickers targeting them.

In their report, 'Understanding and Responding to Modern Slavery within the Homelessness Sector'[1], it is stated:

The potential link between homelessness and modern slavery is evident from two angles. Homeless people are vulnerable to being tracked or held as victims of modern slavery by virtue of being homeless and having associated support needs (such

---

1 'Understanding and Responding to Modern Slavery within the Homelessness Sector' is a report from The Passage, commissioned by the Independent Anti-Slavery Commissioner, published January 2017

as alcohol or drug misuse and mental health issues), that can impair their judgement or ability to protect themselves. Alternatively, victims of modern slavery are vulnerable to becoming homeless since they do not have support networks and have nowhere to go after they leave safe-house support provision.

The report also highlighted two cases where such victims were targeted. In 2011, twenty-four men, recruited while homeless or in the dole queue, were released from a caravan site in Leighton Buzzard where they had been held in a 'state of virtual slavery', some for up to fifteen years. The following year, James John Connors and Josie Connors, travellers from Bedfordshire, were convicted of two counts each of keeping people in servitude and forcing them to work. The court heard how they 'brutally manipulated and exploited' destitute men. The pair were jailed for eleven years and four years respectively, and in the sentencing remarks of HHJ Michael Kay QC, he stated 'the homeless, addicted and isolated men who sleep rough and beg on the streets were potential workers who could be exploited for financial gain'.

Another high-profile case which made headlines around the UK was that of the Rooney family, when in 2017 eleven members of the same traveller family were jailed for a total of 79 years. They had been running a driveway resurfacing company in the Lincolnshire area, and targeted vulnerable men from the streets and from hostels and shelters. Many were homeless, while others had learning difficulties or addiction issues. One victim had lost twenty-six years of his life to their cruelty.

Calls to the Helpline 'demonstrated significant links between homelessness and modern slavery' with 'English victims the most common among homeless people recruited into exploitation'. Over 350 potential victims were homeless either before, during or after they escaped from exploitation, and were involved in 276 cases of modern slavery, comprising 7% of all modern slavery cases reported.

The report found traffickers target homeless people for exploitation, with labour exploitation most common. Locations of recruitment included homeless shelters, and public spaces such as streets and parks. Victims were then forced to commit crimes for their exploiters, mainly forced begging.

After hearing so much about the work of the Modern Slavery Helpline, how it acts as a conduit between concerned members of the public and potentially the authorities, as well as being contacted by victims themselves, I was keen to meet the team who field the calls. I wanted to hear from those who were likely to have a daily impression of the scale of slavery on the streets of the UK.

Once permission was granted for me to visit such a sensitive location, I was expecting to receive the address of a London HQ, or perhaps a major city elsewhere in the UK. I was wrong.

The Helpline is based in an anonymous village, well away from the buzz of city life. It could not be based in a location more at odds with the image of the work it does. With a tiny train station, quaint pubs and a bustling market square, this village seems somewhere I'm more likely to bump into Miss Marple than to have a brush with human trafficking. However, tucked away behind the obvious affluence is a building which holds twenty staff and is often the first port of call for anyone who has concerns about potential victims.

In February 2019, one of those tip-offs led to a couple from Bristol being found guilty of slavery offences after keeping the victim in a cupboard under their stairs. Ion Boboc and Christiana Tudor-Dobre were convicted of requiring a person to perform forced labour, and fraud, and were exposed after a concerned neighbour called the Helpline.

The couple controlled their victim's finances, stopped him from eating or drinking in the house, made him use a hosepipe in the backyard for drinking water and forced him to use the wood when he needed the toilet. When the police discovered him, he had been living and sleeping under the stairs 'like

Harry Potter', while all his documents were found in the couple's bedroom.

During the case, it emerged the victim worked full-time earning around £300 a week, but was given money only for his bus fare, £1 a day for biscuits and £10 a week for cannabis. The officer on the case thanked the anonymous member of the public for calling the Helpline, saying without that information the victim would still be being abused. In April 2019, Boboc was sentenced to four years two months in prison, while Tudor-Dobre received three years seven months. Both were issued with Slavery and Trafficking Prevention Orders.

Though the team at the Helpline allowed me to visit the premises and speak to call handlers, due to the sensitive nature of the calls it was agreed this would be carried out discreetly and for as brief a time as possible. I was met by Rachel Harper, the warm and engaging manager of the Helpline. As she's from the US, it made me smile that she now found herself tucked away in such a quintessentially British location.

She explained how the Helpline had grown in the last few years.

'Since the launch in October 2016, Helpline calls have continued to increase steadily from about 50 calls in the first week to about 170 calls per week on average in July 2019. In the first quarter of operations, the Helpline opened about 350 cases, while in quarter two of 2019, 1,750 cases were created.

'Since 2016, the Helpline team has almost doubled. Webforms have been developed, and in July 2018, the Helpline launched the Unseen app with direct channelling to report into the Helpline and guidance about signs of exploitation. Collaboration and visibility have significantly grown. The Helpline team began by introducing its project and remit to key stakeholders over the phone when establishing bespoke referral routes into police forces or Local Authorities. Now it's the key call to action for many local and national awareness campaigns running simultaneously. Additionally, the Helpline also supports a business portal, to better collaborate with businesses on cases that might indicate exploitation in their supply chains.'

I tucked myself away in a meeting room and was soon joined by Thomas, one of the Helpline supervisors. He explained that while most calls can come from the public, from lawyers, businesses, Local Authorities and even the police, some do come from victims.

'I believe about 10% of calls are from victims themselves. To try to help someone in that situation, we take a victim-centred approach. From our perspective that means – assuming the caller is an adult, as there are different rules if it's a child – we try to find out what help they want. We ask them about their situation, explore with them the options of help, perhaps getting the police to go in and extract them from the situation. Occasionally they are leaving a situation *right now*, and they want advice around safety planning. Other times they may just want to talk and tell you about the situation they're in, but they're not yet ready to leave that situation.

'In that case it could be about agreeing things with them to help them get through their day, and agreeing times for them to call you back when it's safe for them. If they have a window in which it's safe for them to call you, then you can say, "We won't take any action now as we respect it could make things worse for you, and you don't want that, but in a week's time you'll call us and we'll talk about it further". There was one case where we were in communication with someone for three or four months until that person was ready to be extracted.'

The training to become a Helpline Advisor is intense: a ninety-minute interview with a role play, then five weeks of training (including being schooled in legislation and how to protect themselves from the secondary trauma of the job) and a final test, before being allowed to handle the calls and webforms which inundate the team weekly.

I then spoke to Katie, one of the newer recruits, and asked her about the emotional toll of dealing with calls and if, despite the training, she found herself distressed by them.

91

'Yes,' she answered immediately. 'What you're hearing is over-whelmingly upsetting. It can also be confusing, because you don't know what the caller is going to say, you don't have all the infor-mation, and there can be so *much* information – especially on an interpreter call.

'What's more concerning is if the caller is a victim and they're not giving you all the information you require. They can tell you they were trafficked from Libya to so-and-so, and you're trying to get those hard facts, but it's really difficult when they're reluctant to speak or they don't understand what you're asking them.'

Though the team are trained in how to look after their own emotional well-being, it seems they're equally supportive of each other, as Katie explained.

'I'm somebody who's quite warm and I want to help people, and that includes my colleagues. So having that support is really important. To be able to say "I've had a really bad call, I just need to take five minutes out". It's so important to have a really good team around you, which we do.'

It's clear there are big plans ahead for the Helpline, as Rachel explained.

'The Helpline plans to continue providing expert advice regard-ing options and offering support to those who may be suffering exploitation, as well as receiving tip-offs confidentially from members of the public and supporting front-line professionals. The Helpline will also continue to review its extensive data and publish reports in order to influence society, enabling better informed responses. Next steps include expanding the ways people can access the Helpline. The team are also working with key technology support groups to make best use of technological advancements to identify trends in the data and serve those in need.'

After spending a couple of hours with the Modern Slavery Helpline team, I was keen to meet the founder of the charity which created it – Andrew Wallis OBE. Justine Currell, a director of Unseen and the woman who launched the Modern Slavery Helpline, joined us by phone. Both were key contributors to the creation of the Modern Slavery Act.

Unseen is based in a part of Bristol which seems, at first glance, to have missed much of the gentrification of the city, but after a brief walk around I can see that the overpriced coffee bars and organic brownie stores are definitely creeping in between the sex shops and run-down charity shops.

I was greeted at the office by Andrew, the tall, friendly but intimidatingly intelligent CEO, and he talked me through the early days of Unseen. Launched eleven years ago, partly in response to a conversation Andrew had had with a police officer regarding the need for housing provision for victims in Bristol, Unseen began by securing the funding to set up the first safe house. But it was an 'apocryphal' meeting Andrew attended at SOCA (Serious Organised Crime Agency – the predecessor of today's NCA) in Birmingham which really shaped its future.

'We had NGOs, Police, Government, SOCA and so on, all sitting in a room talking about how we share data and intelligence in order to understand the issues. It just turned into a shouting match, as nobody trusted each other. Nobody was prepared to share data. I came out of that thinking, we've lost sight of what we're trying to do.

'So from day one with Unseen, it wasn't just about safe housing, it was how do we stop slavery in the first place? If all you do is provide safe housing then you're just accepting the status quo. You're accepting that bad things happen. That's how Unseen started, and then from there we became more engaged with policing and SOCA, then the Home Office.'

In 2011, Andrew was asked to chair the Centre for Social Justice's report *It Happens Here* (a two-year review into the UK's response to modern slavery). At the same time Justine joined the Home Office to work on anti-slavery policy. Shortly after-wards, they were both working on the creation of the Modern Slavery Act.

As Andrew explained, 'We were engaged from outside the Home Office to work on the Act, and Justine drafted the Act inside the Home Office.'

Justine took up the story.

'I was a Senior Policy Advisor in the Home Office. I transferred from the policing side to take forward work around human trafficking. This was prior to the Modern Slavery Bill. We had the CSJ report, and the Prime Minister at the time, David Cameron, promised legislation. The Home Secretary at the time, Theresa May, said the Home Office would take it on. I was given the task of drafting the bill, and I had only one other person working with me then, so it was a little bit of a "blimey" moment.

'As a Senior Policy Advisor you must identify not only what you think needs to go in the bill, but who you should engage with, and how you will engage with them. That includes a range of "vociferous stakeholders" – the NGO sector, the range of Government departments involved, such as the Ministry of Justice, on occasion the Department of Education, and of course Business, Innovation and Skills as it was at the time. It also included SOCA, which turned into NCA, the Border Force and colleagues within the Home Office. You start to pull together a plan of what you want in, who you want to talk to, what the proposal is and how you think you might get there.

'Then there's a lot of negotiation with the Home Secretary, senior and junior ministers and then a wider range of politicians they want to bring in. They were talking to Frank Field and others.

'We had three months to develop a draft Act. A lot of the stuff that I proposed initially wasn't in that first draft. I had about seventeen areas in mind, many of them referenced in the CSJ report, but there were very clear steers from ministers about what they did and didn't want.

'For all of us working on the Bill, there was a clear consensus that something needed to happen. The Commissioner had to have greater powers and we wanted more on victim support, but there's always a negotiation process. We didn't get Transparency in

Supply Chains in when we first introduced it, it took me another three or four months to get Number 10 to agree to that, and for Business, Innovation and Skills to be on the same page. That provision in particular took a lot more negotiating than many of the others.'

Andrew added, 'What you've heard from Justine is that there was a lot of horse trading. We were limited in time from when the report came out in 2013, as we were on a Fixed Term Parliament. Given we were not going to achieve perfection, we had to decide what, pragmatically, we could get in. We saw a real opportunity for the UK to lead here again, and that was said clearly in the CSJ report, so the politicians jumped on that.

'It was ironic. The only thing that makes the UK legislation world-leading is Section 54 (Transparency in Supply Chains), so that's why politicians now talk about "world-leading legislation". Take Section 54 out of it, it's not world-leading in any shape or form. But what it has done is shift the agenda, because modern slavery is an emotive term. It enabled Policing to know better what they were dealing with, as the legislation had been expanded, but was now all in one place. The media had an easier hook to use. Politicians had something easier to hang it on. Businesses were able to say, "We don't want to be associated with that". They under-stood the issue of forced labour within supply chains.

'Modern Slavery is not a technical term. It's an umbrella term. The Achilles heel of that umbrella term is that it's getting stretched and stretched. There's a danger it becomes too broad. But the Act definitely shifted things.'

Considering the knowledge and understanding Andrew and Justine have built up over the last ten years, I asked them what they considered to be the scale of slavery on the streets of Britain.

Andrew was unequivocal. 'Anyone who says they can give you a definitive number is lying. The only reliable figures we do have are the NRM figures. What we haven't got is a baseline that helps us know whether the numbers are rising or falling. How do you quantify a hidden crime? My view is that you're chasing the end of a rainbow. You'll never get there.

'Whenever every police force can say, hand on heart, they're actively looking for it everywhere, all the time and all their officers are trained, and you can say the same of all the other blue light agencies, *and* you've got a level of understanding among the general population, *and* they know what to do when they see it – when those indicators are all in place, then you have the potential to know what the baseline is.'

8

THE COURT CASE

BIRMINGHAM, MAY 2019

It is a very strange thing, to come face to face with a trafficker.

As Ignacy Brzezinski and Wojciech Nowakowski[1] walked into the courtroom, I realised that through all the time I have spent with survivors, the police and front-line charity workers, the actual perpetrators of this crime had, in my mind, become shadowy figures operating in secret, immune to the destruction and devastation they left behind them. Anonymous, widespread, and too great a force for me to even comprehend.

As part of Organised Crime Groups, or smaller more ad-hoc gangs, the men (for they are mainly men) who facilitate this £100 billion crime, would, I assumed, be physically intimidating, and somehow impressive. Their stature would match their cruelty. So when the small, scruffy, worn-looking men walked – or in one case limped – past me into the dock at Birmingham Crown Court, I was struck by how such weak-looking individuals could be behind the biggest case of modern slavery the UK has ever seen. Pathetic in appearance, yet responsible for the abuse of in excess of 300 victims.

I was in Birmingham to interview one of the UK's leading prosecutors of modern slavery. If you were ever to scroll through

---

1 Details of their convictions are laid out later in this chapter.

my journalist's notebooks, under the sections on human trafficking and modern slavery you'd see the name Caroline Haughey scribbled every ten pages or so. Police officers and those who work with victims have all told me, time and time again over the last few years, that I must meet her.

I could see why. One quick Google search of her credentials and a couple of YouTube videos later and I was straight on to her London chambers to arrange an interview. I was sceptical it would happen, but twenty-four hours later I got an email from Caroline herself, saying she'd be happy to be interviewed – and perhaps I'd like to do so in Birmingham while she prosecuted her current case.

Caroline collected me from a coffee shop across the road from the court, and she recognised me before I saw her. In my defence (Your Honour) she couldn't have looked less like my stereotypical image of a barrister. She was tiny, and though she was wearing smart black trousers, they were paired with a bright pink jumper. She was warm, incredibly modest about her achievements, and as apologetic about me coming to her as I was grateful to her for squeezing me into her schedule.

By the time we were in the courthouse, and she had been greeted with affection by every security guard in our path, she had explained that the case she and her 'brilliant' team were prosecuting was subject to reporting restrictions, and was the second of two cases she had been fighting. As the numbers of both victims and defendants was so large, there was no courtroom available to house all those involved in one trial. So the cases had been divided, and both were to be kept out of the public realm until the second trial had reached its conclusion.

As we reached the private rooms feet away from the court itself, which Caroline and her fellow barristers had used as a base for the previous nine months, I was reeling from the speed and amount of information I had been given.

Three hundred victims. Ninety-two willing to testify. Eight people standing trial.

The office was stacked with folder upon folder, box upon box, the walls decorated with posters listing names in different colours, clearly full of crucial information but at first glance meaning nothing to me.

Caroline had to zoom off to a brief meeting. While I was taking in my surroundings, the stylish pink jumper had been replaced with a barrister's white collar and Caroline switched from sassy coffee buddy to the image of her I'd seen online. I was then whisked out of the room until someone else could sit there with me. No chance of a journalist being allowed to stay unobserved with all the case material!

Before long I was back in the small room, joined by two more junior barristers and then two of the police officers who had investigated the case. They later told me it was such a huge operation it was the only case they'd worked on over the last four years. I was stunned that Caroline had the time or headspace to contemplate an interview during this period, so I sat as unobtrusively as possible, drinking coffee and hoping I wasn't getting in the way.

The day I was there didn't appear to be a normal trial day, with the jury, defendants and legal teams in a courtroom before the judge. Instead, the day seemed to be spent dealing with submissions on law, with all the relevant camps tucked away in their offices, then sweeping in and out of each other's workspaces, wearing gowns and referring to points of law, or very specific questions on certain individuals.

Caroline's more junior barristers appeared to be writing documents focusing on very detailed parts of the case, grilling the two police officers on addresses, timelines and details of the case.

From what I was told, I gathered that a gang had been recruiting men from a small village in Poland to come to the UK to work. It had been a constant, massive operation, going back years. Once in the UK, successive groups of 'workers' were taken to properties within the same few streets in Walsall and West Bromwich. One of the gang would then take the men to a local high street bank, and act as a friend and translator while setting up bank accounts on their behalf, using addresses controlled by the gang. They were then taken to a nearby recruitment agency, where they were set up on the system and were allocated jobs, with the traffickers going on to pocket all the money, and the victims living in absolute squalor. They also registered victims for national insurance and claimed benefits without their knowledge.

I asked one of the police officers about the role of the recruitment agency in this crime. Would they be culpable for their part in this? As it turned out, the agency had been infiltrated by one of the women involved with the gang, as to not arouse suspicion.

As is so often the case in modern slavery crimes, the victims were told they owed 'debts' for transport, rent and living expenses.

As I was talking to the team, a cryptic comment from another interviewee, Susan Banister from the charity Hope for Justice (see Chapter 17), suddenly made much more sense. I'd been to Manchester to meet her a few weeks before, and as we were wrapping up, she mentioned 'a huge case in the West Midlands' which she couldn't talk about, but which clearly meant a great deal to her. As I learned more about the operation, I realised it was Hope for Justice which had been at the centre of cracking open this entire case.

The victims had been living in such extreme poverty they were forced to rely on churches and soup kitchens to eat. It was in a soup kitchen that one of Hope for Justice's Community Outreach workers started to be suspicious. He was seeing countless men from the same area of Birmingham (who were also from the same villages in Poland) all supposedly working, yet living in squalor. Increasingly alarmed, he learned what he could about their lives, then reported to Hope for Justice. They alerted their West Midlands Investigations hub, before the police became involved in 2015. Hope for Justice later said that fifty-one victims eventually made contact as trust with more and more men was built up.

One trial had already taken place, with all the defendants being found guilty, including two women working in the recruitment agencies 'hiring' the men.

In the midst of the legal wranglings going on that day, Caroline managed to squeeze in some time to talk to me during lunch in her office, while taking calls and dealing with countless knocks at her door.

One of the reasons I was so keen to talk to her was because she had been at the forefront of Britain's fight against modern slavery, from prosecuting cases before the Modern Slavery Act came into being to contributing to the formation of the Act itself, and witnessing how the Crown Prosecution Service had evolved in the wake of this not-so-new crime.

According to statistics from the CPS from August 2018, and their first Modern Slavery Report, charges for modern slavery offences rose by more than a quarter between 2017 and 2018, with 239 suspects charged, a 27% rise from the previous year. Referrals to the CPS from police and other agencies rose by a third to 355, the highest ever recorded.

The Modern Slavery Police Transformation Annual Report of 2019, in its section on the Crown Prosecution Service, noted:

> During 2018, the number of modern slavery offences charged and prosecuted by the CPS was the highest it has ever been – at 399. The conviction rate remained at 65% which is within the average expected by the CPS. There was also a marked increase in the average number of victims giving evidence and being supported at court which is reflective of the greater complexity of these cases, and contributes to an increase in the length of time that trials take.

As I found a spot to sit in between piles and piles of boxes and folders on the case unfolding before me, Caroline settled down at her desk to answer my questions. She was alert (though I can't imagine she gets much sleep) and drinking from the travel cup which today didn't seem to be far from her grasp.

I began by asking her how she had become the go-to barrister for modern slavery cases. She was genuinely (and unsurprisingly) one of the most articulate people I'd ever met.

'I've always had an interest in this area. My thesis at university was on the decriminalisation of prostitution so I've always had an interest in looking at crime from a slightly holistic perspective, as opposed to a practitioner perspective. I certainly wouldn't describe myself as an academic, far from it, I am a "go to court" girl.'

In 2011, Caroline was asked to prosecute the UK's first-ever modern slavery case, of a pensioner accused of trafficking and exploiting an African woman she used as a slave. It wasn't the most straightforward case.

'We were stymied because we were limited to working just with the legislation in force at the time – slavery didn't exist in UK law. I relied on trafficking legislation. I could prosecute on how the victim got here, but not what happened to them when they were here. That was very difficult, and it made me frustrated. But that's the law and you have to do your best and work with what you've got. It was very challenging, but it also taught me that allowing someone to tell their story of what's been taken from them restores ownership of their lives, in part, and goes a long way to restoring their human dignity. The victim was a remarkable woman, and so thoroughly honest and good.

'The defendant – Saeeda Khan – was acquitted on appeal because the judge was dealing with difficult legislation, and the Court of Appeal disagreed with his interpretation. We went for a re-trial and the jury didn't buy it – because I couldn't prosecute what happened to the victim in this country, I could only prosecute the journey in, and that's very difficult. So I spoke very publicly, and on numerous occasions, on how the law should change.'

Not long after the Khan case, Caroline prosecuted Rebecca Balira, an HIV expert accused of keeping a woman as a slave. She was jailed for six months and ordered to pay the victim £3,000.

'That was the second-ever prosecution, August 2011. It snow-balled from there. I remember giving a lecture on a human rights report on trafficking, and someone asking me the question, "What did I want?" I said, "If I can have ten things, anything I want, then I'd like a collaborative Act. I want to change the law, first and foremost. I want the Government to stop making it acceptable to traffic people, because you only get fourteen years. And if you traffic a kilo of coke you get life. We're sending out the wrong message." I didn't realise that the person who asked the question was an advisor to Frank Field, who along with Baroness Butler-Sloss, had been asked to do an All Parliamentary Report on Modern Slavery.

'I assisted them with that. Then we had a meeting with the Home Secretary, Theresa May. She was clearly very engaged with this through a woman called Fiona Hill, a special advisor, who was in my view instrumental in this piece of legislation making the books. Theresa May was passionate about this, and particularly well briefed on it by Fiona. This was her policy and she really pushed it, and it was a game changer within the UK, even the world. Whatever else her legacy may be, she can go to her grave truly proud of this.'

Caroline was then invited to make observations on the drafting of the Modern Slavery Act, which came into being on 31st July 2015.

'I was still in contact with the Home Office at the time, who were always asking me, "How is this going? You've been doing cases under it, what are your thoughts on this? Is it working?" So there was keen interest from the Home Office, and passion in ensuring that it was fit for purpose.'

Despite the praise the Modern Slavery Act won here and abroad, one of the main criticisms has been the relatively low number of prosecutions considering the bespoke legislation. I asked Caroline if the length of time cases took to get to court had an impact. She agreed.

'People are frightened by new law and how to use it. As a concept it's pretty alien to think that in the twenty-first century people are kept as slaves. It's hidden in plain sight. A drug is a drug is a drug, you can't pretend it's anything other than it is. But you can hide a victim in plain sight, and that makes prosecutions challenging.

'Often complainants do not want to acknowledge that they have been de-humanised into a slave because it's shameful. Many of them have mental health problems or addictions which is why they were exploited in the first place, because they were vulnerable. So, I understand and am sympathetic to that, but I think there is, on occasion, a failure to understand why that comes about. Perhaps I do get to see that as I am one of the individuals among many who has to make decisions as to who to prosecute and when.

'The tragedy of this all is there are 42 million people, it's understood, who are the victims of exploitation – be it sexual or labour – and trafficking in the world. That's the combined population of Tokyo, London and New York. If I said that they were the victims of terrorism, people would have a very different view. This is a very unpopular, unsavoury form of offending. But it could happen to any one of us. It's not about social class. It's not about poverty. It's not about which side of the blanket you were born on. If you are vulnerable you are at risk. And that vulnerability can manifest itself in so many ways.

'I think it's one of the greatest achievements in my life to be a part of this, and it's been a privilege to see the evolution of a piece of legislation that's protecting people.'

Though there was no doubt that the birth of the Modern Slavery Act solidified the UK's response to the crime, I was still disturbed by victims facing arrest, or being sent to detention centres.

'I think we are getting better at this, and I think people forget it's not the fault of the police if they don't identify someone, because if they don't self-identify it's very hard to engage with them. One of the mechanisms by which exploitation of non-British citizens happens is by saying to them, "You can't trust the police here, they're like our police back wherever we're from. You can't

104

walk outside the house without your ID card, you'll be taken and put in a holding centre and you'll be arrested and deported".

'They use fear and lack of knowledge as one of their means of control. When someone is recovered, it takes them a long time to engage with the police process. So, I don't think any blame can be laid with the police.'

We began to touch on the case Caroline was in Birmingham to prosecute. I was trying to get an idea of when in the process someone in her role would become involved.

'It depends. Some of the cases have already been investigated and charges laid so I'm instructed to prosecute the case. On this case I was brought in very early to decide whether it merited further investigation. I've been involved with this since October 2015 so it's been four years in the making. It needed it; this is enormous.'

We were interrupted as the food from the local coffee shop arrived, but Caroline was happy to stay in her office to carry on talking. I asked her how hard it was to switch off from what she was seeing every day.

'It gets under your skin. You can never turn this off, but you have to do your best. I've heard stories that horrify me. In ways I can't tell you. I've had complainants give evidence about being locked in a room for six months, raped orally, vaginally and digitally every day by the same man. I've seen the conditions in which human beings are being kept. Dogs are treated better. I've seen the desperation of a human being who just wants to make their life better and do their best for their family, to pay for a heart transplant for their daughter, to earn a living. Not one single complainant in any of the cases I've done, and I must have dealt with hundreds upon hundreds of complainants, ever came here to milk the system. Ever. All they wanted to do was do a job and get paid for it. And I think we're all entitled to that.

'What horrifies me is the scant regard for a fellow man by another human being. If I can make things better for other people then it's my responsibility to do so.'

One of the things which makes a prosecutor's job so hard, and can be a factor in the speed (or perceived lack of) convictions, is the issue of victims not wanting to testify. I asked Caroline how hard it was to work on a victimless prosecution.

'My priority is the safeguarding of the complainant. If a victim says they don't want to do it, but they're safe, then 90% of my job is done. I have to deal with it on a case-by-case basis. I have done victimless prosecutions. It's really hard, but you have to look at all the lines of evidence. The evidence in trafficking cases and exploitation cases is as much about what is *not* in existence as what *is*. If I google my name, I have a digital footprint. These people don't. They don't have access to Facebook. They don't have medical records. You start peeling away the layers of their existence, and that's often the indicator. You can show things; you can paint a picture.

'In my closing speech in Operation Field, which was a Vietnamese case, I said to the jury, "Members of the jury, when these young women were searched, when they were found in the nail bar, the entire sum of their possessions was a purse with a sanitary pad in it and a bus ticket. Look in your own wallets and what do you have?"'

When I asked Caroline about the scale of modern slavery in the UK, and if she had ever got to the point of being shocked by what she heard, she answered immediately.

'This has shocked me. This case has shocked me by its volume, by its inherent sophistication, by its reach. This is an Organised Crime Gang who happened to be predominantly one family, but whose tentacles and reach are extraordinary. We've got at least 300 people. We had a witness from Hope for Justice who said the homelessness in his area dropped by 80% when this case was investigated. So when they started making arrests in Operation Fort [the Brzezinski/Nowakowski case], the number of homeless people visiting him dropped by 80%.'

Having been in the courtroom earlier that day, face to face with the traffickers, I told Caroline how surprisingly unobtrusive and unimpressive I thought these gang leaders actually were.

'They're human, and they have human frailties. I'm sure in parts of their life they could be good people. But not in the treatment of their fellow man. I'm interested in human beings – the who and the what. But the why is just as important. As far as the defendants are concerned, for me they are simply a case. It's not personal. It's never personal. Once it's personal you've lost sight of the real world.'

I wanted to know, considering how many cases Caroline had been involved in, if she thought there was any such thing as a typical perpetrator. Her answer surprised me.

'No, but more women commit this crime in my experience than any other. Every single indictment I have done, there has been a woman in the indictment. Often key, or second or third down the chain. That's unusual.'

Considering Caroline has witnessed the entire spectrum of cruelty that man can inflict on his fellow human, I asked if there was anything that still got to her.

'Yes, the rapes. Sexual violation. Of course I know it goes on. But when you cross-examine the person who does it, and their response is so . . .' she paused for a long moment, and sighed, '. . . indifferent . . . that I find difficult. That I find very difficult. There are some very nasty people out there, profoundly evil people whose arrogance and greed enables them to, without remorse, sneer at, degrade and own and keep the lives of others.

'I've always said this kind of behaviour is tantamount to murder, without stopping their breath. I don't understand that. But my job is to be the conduit for the evidence.'

During the time the Birmingham case was being investigated, a number of other UK prosecutions were achieved.

Lanarkshire
In Lanarkshire, Scotland, a five-week trial in 2018 saw three men from a Gypsy Traveller family found guilty of 'abduction, violence and intimidation' against men who worked for them. The court

heard how Robert McPhee, his son-in-law John Miller and James McPhee preyed on eight vulnerable men from troubled backgrounds. The victims were promised work but received little or no pay. One told how he was battered and 'taught a lesson' when he tried to get away. One lived in a caravan with no water or toilet, another was 'left cowering like a dog' due to the abuse. McPhee, Miller and McPhee were found guilty of more than twenty charges between them, dating from 1992 to 2016. They, plus another man who pleaded guilty, were jailed for a total of 29 years.

Belfast

In 2018, two Romanian brothers were jailed for trafficking and controlling prostitutes in Belfast, in a landmark case for Northern Ireland. It was the first conviction and sentencing for a human trafficking for sexual exploitation offence in Northern Ireland, and also the first human trafficking conviction in Northern Ireland where the victims did not have to provide any evidence as part of the investigation.

Decebal and Spartacus Mihai were accused of being part of an 'extensive' UK-wide criminal operation, and after pleading guilty were sentenced to four years and three years respectively. The female victims were in their late teens, and the judge said they were 'vulnerable and isolated because of their limited grasp of the English language'.

DCI Mark Bell of PSNI (Police Service Northern Ireland) said, 'Victims of human trafficking experience the most horrific of ordeals. Their captors subject them to a degrading life which violates their human rights and denies them their rights to life, freedom and safety.'

Glasgow

In October 2019, four people were found guilty of trafficking women from Slovakia to Glasgow – with one victim sold for £10,000 on Argyle Street. Women were forced into prostitution and sham marriages, after being moved into flats in Govanhill over a six-year period. Vojtech Gombar, Anil Wagle, Jana Sandorova and Ratislav Adam were caught after a five-year police operation. Officers described the crimes as 'despicable'.

London

In June 2018, the case of London-based Josephine Iyamu made headlines around the world, after the British nurse was convicted in Birmingham of trafficking Nigerian women to Germany in order to work as prostitutes. She subjected them to 'voodoo' rituals, making the women hand over money to her during 'juju' ceremonies – an act designed to terrify the victims and give her complete control. She was jailed for fourteen years and was the first British National prosecuted under the Modern Slavery Act for trafficking victims from *outside* the UK.

Ilford, Essex

In June 2019, three men from a Romanian organised crime group were given sentences of 28 years for modern slavery and Proceeds of Crime Act offences. Valentin Lupu, 25, Grigore Lupu, 39, and Alexandru Lupu, 43, worked with other (unknown) gang members, trafficking victims into the UK to exploit them within the construction industry. Thirty-three potential victims of human trafficking (twenty-four men, four women, and five children) were recovered from four London addresses and taken into safety. The Lupus made more than £1.2 million in the three years they were active, in an operation which was busted by a Joint Investigation Team made up of the Metropolitan Police's Modern Slavery and Kidnap Unit, the CPS, Romanian Police and Prosecutors, Europol and Eurojust. In a case which sounds all too familiar, victims were deceived into travelling by being promised pay of £500 per 30 days. Once in the UK, they had their identify cards confiscated and were forced to stay in overcrowded and run-down properties in East London.

After my interview with Caroline, I was doubtful, because of the complicated nature of the trials, that any of the court material from my day with her, or the case itself, could be included here. However, while I was still writing, the news broke. The story was out there, and reporting restrictions had been lifted.

The entire human trafficking gang was found guilty of modern slavery offences, in the UK's largest modern slavery investigation. More than 300 suspected victims, many of them homeless, addicts, or targeted as they left prison gates in Poland, were tricked into coming to the West Midlands to work. Once in the UK, they were abused and exploited. Ninety-two victims were identified, and a staggering 88 of these accounts were heard in court.

The Polish gang made, at the most conservative estimate, £2 million from exploiting those victims, over five years, with one driving round the Midlands in a Bentley, while the workers were living in rat-infested houses and forced to work in a range of roles in businesses from recycling centres to poultry factories. Their ages ranged from 17 to 60, and when one worker died (of natural causes) at one of the gang's addresses, his ID and personal effects were taken from his pockets before paramedics arrived.

If they were paid at all, it was only 50p an hour. The victims were forced to rely on food banks (or the soup kitchens which would eventually save their lives), and one man explained how he had to wash in the canal because there was no other way for him to access water. They lived, and I use that term loosely, across different addresses in West Bromwich, Walsall, Sandwell and Smethwick, often four to a room with not enough mattresses to sleep on. Some premises had no working toilets.

The level of physical violence shown to victims was shocking.

One man made the mistake of complaining to his captors, who broke his arm and refused him medical help. When he was then unable to work, they threw him out on to the streets. Another was threatened with the removal of his kidney: he was stripped naked in front of other victims and then covered in the surgical chemical iodine, as the gang yelled warnings at him to keep quiet. A normal threat was to put men into a car and tell them they would be driven to a forest and hung from a tree by their testicles.

While the convictions were an incredible feat, there were two names in the reports of the trials which stood out for me: Ignacy Brzezinski, 52, and 41-year-old Wojciech Nowakowski. These were the men on trial in the second case, the men I came face to face with in court.

Ignacy had absconded. Granted bail because he'd broken his leg in a fall (in court), he then disappeared. In his absence he was sentenced to eleven years in prison, with Judge Mary Stacey saying, 'As the head of the family, he set the tone of the operation, and also enjoyed the fruits of the conspiracy, riding round in his Bentley with a fleet of high-performance cars at his disposal.'

He was later found and arrested in Poland.

I was shocked to learn that Nowakowski, who was jailed for six and a half years, had once been a victim of the gang. He had endured what other victims had, yet went on to become a 'spy and enforcer', 'enjoying power over the others'.

The police team, led by Chief Inspector Nick Dale, explained how each defendant played a role in the trafficking operation.

Ignacy Brzezinski was the head of the family, controlling cards and bank accounts and renting addresses, as well as dealing with recruitment and providing what could be loosely described as jobs and/or accommodation.

Marek Chowaniec, 30, of Walsall, was the 'respectable' face of the gang, the member taking victims to open bank accounts and join the recruitment agencies. He too controlled addresses and living conditions, handing out tiny amounts of money to the victims from their hard-earned wages. He was jailed for eleven years for trafficking, conspiracy to require another to perform forced labour, and money laundering.

Marek Brzezinski, 50, of Tipton, travelled to Poland in order to find victims, and was jailed for nine years, again for trafficking, conspiracy to require another to perform forced labour, and money laundering. He controlled one specific address and took men to and from their work, ensuring they were constantly under the control of the gang.

Justyna Parczewska, 48, of West Bromwich, Ignacy's wife, was described as having a 'matriarchal' role, welcoming new arrivals and giving them cups of tea and food at her home. She too controlled bank cards, and CCTV evidence reflected her multiple use of bank cards at different machines around Walsall. She was jailed for eight years for conspiracy to require another to perform forced labour, and money laundering.

Julianna Chodakowicz, 24, of Worcestershire, was jailed for seven years. She was the gang's insider at a Worcester employment agency and signed up dozens of the victims. Natalia Zmuda, 29, of Walsall, also escorted victims to job centre appointments and controlled their bank accounts. She got four years and six months.

Jan Sadowski and Wojciech Nowakowski (both 26) met the arrivals in the UK. Sadowski got three years, and Nowakowski six and a half, and both were convicted of trafficking charges, conspiracy to require and control another person to perform forced labour, and conspiracy to acquire, use and possess criminal property.

The judge described the case as the 'most ambitious, extensive and prolific' modern-day slavery network ever exposed in the UK.

Caroline later told me, 'This case both horrifies and fascinates in equal measure. It is fascinating in its size and complexity. But it is horrific that in twenty-first-century civilised Britain, vulnerable men and women, seeking to earn a proper wage (all they expected was between £250 and £300) were deceived, violated and abused by a group of people whose sole motivation was greed.

'It is remarkable and horrifying that this happened in plain sight, in the twenty-first century, but we have made a change, we have safeguarded the vulnerable, we have disrupted the gang and we have punished the offenders. We are sending a message that this conduct, this criminality is not tolerated. It makes me proud that our legislation, our police, our charities and our criminal justice system have gone some way to giving back these victims their voice and their dignity, and I am hugely privileged to be part of that process.'

9

SURVIVORS AND THE SYSTEM

It had become clear to me, witnessing Elena's experiences and hearing from The Salvation Army, Caroline Haughey QC, and support workers directly providing care to survivors, that the men, women and children who had experienced exploitation of any kind were victims with unique and individual needs.

In a country whose Government claims to be a world leader in spearheading the fight against modern slavery and human trafficking, you would expect survivors to be cared for within a compassionate, flexible and victim-centred system. However, those who work with and on behalf of survivors every day, and who have spoken to me for this book, would question that. The system within which survivors are expected to navigate is extraordinarily complex.

Unlike any other victim of crime where the police investigate and refer victims to associated support where appropriate, survivors of trafficking and slavery are dealt with through the Home Office. A police investigation may run alongside this, but the need for a Government department to officially declare someone a victim is a process unique to the crime of modern slavery.

From the moment a victim is identified by a First Responder, if they choose to enter 'the system' (the National Referral Mechanism) it is the Home Office which will decide if they are indeed a victim of trafficking or slavery, and it is the Home Office which will decide their fate. This is a two-fold issue if the potential victim is also pursuing an asylum claim.

The NRM is based on the system created by the Council of Europe Convention on Action against Trafficking in Human Beings, ratified by the UK for our own purposes, but not created by the UK. Within that framework, the Home Office has chosen to make decisions which have directly impacted the well-being of survivors. In 2017, the Government announced a raft of alterations to this system, which began to trickle down to the front line over the following couple of years.

As we discussed in Chapter 2, first and foremost, the decisions on victims' Conclusive Grounds are made by the Government department responsible for keeping immigration figures low and implementing the 'hostile environment'. At the time I started writing this book, there were two 'Competent Authorities' (decision makers) for potential victims. For potential victims from the EU, the National Crime Agency would decide the outcome of the Conclusive Grounds decision. For non-EU potential victims, UK Visas and Immigration would decide their fate. It was a distinction deemed unfair and concerning, that a survivor's immigration status would take precedence over their status as a victim. It was feared that negative decisions would be a more likely outcome, given the Government's wish to keep to immigration targets, with the care of the individuals themselves being secondary to that.

In spring 2019, this changed. There became only one Competent Authority: the Home Office. Many contributors have told me it's too early to tell what, if any, difference this will make to Conclusive Grounds decisions, but they fear they will still be based on the immigration status and the country of origin of the victim.

The day after these changes came into play, I was in Bristol with Justine Currell and Andrew Wallis from Unseen. Because they both work on the front line in anti-slavery work and were involved

116

in the creation of the Modern Slavery Bill, I was keen to know their thoughts on the changes to the Competent Authority.

Justine told me, 'This is called moving the deckchairs. I think there's [a] lack of strategy and a lack of understanding what the end game is. If you take away the NCA and Immigration from the process and transfer it all to the Home Office, that maintains a very close link with immigration whether the Government want to admit it or not. The people who are making those decisions – half of them are probably still the same people who were making them three days ago. Do you have a different mindset when you've got the same people making decisions?

'We need to look at the NRM as a means of accessing support and helping somebody recover and move on, rather than it being an identification and number counting process, which historically it has been. I was really hopeful we might get some fundamental changes, but I think the changes have been done piecemeal, and I don't think there's a real understanding of how the whole system works.'

Andrew added, 'I think that's key, and I think it's fundamentally about what we are trying to do when we identify someone as a victim of this crime. In the last eleven, nearly twelve years now, when we ask the question, "What is the journey we want this person to go on?" we should be saying we want to go from the identification of someone who is a victim of a crime all the way through to complete resilience. *That* should be our ambition.

'The NRM was the response to the EU directive about identification, providing 45 days for reflection, then "Thank you very much, now go and get on with your life". It's a totally inadequate and unambitious response. You've got to start asking yourself what are the outcomes for these people, and what are the outcomes we want?

'If you intervene correctly in someone's life and invest in someone's life – and we know this from every other early intervention programme that's gone on – then actually their outcomes and life

117

chances are so much better. They can contribute to society. It can take a long period of time because you're dealing with some people who have suffered severe trauma, but there doesn't seem to be the breadth of thinking to do that.

'There is no coherent plan, setting out what will happen for people, with proper costings, to deal with this. And that's what I mean about an unambitious and a non-world-leading response. It's a lack of strategy. I don't know if it's partly because of the dreaded B [Brexit] word. Even the NRM issue intersects with so many other different Government departments. So there are restrictions such as, if you're in the NRM you can't work. Just think of the crass stupidity of that! Most people end up in this situation because they were seeking economic advancement, and then we disenfranchise them from that process. It's deeply intertwined with the asylum process as well.'

Another area which has given cause for concern to those supporting victims is the financial entitlements offered to them. This is a complicated matter, with Judicial Reviews in play over the last couple of years, trying to bring clarity – and parity – to the situation, after the Government decision to cut financial support was deemed unlawful by a High Court judge.

All victims had been receiving £65 a week. Then on 1st March 2018, the Home Office slashed the weekly support that *asylum seeking* victims of trafficking received to £37.75. This was to bring them in line with what *non-trafficked* asylum seekers received. This was done with no warning or consultation with those caring for victims.

Two victims of trafficking, represented by Wilsons Public Law team, challenged the decision after the cuts left them struggling to attend key appointments and support sessions, and for one of the victims, unable to maintain the strict diet needed to coincide with HIV medication, after contracting the virus as a direct result of her exploitation. The cuts had a direct impact on their mental and physical health, and their recovery.

In October 2018, the High Court heard a Judicial Review on the changes, and the following month the judgement was handed down. Mr Justice Mostyn ruled that the Government had acted unlawfully in reducing the payments and ordered back-payments potentially exceeding £1 million. He said, 'The very substantial cut imposed unilaterally' by the department was taken on a 'false basis and could not stand'.

He also referred to the fact that the Modern Slavery Act was still missing crucial guidance on how victims of modern slavery are to be supported (Sections 49 and 50), writing that the Home Secretary has 'an absolute duty immediately to issue the guidance that Parliament required [of] him' adding any further delays are 'completely unacceptable'.

Forty-five is a number which comes up a lot in discussions about the care of victims. Simply put, there are two periods of 45 days which are key in the entitlements of survivors.

In England, Wales and Northern Ireland, once a potential modern slavery victim has been accepted into the NRM, they are entitled to 45 days of 'specialist, tailored support', also known as the 'reflection and recovery' period. In Scotland, as of April 2018, this support period was doubled to at least 90 days. In the UK, therefore, we actually offer more than the Council of Europe Convention on Action against Trafficking in Human Beings – which provides only 30 days of support.

The 45 days' time limit is supposed to provide care for victims in the period between their *positive Reasonable Grounds decision* and the *Conclusive Grounds decision*. However, that's working on the assumption that the Conclusive Grounds decision arrives in 45 days. It doesn't. One of the main criticisms of this period is the waiting times victims have to endure until a decision is made. Victims are told they have 45 days of support, and their anxiety typically increases as the date gets ever closer. Therefore as Day 45 passes with still no news, Day 46 is referred to by specialists as the 'cliff-drop'.

In the NRM figures released in 2019, the number of survivors within the system who had not yet received a Conclusive Grounds decision from the Home Office was included. Some had been waiting *six years*.

The numbers are as follows:

2013 – 4
2014 – 69
2015 – 208
2016 – 398
2017 – 1,613
2018 – 3,867

There is another area of victim care which has recently been in a state of flux due to court cases and legal wrangling with the Home Office, and is another aspect of the NRM which has come under fire.

Once the decision on a potential victim has been made, it's time for them to enter a new phase of their recovery. Until 2018, and the onset of the NRM reforms, a negative decision would see someone exited from support services in 48 hours, and a positive decision would give a victim fourteen days of 'move on support'. However, from 2018, these time frames were extended to nine days exit period and 45 days move on support.

In April 2019, two victims of slavery (and their representatives at Duncan Lewis) sought a Judicial Review of the 45-day time limit, and a High Court judge deemed the level of support available in England and Wales could indeed be unlawful. By June, the Home Office conceded the 45-day policy was unlawful, and also incompatible with the Trafficking Convention.

The Home Office agreed that support should be provided appropriate to a survivor's needs, and committed to creating a system based on this principle. Expert stakeholders would be involved in the scheme's development and, in the meantime, the

45-day rule would not be reapplied and no restriction on care for victims based on a timeline would be applied.

The Government then released its policy in response to this – the Recovery Needs Assessment – outlining how it would decide how a victim would carry on getting the support they needed. The policy has certain limitations: the ultimate decision will be taken by the Government, and the only people who can request that support carries on are those working for the Government providing support. Neither a victim, their lawyer nor a charity not under Government contract to provide support can request an extension. The decision time taken to extend support is not made clear either, as the policy simply says if a decision is not made in the 45 days the victim will continue to receive support until a decision is made and transition arrangements are in place.

Legal charity ATLEU (Anti-Trafficking and Labour Exploitation Unit) responded to the policy saying, 'We welcome the Government's shift towards a consideration of victim needs when thinking about support. It remains to be seen how it will work in practice but the policy as drafted raises concerns. It appears to take an overly narrow view of victim needs and not be wholly victim-centred. Victims are also denied direct access to the application process and have no right of appeal if a decision is wrongly made . . . The policy also raises questions that we welcome clarification on, for example, the right of a victim to go back into support if needs come up after they have exited and how they can access this process.'

SUPPORTING SURVIVORS

To help me get to grips with not only a very complex system, but one which is currently in a state of flux, I met Kate Roberts from the Human Trafficking Foundation (HTF) to talk me through the endless changes facing victims and front-line organisations. HTF was set up in 2010 by a cross-party group of MPs, growing out of the All Party Parliamentary Group on Trafficking.

Over coffee in East London,[1] Kate explains the background to HTF.

'The idea was to set up an NGO which would act as a bridge for all the people working on the front line, and policy makers. It would ensure policy makers and parliamentarians understood the issues around supporting victims – because as we know there has been a real disjoin between the people who are doing the work and the people who are making the decisions. So that was what HTF was set up for, and that's what we continue to do.

'Although we're very small, we focus our energy on bringing people together. Obviously we work with NGOs, but one of my colleagues is also working with the London Local Authorities, trying to help them understand their statutory duties, that they have a legal obligation to support victims of trafficking, but also working with them to do this in a positive way. She's had a really good response, because again I think there has been a lack of leadership.'

I asked Kate if she thought the UK was doing enough for victims.

'We're spending a ton of money. The Care Contract is worth millions, but what is it actually doing? I think it's clear that at the moment we can't show any real outcomes for survivors. If you look at the NRM and the large numbers of referrals in, – going up about 30% each year – we still can't show what happens to people after they leave. Clearly we're not doing enough because it's not survivor focused.

'If it were, the annual statistics would show how people have moved on with their lives. The whole focus has been on identification, which tells you little about the victims themselves. The figure we see in the NRM is referrals *into* the NRM. In the columns of figures, the largest column is the number of people waiting for

---

1 This interview took place before the Government brought in the extension of recovery time for victims, and before Section 49 of the Modern Slavery Act was published

a decision, so they are the people in limbo for years maybe, just waiting. Their lives now controlled by the NRM. They can't do anything. They just have to wait for this decision without knowing how long it could take. I think that's really controlling. It's certainly not the way to begin to recover from slavery. This torture of waiting, often when people also have an asylum claim, or other similar issues going on – you can't begin to rebuild your life and unpack what's happened to you on that basis.

'I'm in touch with a lot of domestic workers from my previous job and whenever I go to meet them, they hear about other people who have been in the NRM for two years, and they don't want that. They've experienced horrific abuse. They don't want to engage with a system which does that.

'I think it's very clear that the Government-funded systems we have in place are not designed with survivors' recovery needs in mind.

'HTF wrote "Life Beyond the Safe House" in 2015 highlighting this cliff edge that people are dropping off. You spend all this money identifying people, but for what? I've met police officers who've referred the same person into the NRM *three* times because they've gone back into exploitation and been picked up again by the police. So even if you don't care about the people themselves – that's expensive and stupid.

'We were obviously very pleased when move on times were extended from two weeks to 45 days. It's still not enough, but it's great that there's recognition that people need time to move on. It's a step in the right direction. However, that was used to justify the cuts in subsistence rates, because they said they had to pay for it somehow. They turned round to NGOs and said they were the ones who asked for it. Well, no one asked to cut subsistence rates, we didn't say take the money from the victims' pockets.

'What we said very clearly *against* subsistence cuts was that keeping people in destitution for longer is not a *recovery* period, you're not extending their *recovery* period. Obviously if you're trying to work out how many lentils you can buy, you're not thinking about recovering. You need to be able to travel to see your therapist, to make friends, to see people, to live a life. But how can you?'

When the Modern Slavery Act came into force in 2015, many NGOs criticised the legislation for not doing enough to protect victims, with key sections on the care of the most vulnerable essentially to be filled in at a later date.

Kate was clearly still passionate about this.

'The Modern Slavery Act doesn't cover victims. The problem is that the Modern Slavery Act . . .'

She paused to consider her words very carefully.

'Everyone welcomed the Modern Slavery Act but the NGOs were concerned that there was such a focus on prosecutions. The section on supply chains was seen as a real win. Though people now are saying even that didn't really have teeth. I think all I can say about the Modern Slavery Act is that it was good, but it's not at all controversial of me to say it did not go far enough. At the time it was decided that it was better to have an Act than not.

'Sections 49 and 50 of the Act were left undeveloped[2]. They were to make provision for statutory guidance for victim support and regulations on victim support. They're blank still. Four years later there is no statutory guidance on regulations on victim support.'

It was this lack of clarity in the Act which affected the recent court case into victims' subsistence rates.

'It's all interlinked. In the subsistence case, the judge said, "If there was guidance we wouldn't be in court". What I think the guidance was meant to be is a mandate, so anyone can look at it and know what victims should be entitled to.

'Without this guidance, support entitlements are not written down anywhere. It's why everyone's confused. Victims don't know. Adults are supposed to give "informed consent" to go into

_____

2   This interview took place before the Victim Support Guidance in Section 49 of The Modern Slavery Act 2015 was finally published. Section 50 is yet to be completed.

the NRM. You don't even know what you're going to get in the NRM! No one knows. Nothing's written down and this is why everyone has been traumatised going to court, spending loads of public money going to court, because nothing's been decided. The judge is reduced to saying, "I cannot believe there is no guidance. Why are we even in court?"'

In spring 2019, I travelled to Manchester to spend the day with Hope for Justice. While there, I was introduced to Rebecca Kingi – an Independent Modern Slavery Advocate and a New Zealand qualified solicitor. She's in her mid-twenties, a passionate, fast-talking dynamo whom I could imagine breaking down any barriers possible in order to help her clients. She was the perfect person to talk me through what victims are entitled to once recovered, and where the faults in the system lie.

'Once someone has come out of exploitation, we say rescue is a process not an event. Because there are so many legal and personal issues that remain unresolved. To prevent the risk of re-trafficking and re-slavery, and to ensure that person has hope for their future, a lot of care and work needs to be done.

'It's not easy for survivors. It can be a complete mess, to be blunt. There's a huge need for independent advocacy for each victim so that they can navigate the system, and also (if they want to) to be able to be supported through a criminal prosecution.

'Any restoration process means long-term support and advocacy for survivors. A lot of our clients are with us for a number of years because it's not just a matter of 45 days then, right, you've had your time in the safe house, you're fixed to get on with your life. I think it's unrealistic to expect someone to recover from modern slavery in 45 days, and the reality is that most of the legal issues won't be sorted out in that time either.

'We're separate from the Home Office Victim Care Contract. We're independent. We're not an NRM safe house provider. Once the victim has gone through the NRM (they've gone to the safe house, say, had a positive reasonable grounds, then perhaps waited a very long time before their Conclusive Grounds [decision] came through), it's at that point the Advocacy Team will work with survivors. It's at that point, we have found, many victims were left and just dropped out of the system altogether.

'If they get a negative Conclusive Grounds decision, we would want to look at whether that should be challenged. Identifying whether someone's a victim or not is complicated, and there have been many cases which needed to be legally challenged.

'Unfortunately, in our view, that system is broken, because the only option is Judicial Review or an informal system with the Home Office where the First Responder or the Victim Care Provider can submit a reconsideration request. That in itself is quite complicated.'[3]

Rebecca couldn't have been clearer about her thoughts on the challenges facing victims and their recovery in the UK.

'Immigration status is essential to victims' rights. It's the key ingredient and without it they can't unlock any other support.

'Victims who are British nationals don't face that initial barrier of securing immigration status (that's not to say British nationals don't also face barriers in getting support). For victims who are not British nationals, our big push for change would be for them to be automatically entitled to a grant of Leave to Remain status, even if it's for a set period. EEA nationals need this too; EEA nationals don't automatically have a right to reside unless they have a grant of leave or are exercising their Treaty rights – so that pretty much means you're working or you have attained worker status. And post Brexit it's going to get a lot harder for EEA nationals as everything is changing.

'We are always trying to get immigration solicitors to fight for Discretionary Leave to Remain for EEA nationals, but we're finding it's getting a lot harder for people to get that. It's leaving a lot of people very vulnerable. They're relying on their rights as an EEA

---

3   Since this interview took place, the High Court has deemed this policy unlawful, and the Home Office agreed to no longer refuse a reconsideration.

national, but unless we have clear evidence they've been working (which naturally many victims don't) we end up battling with the DWP and Local Authorities for agreement that they're eligible for Homelessness Support or Homelessness Credit or other Welfare Support.

'Our advocacy with EEA survivors involves advocating for EEA nationals to receive the support they are entitled to from the state, based on their EEA rights and wider rights as a victim of trafficking. Our position, which is legally correct, is that exploitative work can count as genuine and effective work, which means that person has been exercising their Treaty rights and therefore has a right to reside. Of course, these arguments become a lot more complicated if someone has been in a safe house for a couple of years. That's not to say an EEA national can't claim asylum but it's a lot harder because I guess the Government's position would frequently be that there's not a high risk involved in an EEA national returning to their country of origin. Whether that's the case in practice . . .

'The third category, who would go down the asylum route, is the non-EU survivor. That's another really complicated legal battle. As an asylum seeker you may be eligible for asylum support accommodation, so that immediate risk of homelessness may not be as prevalent perhaps if you've got asylum seeker status and are eligible. However, victims have a legal right to safe and secure accommodation, and I think asylum support accommodation is not suitable for many victims yet they are continually placed there instead of in safehouse accommodation.

'We want to work with the Government in terms of safe house providers because a lot of people are doing the best that they can. There's a lot of room for improvement but we're not the only charity banging on about the need to look after victims post-rescue. If we want to see people have hope, have a future where they're not going to be in the same position of vulnerability that they were pre- and after rescue, they need advocacy in all these areas.'

*

After speaking with both Kate and Rebecca it's clear to me that there are two key areas which need to be improved in order for victims of slavery to not only survive, but to thrive, within the UK.

Firstly, they need to be able to secure a clear and compassionate immigration status based on common sense and victimhood. This level of security would then go a long way to accomplish the second priority – the need for time and resources in order to recover in a safe and secure environment. Currently victims are being rushed through a process with no record of what happens to them when their time is up and they come to the end of the formal process.

As long as the fate and care of victims is being decided by the arm of Government tasked with controlling immigration figures, there will be question marks over how well the UK can state it protects survivors of modern slavery and human trafficking. Many of the stories which appeared in the press in the summer of 2019 did little to reassure front-line workers that victims were safe once they were in the NRM.

In July 2019, an open letter in *The Independent*, signed by twenty charities, accused the Home Office of covering up the fact that trafficking victims were being detained in immigration centres. As reported in *The Independent* and *The Guardian*, a Freedom of Information request revealed 507 victims were being held under immigration powers.

Frank Field MP requested the data via a parliamentary question to the Home Office, but was told by Caroline Nokes, the Immigration Minister, that there was 'no central record' of this and that the department 'did not collate or publish the data requested'. When data mapping project After Exploitation obtained the numbers, it was reported the figures had been requested by MPs on numerous occasions, but that Home Office ministers continually claimed no such data was held. More than twenty charities then went on to sign an open letter once again pointing out and condemning the ongoing conflict of interest between the Home Office's immigration policy and its duty to protect trafficking victims.

The Independent also reported several cases of victims within the NRM being held or threatened with deportation, including a Chinese woman held in Yarl's Wood for six months. The paper reported that the day before her case went to court, the Home Office conceded her detention was unlawful. It even went on to admit she was entitled to compensation for the time she was held. Also in the summer of 2019, a report from the Labour Exploitation Advisory Group (LEAG) was equally damning, claiming identified victims of trafficking and slavery were being knowingly moved to detention and removal centres 'for protection', going on to accuse ministers of, once again, prioritising immigration over victims' right to support. In one case from the report, the Home Office endorsed the detention of a male victim of slavery saying his entitlements (safe house accommodation and financial support) could be met in detention.

Quoted in the press at the time, Emily Kenway from Focus on Labour Exploitation (FLEX), said locking people up when they have experienced the trauma of being trafficked was clearly at odds with the Government's own aim of reducing harm caused to victims, adding, 'This leads to cases like those exposed today, where victims are treated as offenders and their immigration status is prioritised over their right to support.'

A Home Office spokesperson said, 'The Government is committed to protecting the vulnerable and treating those in detention with dignity and respect. This includes identifying and supporting victims of modern slavery.'

The criticisms aimed at the Home Office were not new. In 2018 the Government was accused of not fully understanding modern slavery, and of having a strategy which was yet to result in coherent action.

A report from the Public Accounts Committee revealed that while the Government had good intentions there was no measure of success in place, there were clear inconsistencies between police forces in fighting the crime, and as well as having no clear idea of how many 'modern slaves' there are in Britain, the Government also failed to record outcomes for those who *are* in the system. Waiting times for victims on decisions about their status were also criticised, as was the monitoring of support services, and the hands-off approach to businesses engaging with transparency in supply chains legislation.

At the time the Home Office replied with this statement:

> The Public Accounts Committee recognises that the UK is ahead of many countries in responding to modern slavery and the government's Modern Slavery Taskforce will consider its recommendations carefully.

These concerns were echoed once again after the Home Office revealed in August 2018 that modern slavery costs Britain up to £4.3 billion a year. At the time campaigners said the figure was likely to be higher, as the Government was underestimating the number of potential victims living within the UK.

Not long before the criticisms from the Public Accounts Committee were revealed, Theresa May's Modern Slavery Strategy came under fire in a very critical report from the National Audit Office (NAO), saying it had failed victims. The report in December 2017 stated:

> Until the government is able to establish effective oversight of the modern slavery system as a whole, it will not be able to significantly reduce the prevalence of modern slavery or show that it is achieving value for money. The Home Office has an incomplete picture of the crime, the victims and the perpetrators. Accountability within the Modern Slavery Strategy is unclear, oversight of victim support is inadequate and few cases have led to prosecution. The NAO also finds that the Home Office has limited means of tracking its progress and there remains much more to do to ensure victims of modern slavery are identified, protected and supported effectively.

In spring 2017, the Work and Pensions Committee found that there were 'inexcusable' failures in the UK's Modern Slavery Strategy which essentially left victims living in poverty and limbo, while allowing their traffickers and abusers to escape unpunished. The inquiry[4] had come about at the request of the UK's then Independent Anti-Slavery Commissioner, Kevin Hyland OBE, who wrote to the Committee expressing his concerns that the support for victims of modern slavery was inadequate.

The inquiry found:

- Front-line support is weak and uncoordinated and instances where a person is re-trafficked are not even recorded.
- The current mechanism for identifying and supporting victims means, once identified, they have no automatic formal immigration status or rights and are often faced with a total lack of understanding or even recognition of their situation.
- The lack of proper support for victims is having a negative impact on the number of successful prosecutions of slave masters.
- No data is collected on victims once they leave the NRM and the collection and recording of data is 'generally substandard'. The Government does not monitor the re-trafficking of victims – an 'unacceptable' situation.
- Reform to the NRM must include the recording of instances where victims have been processed through the framework more than once.
- All confirmed victims of modern slavery should be given at least one year's leave to remain with a personal plan for their recovery, which should act as a social passport to support for at least the twelve-month period of leave to remain. Committee rejects the argument that this would create a pull factor to the UK, for slave masters or victims.

---

4   Work and Pensions Committee's Victims of Modern Slavery, April 2017

The Chair of the Committee, Frank Field, gave a brutal assessment of the UK's response to caring for victims:

> While we applaud the leading role the UK has taken in tackling this 'barbaric crime', as the Prime Minister has called it, when you consider what is at stake, there is a shocking lack of awareness and co-ordination in the front-line services dealing with modern slavery. What these people go through is unimaginable, and yet it is happening, here, now, and our response seems almost lackadaisical: a paper exercise earning you recognition as having been enslaved, which then entitles you to almost nothing as far as we can see. We don't even record instances where the same person is thrown back into this hell, even though that is surely the clearest sign of the failures in our response. No society worth its salt can allow this to continue, or fail to support those who fall victim. The Prime Minister now needs to open up a further front in her Modern Slavery Act. The incoming Government must conduct an urgent review of our national response and put in place some basic minimum safeguards, status, that will allow a person to begin to rebuild a life, testify against their abuser if they feel able, and above all, be protected from the unimaginable but real possibility of falling victim again.

It was Frank Field MP, along with Baroness Butler-Sloss and Maria Miller MP, who was to lead the review of the Modern Slavery Act, which was launched by the Home Office in the summer of 2018 to 'ensure our world-first legislation keeps in step with this crime'.

By summer 2019, the results of the review were made public.[5]

---

5   See Chapter 19.

10

ELENA'S STORY: LONDON (2016)

It was my beautiful day. The most beautiful day in my life.

'Elena', on the birth of her child

Elena's first night in London was spent in the doorway of a Home Office building.

She was heavily pregnant, exhausted and afraid. After the lorry driver had rushed her out of the back of his vehicle, she appears to have wandered for quite some time. A woman had found her walking the streets and told her she needed to go to the Home Office.

Elena earnestly explained to me, 'When I come here in the middle of the night, she tells me the way to go to the Home Office. She left me there to go to her job, to go on her way. She didn't stay with me.'

Once the stranger had left Elena, the night passed slowly.

'In those moments I was so tired, I had not eaten. I had a lot of pain in my stomach, and I was worried that something was happening to the baby after all the stress and tiredness that I was experiencing myself. In those moments the city was quiet and there was little movement. I just wanted a bed where I could sleep, and I wanted something to eat. At the same time I was

133

both worried and frightened as I didn't know where I was going and if I was going to be supported by them. I didn't know anything.

'I slept on the ground for two hours until it become light outside and then I waited for the morning to seek help from the Home Office. They opened the doors to me and I am grateful. They started their procedures to carry out their work but I continued to have pain in my stomach during the entire day. I had two short interviews and they asked me lots of questions.

'They were very, very nice with me. Other ladies, they tell me the Home Office was rude, but with me, no. They were good. They give me a sandwich. Every time I was hungry they bring me food and juice. I can say that most of the workers treated me well on that day, I was given food and I was sent to the hostel earlier than they were going to take the other people.

'I entered the Home Office sometimes around 8am and after being inside there for eight hours they decided to take me by taxi to the hostel where they were taking people who didn't have accommodation. In the hostel I had a bed, sharing a room, just one room, two beds, sharing with another lady. And then I was waiting.'

Elena began to settle into the anonymous hostel somewhere in London and started to find her feet. Despite her advanced stage of pregnancy, and the fact she had experienced such trauma, she was determined to find the help she needed.

'Then at the hostel where I was, the workers gave me the addresses of some churches so that I could get some clothes for the baby and for myself and the hospital address. I was forced to find them myself after a few days as in the first few days I didn't have any money to put in my Oyster card in order for me to get to these places. But after a week in this accommodation where the Home Office had taken me, a charity came and supported me with some weekly money and offered me help to find a solicitor. They helped me with this part, whereas for therapy with a psychologist I was helped and referred by my doctor.'

During this period, Elena also managed to seek medical treatment. She was almost ready to give birth, but the distress of the past few months had clearly taken its toll.

'It was not good for me. I had pain in my belly. I went to see a doctor because in all the eight months I had seen just one doctor once. In that time I don't have any idea how is my baby? Nothing. I live one month and a half in shared room, with other ladies, from different countries. In that hostel we can leave the room, but my English was not very good so I just stayed in with other people. But when it comes to being given help after for things needed for my baby I was helped by Christine, a noble lady who stayed so close to me. All the stuff for the baby was brought to me by Christine from charities.'

Elena was in London only a few weeks before her baby was born. From those early months in the brothel, when she knew she was pregnant and was so terrified, to the strength she found to escape in order to save her life and the life of her child – there was no question the young woman had been on an emotional and physical rollercoaster. But whenever I talked to Elena, it was clear that the moment she met her child had shaped her life since then.

She wept as she relived that day.

'When the baby was born, it was my beautiful day, the most beautiful day in my life. I went to hospital with pain, it started slowly, slowly. Every five minutes. But I was very calm. I go to reception of the hostel. I told them, "I need an ambulance because my baby is coming. I need to go to hospital or my baby will be born here. Please take me to hospital!" They sent me to hospital. An Albanian lady from the hostel, she came with me. She helped me. She came to hospital, but did not stay with me. So I was alone, with much pain. Very stressed, very scared for my baby.

'I stayed two days in too much pain. Then I have epidural in my back, very strong injection. I still have pain in my back from that injection.

'The baby was born and it was a very, very happy moment for me. I just cry. My baby was so quiet, not crying too much, lying

135

on my breast and sleeping. It was the most beautiful moment in that year – one year that was very bad in my life. When the baby came, my life changed. I couldn't believe it when I first saw my child, perfect down to the fingers and toes. From that moment on my heart was filled with love. I am stronger now. I am not thinking a lot about what I went through, but it still hurts when I think of it.'

Before her child was born, Elena was sharing a room with another Albanian woman, but after she returned with her baby she was given a single room.

Staying in the hostel was not a long-term solution. She needed a permanent home while waiting to hear from the Home Office about her NRM Conclusive Grounds decision and her asylum status.

When the baby was a couple of months old it was suggested Elena move to another city. She was told it was five hours away in the car, and as a new mum, on her own, she told me how nervous she was about making such a move away from everything she had come to know. 'I was like, oh my God, where am I going? I was very scared.'

It was decided the move to a new city was unhelpful, but Elena was to be moved away from the hostel. Her next accommodation came in April 2017, but that wasn't to be permanent either.

'I stayed in a shared accommodation with two more ladies. We stayed there for just three months before they told us that we needed to leave the property and go to a different house with the same women I was sharing. I was grateful to have a room as I could have been out in the street somewhere. I feel safe because other people don't have a room. I think it's good. Many people stay on the street, so I am lucky. We are safe and they support us. But it's not a big house. It is six rooms, six ladies. Every lady has children. There are thirteen people there. Two showers. Very small rooms, very small kitchen. If we go in the kitchen at the same time, we can't do anything so we go in at different times for cooking.'

Although Elena was grateful for the support she had been given, there was no question her life was challenging – emotionally, practically and financially.

'For the house we don't pay anything. The Home Office gives me an ASPEN card, £75 a week for me and the baby. I think it's £37.50 for me and the same for the baby. I have had that amount of money for three years, and I manage on it. For me it's good. I am grateful to have whatever amount I am offered. Maybe it's not enough, but if you manage the money it's good. All the other people have the same.'

Elena relied on local churches and charities for clothes for the baby and herself. Her daily routine, while living in the limbo of waiting for her Home Office decision, centred around looking after the baby, attending legal and health appointments, and visiting playgroups and drop-in centres where she could try to make friends and accesses services which could help her. She was proud that she was able to find a community while she was an asylum seeker in London.

'I know the shops here and the streets here, and the playgroups. I know more people here. I am glad to be here. I make friends, especially in the church or playgroup. Not many, as I don't trust too many people, but I think I have two or three ladies I see regularly. The routine has been the same. Looking after my child. Going to appointments. Waiting for the decision is very stressful. Every single day. But we have to wait. We don't have any other choice. The stress in my mind [when they say] "we don't have any news today, we don't have any news today".

'The first year was very, very difficult. When I came here my English was very bad. I knew just five words then, no more. But when my baby was born I felt I had the strength to find everything I needed. Slowly, slowly I found everything I needed.'

11

THE COMMISSIONER

The first time I met Kevin Hyland OBE was on a train to Gatwick. The third time was on the Victoria Line platform at Victoria Station. So it seemed fitting that the fifth time was in a café at an airport in Ireland.

The UK's first (now former) Independent Anti-Slavery Commissioner remains an incredibly busy man so the only way we could meet face to face was for me to fly to Cork and meet him at the airport between his flights. It all felt very *Bourne Identity*.

We met in the small coffee shop in the entrance of Cork airport, and after being used to seeing him in a professional capacity, in smart suits and ties, seeing him in a casual shirt and jacket was a bit like seeing a teacher out of school in the summer holidays. An ex-Metropolitan Police officer with thirty years' service under his belt, Kevin was appointed to the role of IASC in 2015, after the position was created by the Modern Slavery Act. His role as the Independent Anti-Slavery Commissioner put him on the map politically, but long before he moved into such a high-profile role, Kevin was fighting trafficking on the streets of London – before politicians realised the scale of the crime the country was facing.

At the end of 2009, when he was still in the Met, Kevin was given the job of running their Vice Teams, tasked with looking at prostitution and organised criminality. Though forward-thinking at the time, it was the very early stages of the UK beginning to understand the extent of trafficking within the country, as Kevin explained over coffee.

'The Met had a small trafficking team working out of Scotland Yard, and the UK had just signed up to the National Referral Mechanism which was then being run by the Poppy Project. SOCA was looking at the NRM decisions. The whole thing was being created without a structure that reflected what this really was, which was serious organised crime involving groups that were way more complicated and technical than was realised at the time.'

Kevin and his team started to fill in the gaps.

'I asked for every single crime in London that was classified as human trafficking or related to human trafficking. As a result, I was given reams of crime reports going back to when the legislation had come in in the UK, going back to 2003 and the Sexual Offences Act. Then there was other legislation which looked at human trafficking in 2004 (the Asylum and Immigration Act which criminalised trafficking).

'When I started looking through this I could identify where there were suspects and missed opportunities and I moved the team on to looking at them. Very quickly we focused on one operation which was investigating a Thai gang. We carried out raids in East London, early in the morning. We'd been given advice on what victims looked like.

'There was a small Thai woman who looked like a girl but she was only eighteen. She'd been in the premises for six months. She'd had to have sex with many men every day and she was living in terrible conditions. Of course we'd been told victims will never talk. I had two well-trained specialist officers with us who said, "Gov, she's happy to talk to us, let's take her away to a victim suite and get her support". By the end of the day they had statements from her, and they'd given her guarantees that we'd support her under victim protection. She wanted to go back home to Thailand and we were going to organise that. We placed her into support.

'The offender was a Thai woman who lived upstairs and ran a string of a brothels. Then I looked at how connected this was. She had people recruiting for her in Bangkok, she had a staging post where they used to get false Romanian passports and visas. They were taken on to Belgium and then she brought them into East London. All that had been looked at previously was the bit in London, not the whole network. The victim came back for the trial, and because of that the perpetrators pleaded guilty and got six years.

'Then another case came in, where a victim had been investigated by three different police departments in two forces. She'd been raped, but the evidence was "insufficient to charge with rape". She'd been trafficked, but again the evidence was deemed insufficient to charge with trafficking. She'd been subject to all kinds of abuse, but it was deemed "insufficient" every time. I was asked to look at it, but when I went to the meeting it was like playing tennis with six people. Everyone was batting it away. So I said, "Give it all to me". I sat down and read all of it and realised that if we linked all this together and showed it was a continuum of this woman's life, then we would have the evidence. We investigated it, we charged people and we got them convicted, including one who received fourteen years for rape.'

It was on this case that Kevin worked with 'a really good barrister' – none other than Caroline Haughey.

'Caroline and I met and decided we'd do all we could to get this case home. We discussed this "continuum", the small amounts of money involved and how we could prove that. We managed to prove that the first group of people were related to the last group of people, we found documentation in the housing to show that. We showed failings within the police: for example, they said they spoke to the victim and she said she was ok and didn't want to make a complaint. The victim didn't speak English. At all. So there was all this fudge. But we put the evidence together and we convicted.'

Case after case came Kevin's way, working with other police forces and taking on cases where he felt the victims were being lost within what he saw as the police's focus on intelligence gathering.

'I carried out investigations which were a hybrid between serious and organised crime, which is what my background is, and vulnerability, which is also my background. There aren't many police officers I would say who have run covert teams and worked on murders, *and* worked on rape cases.

'What usually happens is that vulnerability sits in one area and you have a certain kind of police officer who deals with that, and you have the other side which is kidnap and another sort of police officer deals with that. Policing over recent years has really become siloed.'

Considering Kevin's obvious passion for hands-on police work and placing victims of trafficking front and centre of any case, his move from the Met into his high-profile role as the UK's first Independent Anti-Slavery Commissioner seemed to be a surprising move towards politics.

The creation of an Independent Anti-Slavery Commissioner role was one of the key provisions of the Modern Slavery Act 2015, and the role centred around 'encouraging good practice in the prevention, detection, investigation and prosecution of slavery and human trafficking offences; and the identification of victims of those offences'.

The remit of the role ranged from 'making recommendations to any public authority about the exercise of its functions', 'undertaking or supporting the carrying out of research' and 'co-operating with or working jointly with public authorities, voluntary organisations and other persons, in the UK or internationally'.

Kevin explained how his appointment had come about.

'When the role was created, the Modern Slavery Bill was being written and I was being asked by ministers for advice. They'd come out on operations with me, seeing the work and hearing from me. I actually wrote the draft Risk and Preventions piece. I gave them draft wording for the bill, I worked with Frank Field, attended the Labour Party conference and held a side event. All of this was going on while I was still a police officer.

'When the role was advertised I applied. The process was robust and very thorough. There was an interview with a board made up of all the devolved administrations. You had to make a presentation on what you would do in the role, there was a written section, and a one-to-one with the Home Secretary. Theresa May appointed me.

'What has always driven me wherever I've been as a police officer is justice. That's the one thing. The role of the police and Government is to protect people from bullies.'

Kevin's first Strategic Plan (2015–2017) was released in October 2015 to coincide with Anti-Slavery Day. His statement was bold and to the point.

'My immediate aims as Commissioner were to see an increase in the numbers of victims of modern slavery that are identified and referred for appropriate support; and, in tandem, to see an increase in the numbers of prosecutions and convictions of traffickers and slave masters.'

The strategy was based on the international framework drawn up to combat modern slavery: the 4Ps – Prevention, Protection, Prosecution and Partnerships. It also tied in with the Government's strategy of Pursue, Prevent, Protect and Prepare.

Kevin's priorities were outlined as:

- improving identification of victims and enhanced levels of immediate and sustained support
- improving law enforcement and criminal justice response
- understanding and promoting best practice in partnership working
- engaging with the private sector to encourage supply chain transparency
- international collaboration

Victims were at the heart of Kevin's agenda. As he said in the plan:

A victim and human rights-centred ethos is at the very core of my outlook as Commissioner. A constant and consistent focus on victims and their needs is absolutely vital. Every stage of the trafficking and enslavement process can involve physical, sexual and psychological abuse and violence, deprivation, torture, manipulation, economic exploitation and abusive working and living conditions. As a result many victims suffer from an array of physical and psychological health problems. I will also be concentrating on ensuring that the unique vulnerabilities of children to trafficking and enslavement are properly addressed.

He went on to highlight concerns over the treatment of victims in the system:

Far too many modern slavery victims in the UK are not receiving an appropriate response. Morally, this is unacceptable. It also limits the law enforcement response, as victims are often the best possible source of intelligence on this crime. I have already identified inconsistencies in the recording of modern slavery crimes and failures to investigate. Claims that modern slavery is 'too hidden a crime' can no longer be accepted. I am determined to ensure that the mechanisms used to identify, track, record and investigate crimes are watertight so that cases do not slip through the gaps.

He signed off his first Strategic Plan with a clear message:

Here in the UK, through the new pieces of legislation that have been passed in England and Wales, Scotland and Northern Ireland, together with associated non-legislative activity, we now have a platform for a much-improved response. But I am clear that this is only the first step, and that only through effective implementation will we see tangible, positive change.

144

As a former serving police officer, and after being the first person to hold the role specifically created on the recommendation of the Modern Slavery Act, Kevin's view of the legislation was of interest to me. He believed it was 'great legislation', particularly in introducing life sentences for trafficking.

He explained how police and prosecutors previously relied on the Sexual Offences Act of 2003, the Coroners and Justice Act of 2009 and the Immigration and Asylum Act of 2004 – all of which included trafficking in the legislation, but were far from perfect when it came to charging many of their cases.

'The 2004 Immigration and Asylum Act had a big flaw. The same person who trafficked the person in had to be the exploiter. Unless you could prove the next person [in the chain] *knew* they would be trafficking, that was challenging to charge and prosecute.'

Perhaps unsurprisingly, considering his input into the process, Kevin also endorsed the Risk and Prevention Orders introduced with the legislation.

'As a police officer you've got an issue of capacity around how much you can do. When you're arresting people and placing them on bail, you may have enough intelligence to say they're involved in trafficking, but you may not have victims who want to give evidence. You may not have enough but there's enough to strongly suggest it, or you have a police force in another country telling you you've got traffickers coming to your country. With the Risk and Prevention Orders, you can apply for orders and ask for what you want. For example, an Order would forbid someone from buying airline tickets for anyone else; from holding anyone's passport; from renting more than one property at a time or visiting a certain geographical area. If they breach the Order you've got them for that, and if their enterprise is pretty big you can prove it pretty easily. However, the Orders haven't been used enough.

'The other thing that needs attention is proceeds of crime. There's lots of criticism about not enough monies being found, but when I was running trafficking teams I'd always get a financial investigator attached. That isn't routinely happening any more. If you have a financial investigator at the beginning of an inquiry, they can tell you where credit cards are being used. You can do surveillance without doing surveillance. You should always do that before surveillance because you can see how regularly someone goes somewhere. One of the cases that we charged without any victims was based on the number of one-way flights being booked: 200 people on budget airlines. None of them coming back.'

I asked him about the many criticisms the Act has received regarding its perceived failure to protect victims.

'It should give victims status. There's a clause in it about the victim, Section 45, which was never finished. There's a desire now to create new legislation. Well, just finish the other legislation. Had all the effort that's gone into creating new legislation been used to get Section 45 right, I think they would have had it fixed by now.'

At the time Kevin and I met, the Modern Slavery Act Review had not been published, and I asked him if he thought it would make much of a difference.

'Well, it's sharpened up the attention. With the main driver of this, Theresa May, moving on – does that mean the political will behind the issue weakens? I hope not.'

One of the other areas Kevin called into question while in the role of Commissioner was the state of the NRM – the framework in which victims of modern slavery are identified and access the relevant help. In an open letter to Sarah Newton MP, the then Minister in the Home Office for Vulnerability, Safeguarding and Countering Extremism, Kevin pointed out two key developments which were crucial in acknowledging the system was no longer fit for purpose.

First was the rise in number of the victims within the NRM, now much higher than in its inception in 2009, and consequently the complexity of their needs had grown and developed. Second, he pointed out that the trends, types of exploitation and the traffickers' modus operandi had changed, and the current NRM was no longer able to fully respond to the crime or cater for the multiple, complex needs of victims.

He said the NRM had become a cumbersome process with little co-ordination among the many stakeholders involved and that the time had come for radical change. In his Annual Report of 2016–2017, he called for complete reform of the system, with more co-ordination, accountability, oversight and monitoring as the existing NRM had many flaws which had been allowed to operate for too long.

The recommendations included providing potential victims with immediate access to support so that an informed decision could be made about their next steps into recovery. He also called for the decision-making process around the status of victims to be moved from the NCA and Home Office into a 'multi-agency expert group', then ensuring that a positive NRM Conclusive Grounds decision would entitle victims to long-term support. The importance of collecting accurate data around identifying victims was also highlighted – to 'feed into the UK intelligence [a] picture in order to improve the response to modern slavery crime'.

The then Home Secretary, Amber Rudd, accepted the recommendations and acknowledged that improvements needed to be made to the immediate support given to victims to prevent re-trafficking, and that long-term support must ensure victims were able to rebuild their lives.

Though the recommendations were agreed in 2017, they're only now starting to filter through, including the National Crime Agency no longer being one of the two Competent Authorities. Instead, all decisions on potential victims are being made in the Home Office.

Over coffee, Kevin shared his thoughts on this interpretation of his recommendation.

'They've kept decision-making in the Home Office. And that's going to break the whole system. I said this should be the responsibility of policing. Policing deals with every other victim. When they're making the enquiry of the victim, they know how to do it. When you're sitting in the Home Office, do you know what an enquiry looks like? Do you know what an investigation looks like? I don't think it should sit solely under policing but what I suggested was it should be funded for the police, with appointed NGOs in there to help and to manage the liaison so there was communication. You'd want Local Authority and immigration experts or lawyers involved.

'What is one of the Home Office's priorities? It's immigration. The same person who's in charge of that is in charge of trafficking. It's unfair. Definitely on the victims, but also on staff. It's unfair even to create an organisation like that.

'I know policing also has a responsibility to the laws of immigration but actually policing is accountable to the public. The police are accountable locally, to a local MP, a Local Authority, a Police and Crime Commissioner, as well as to the IPOC, to Parliament itself, to the Home Office and the National Police Chiefs' Council.

'If you want to make a complaint against the police there is a process. With the NRM, if you're a victim who's been trafficked, you may be waiting four or five years for a decision, and though they may say there are only a few cases still waiting from five years ago, that can be nearly six years! If a trafficker had been convicted they would almost definitely be out of prison in that time.'

A vital aspect of the role of the Independent Anti-Slavery Commissioner is its independence from Government. As it turned out, this became an issue for both Kevin and the Home Office, but in the early stages of his appointment, he was clear as to his aims.

'There were a number of MPs who asked if I was really going to be independent. That was something I was really clear about and why I didn't recruit serving police officers. It would have been easy to get serving police officers into the office, on secondment, but that was never going to work. If you're seconded you're still under police regulations, you still report to a force, so if you say anything negative about the police or law enforcement it's very easy for that to come back on you. You're going to be thinking about your career. It just wouldn't work, so I was not going down that line.

'In fact people were quite surprised when I said the National Crime Agency wasn't doing a great job, or when I said policing wasn't doing a great job. I think people thought I'd come in and be almost a cheerleader. It got people thinking, "Ok, this guy means business". Lots of Chief Constables told me I was doing the right thing, putting pressure on the NCA, on policing and the political world. I was doing it for the right reasons.'

Having met Kevin several times, and seeing his passion for this cause in presentations and when I'd interviewed him previously, now he had left the role I wondered if the expectations he had when he accepted the job matched reality. He used his reappointment process as an example.

'Once the officials in the Home Office got a chance to have some say in it, when it came to the reappointment process, and to influence that, they wanted to reappoint me in a totally different way. This was after three years. For example, Theresa May used to do my annual assessment, one-to-one. It was very high level, very detailed and prepared for. When she was gone, then they decided it was going to be a process similar to that for a civil servant, and my professional development review was going to be done by a director of the trafficking team, someone *I* was holding to account, and whom the Minister had asked me to hold to account. So then *they* were reporting on *me*.

'This was what I said to the Prime Minister when I was leaving. It was as if the worst pupil in the class (the Home Office) was marking the Headmaster. That just can't work. That's when I realised these guys are playing a game. They're playing a game. It's not about looking after people. The priority had shifted.

'When I saw there would be subsistence cuts to the victims, I raised the matter in a meeting in the Cabinet Office. I said this was taking a little from people who haven't got much. To the Government it's nothing. To them it's a lot. That told me where this was going, indeed that was the first thing they did. I wrote publicly to Sajid Javid and I met him about it. I did say, if the Government brings in a much better NRM, and victims' services don't need so much, and they're getting their money for travel etc., then you can consider cutting the overall allowance, because actually they're getting more. But not until that time. I saw the way that was introduced, I was in that meeting, there were lots of senior people there and I was the only voice that dared to speak out, but they railroaded it through.

'The whole role of the Commissioner was to be the person who would challenge these situations, and the legislation was supposed to give me the safety to do that. I provided the insurance policy, because the Government, the ministers, the legislators admitted they had got it wrong, and they needed someone who would be the voice of what needed to happen.

'I saw my role as not being over the top, not being personal (and I don't think I ever was), never doing something that wasn't evidence-based, and sometimes hitting hard. But what I did find was that the backup that was supposed to be there for me, which was the legislation, was just ignored – by the Home Office.'

In May 2018, nearly four years after his appointment, Kevin resigned as the Independent Anti-Slavery Commissioner. In his resignation letter to Theresa May he said it had been a 'genuine privilege' to work with her addressing modern slavery, and praised her 'personal leadership in securing ground-breaking legislation' and her 'global call to action'. However, he claimed that independence was vital for the success of his role, but at times independence had felt somewhat discretionary from the Home Office, rather than legally bestowed. He closed: 'I hope that any future incumbent can be assured the independence I am sure you intended as the author of the legislation.'

I asked him how difficult a decision it was to make.

'It was a gut-wrenching decision to go. There was some real underhand behaviour going on from people who should have been on the side of the fight, but were not. I always thought integrity would be something that could protect you. You only lose your integrity once. You only lose your trust once. I thought, I'm going down a line now where I'm going to be sacrificing my own integrity by agreeing with something the Home Office want as opposed to agreeing with what the law says.

'I met with my advisory panel and we spent hours talking about this. They wrote letters to the Home Secretary and others, then I just thought, I'm selling myself out here if I don't say I've taken this as far as I can. If I go down the way the Home Office want I'm actually just becoming a puppet. I wasn't willing to do that.

'How do we ensure people are responding to this as what it is, which is serious organised crime? People are traded and exploited. There should be some kind of humility. That's the bit I wanted. Some kind of humility. You're getting to something when the UK, no matter what it did, was saying, "Aren't we brilliant?" I was at the UN saying, "I appreciate what the UK's doing, I support it, I'm at the front of it, but we all need to hold our heads in shame. All of us".'

Given his extensive experience, fighting trafficking as a police officer, then as the IASC, I was interested in Kevin's perspective on the ongoing strategies for tackling modern slavery – starting with his advice for his successor (now named as Dame Sara Thornton).

'I think Sara is a formidable person. She's been a Police Chief for a number of years. It comes back to that issue of independence. It may sound as if I'm putting that above the issue itself, but I'm not. Once you lose that independence, you're not then representing the reason you're there. Relationships are important, of course. You can't just go around like a bull in a china shop.

'But if the role is what it should be, then, provided you stuck to the facts, were never personal or a maverick, then you should be able to operate with that independence, just like an MP. Where you can stand up in Parliament and ask questions of your own side. That's why we have a democracy, so people can openly criticise without fear or favour.'

If there was anyone who could give me an overview of the scale of modern slavery, in the UK and beyond, it was Kevin. I told him I appreciated putting a figure on the number of victims was complex, but I got a comprehensive answer.

'I would say this has become part of daily life in as much as our mobile phones and computers will have cobalt in them, mica will be in make-up and shiny material, and those elements will definitely be tainted by modern slavery – children down the mines, abuse in other parts of the world – so the connectivity of it is exactly as it was back in the time of the transatlantic slave trade. But the demand for materials is much higher. The access to materials is much higher. The way people and products are moved is much quicker, and the number of products is way higher than it ever was. So it's a bigger problem, even if we look at it in relation to the transatlantic slave trade, which was about moving people for products that we wanted.

'So it's the connectivity we must explain to people. There is a demand in the UK, and other parts of the developed world, for services and substances and products that are in the hands of people who are in exactly the same, if not worse, conditions than during the transatlantic slave trade. That aspect of slavery isn't pitched well enough.

'On our high streets, there are nail bars and car washes everywhere. You've only got to look at them to realise that they're not up to the standard of the usual high street business in the UK. Butchers and supermarkets, for example, are governed by strict rules and regulations. So one end of our high street is really well regulated, then at the other end of the spectrum we have foreign nationals providing cheap services which we all find handy, but which are ungoverned.

'Open up an off-licence in your own town and start selling alcohol. Get your booze from France, cheap, and fill up your shelves. You will be closed [down] by the end of the day. The laws and the rules are in place for licensed premises, and the police know how to deal with it. They just come in, serve a summons on you, take the booze away, shut the door and you're out of business.

'Car washes should be required to have certificates showing they are complying with environmental health and health and safety legislation, and that they're paying taxes, and employees are registered. That's all the certificate needs to do. Tesco have done it, with their car washes. You can pay by credit card, they've got a certificate, it's all contracted.'

I mentioned my ongoing concern about reporting car washes but ultimately only managing to disrupt the lives of workers who were willingly working in terrible conditions, purely because it was better than what they were used to elsewhere.

'There are many people who tolerate a lot just to get by, and it's up to us, in leadership roles, to raise their standards for them and to do that in a constructive well-managed way. Does that mean you will have to shut some places down? I'm afraid so.

'The reason [modern slavery] is embedded on the high street is lack of governance. Lack of management. Lack of support. The NRM isn't not working because it's not got the money. It's because it's got no structure. So if we can just push that a little bit more, which I hoped I would do as Commissioner, then we can start to get that change.

'I think the biggest opportunity is with money, with proceeds of crime. At the moment we have to deal with this in the way we would after a drugs deal or an armed robbery. We say the money has been earned from the sale of the drugs or has been taken from the bank, and once we find that money, we can recover it.

'With modern slavery and human trafficking we need to identify money as being tainted. A supermarket in London, a big chain, sells prawns. Those prawns are shown to come from slavery in Thailand. That supermarket should lose all the profit from those goods, and that profit should be used to compensate those who have been exploited and then to fund the global fight against slavery. That pot would soon get £150 billion in it.

'We've created a level of tolerance for this. We're saying to business[es] it's fine "as long as you're looking" without saying how closely they need to look. What they always say is that their supply chains are so complex, it's really hard to find out. If you bought some beef in the supermarket tonight, and it was contaminated, and everyone in the area got sick, they would be able to find out where that beef came from. After the horse meat scandal they had to know where every piece of meat came from, every bit of chicken, every bit of meat. Yet we can't work out where the people are?'

After everything he's seen, with victims, traffickers and in the world of politics, I asked Kevin what kept him going when the fight seemed endless.

'We're never going to deliver equality until it's about reality. We're never going to deal with poverty while we've got human trafficking. We're never going to deal with equality while we've got human trafficking because 96% of sexual exploitation is women. 72% of all victims are women. We're never going to deal with education while there's trafficking. But I stick with it because this is an issue I think we can solve. It's created by humankind so it's got to be ended by humankind. While this crime is there, you can't say we're in a just society.

'When you're that determined to do things, you're not going to drop them just because you're in for a bumpy ride.'

12

POLICING

On a grim, rainy day in Manchester I was standing on a street corner waiting to be picked up by the police. Not just any member of Greater Manchester Police, but a Detective Constable who has been at the coal face of anti-trafficking work (including the second Rochdale grooming investigation) for the last thirteen years. DC Colin Ward is part of Programme Challenger and has been front and centre of Greater Manchester's fight against slavery since 2006.

We'd arranged to meet in the city centre, so that he could talk me through his experiences combating the crime while giving me a tour of some of the sex trafficking hotspots. As soon as I jumped in the police issue people carrier, the weather turned even worse. It seemed to reflect the changing environment, as we headed away from the smart, modern part of Manchester which I've seen change considerably since my teenage years, to the industrial, Lowry-like appearance of the more run-down areas of the city. Hail the size of golf balls battered the car windows, and it suddenly felt like mid-winter rather than spring.

Colin began to explain how he had found this unique path within policing.

'In 2006 I was a detective in a regular CID unit, and there was a job in Lancashire where a young Czech girl had been kept above a curry house and repeatedly raped. During the enquiry it was discovered she was from Manchester, so I got involved in that case. While that was happening, a new unit was being set up in Manchester to deal with cross-border sexual offences (serial rapists, international sex crime, potentially online stuff) and human trafficking, but that was really in the small print. No one had a clue about it at the time. I knew a little bit about it, because of Morecambe Bay.

'I moved into this unit and from day one, I had job after job after job on human trafficking. No one had looked for it before, so it grew from there.'

Thirteen years later, Colin was still running anti-trafficking and slavery cases. Without my even asking him why he'd stayed in this area so long, he offered: 'I suppose because one of the first victims I met . . . well . . . the impression it leaves on you . . .'

Colin's team grew, and the Modern Slavery Coordination Unit was established in 2015, a section of Programme Challenger, a few months before the Modern Slavery Act came in.

'By 2013, I was still the only one dealing with this in Greater Manchester Police, and I kept going to the bosses saying, "I can't cope with this, we need more. This is growing and growing and we're not doing enough".'

He was incredibly passionate as he talked, and I could imagine Colin being brilliant at his job. In his forties, tall without being intimidating, he was calm with a warm northern accent. He'd clearly seen more than any human would wish to, but you got the feeling he let it sit comfortably alongside him, to spur him on to do a better job – rather than being eaten up by the misery.

'Challenger was set up after the murder of two policewomen in Hyde (the Dale Cregan case) and that was a multi-agency team because we had realised teams weren't talking to each other. DWP, Immigration, NHS – none of us were talking to each other as much as we could. That happened to coincide with the Modern Slavery Act coming in, so it was a good time to move how we were dealing with it in GMP.'

*

Before we started our tour of Manchester, we stopped for coffee in a part of the city I didn't even know existed, and tried to keep our voices down while carrying on our conversation.

From all my conversations with Colin before meeting him, I was confident he was a no-nonsense kind of bloke, and if he didn't want to answer a question then he wouldn't. So I risked broaching the subject of how he dealt with such tough cases emotionally.

He paused. 'It's a strange one.'

He seemed to be searching cautiously for the right words.

'About a year before I went into slavery work, I dealt with the murder of a child – three years old. And that was the most traumatic . . . The kid died in front of me in the hospital. The injuries were horrific. It was a game changer for me. I saw how horrendous that was, and everything else now affects me differently.'

Back on the road, Colin told me he was taking me to meet Tina. She worked for a charity which helps the city's sex workers.

Tina greeted us warmly; she seemed to have a great working relationship with Colin. The centre is tucked away under an arch in an industrial part of Manchester, with the office upstairs, and the downstairs open to clients. There are therapy rooms, a kitchen and open space for service users, and even a clinic.

The space was bright, with artwork, posters and leaflets everywhere. Tina told me a little about what they do at the charity– ranging from handing out condoms to offering a needle exchange (many of the sex workers have addiction issues so they are provided with the right equipment to help keep them safe). As well as the clinic on site, they also offer outreach sexual health work in a van which they take around the city. They offer the women routes out of sex work should they want it, and help with drug and alcohol dependency for those who can't make such decisions due to addiction.

I asked Tina if the team worked with women who were trafficked, or whom they believed to be victims of trafficking.

'We see indicators that would lead you to believe there is some sort of coercion there, but it is all very hidden so it makes it difficult to identify. Women are reluctant to disclose addresses. They'll say they're in a hotel but have no key cards, for example.

'Massage parlours became saturated with women from Eastern Europe about ten or twelve years ago. Especially city centre saunas. We never saw these women on the street. Then about six or seven years ago we started seeing women from Eastern Europe – mainly Romania – coming out onto the streets. It's grown to the point now where we can sometimes see more migrant workers on a session than UK women.

'When we started off we had no interpreter, so we were finding out very little, meeting the women but not having very good quality communication with them. So we now have a Romanian interpreter who does four nights a week. That's how much of a need there is. She's crucial in helping us build up a better picture of what's going on out there. Finding out the villages they come from, and if they've got kids. We're compiling better intelligence on what brought them here.'

I asked her how she would identify a woman selling sex as a trafficking victim.

'You see how often a woman is out. There's a cohort of quite young Romanian women who are always out. No matter when you're out, they're out. They come out at a certain time and they're working 'til the early hours of the morning. They'll get into our van, we're chatting, they're having a hot chocolate and all of a sudden a phone will go. A woman will answer her call, and our interpreter will tell us, "It was a male voice, but I couldn't quite make out what he was saying". But then the woman says in Romanian, "Right, we've got to go now", and everyone just packs up and leaves the van. We've had that a few times. We've even had women whom we have assisted with health issues, and they have still chosen to go back out onto the street.

'Often women will say things that lead us to believe that they don't want to be out working on the streets, but don't disclose any further reasoning behind that.'

'We helped one woman get back to her country of origin. This lady was brave enough to be able to make some disclosures so we could help her. Within this intelligence she told us that often there are males who are seen as boyfriends but they're actually putting women out onto the street. These women were working from say, 8pm to 6am the next day. She also disclosed that some of the men made women stay on the streets until they'd earned a certain amount of money before they could go home. Most of them don't carry their IDs, and they tell us they don't have access to their papers.'

Back in the car, Colin and I were driving around side streets of the city, as he pointed out where British sex workers would be found, and the streets opposite where Eastern European women tended to work. He mentioned pockets of the city around local landmarks and told me about some of the cases he'd worked on – not all of which can be mentioned.

I asked him about the scale of trafficking and slavery on the streets of Manchester.

'The big difference is – we're seeing it now. I always get asked when I'm doing talks, if we have more victims now. I don't think we have. Maybe a few, but I think we're aware of it more. NHS, Immigration, Local Authorities, the media are all more aware, and that really helps. Members of the public are understanding it better now, so we're coming across more victims.

'I don't think the traffickers are doing anything very differently. There are a lot more adult sex worksites, but it's not hard to traffick somebody. They still target people from their own villages. They still target the vulnerable. If you smuggle drugs into a country you can get caught. How easy is it to traffick a person? They walk on their own two feet, they walk through customs, they've got their own ID card. And it's only when they get here that they're controlled, beaten and raped. So I don't think their methods have changed massively.'

What about the nationality of the perpetrators and victims?

'It tends to be that a Romanian will traffick a Romanian, a Hungarian will traffic a Hungarian. Where the changes are happening is that Albanians are realising the Vietnamese are the best cannabis growers in the world. They're getting involved in the Vietnamese gangs now – so there's a bit of crossover. British traffickers tend not to be involved with foreign nationals being trafficked. They may be the owner of a brothel, but that's changed too now with pop-up brothels, with Romanians running the house so they don't need the English madam, they don't need the English brothel owner.

'There are definitely British victims. Look at CSE (Child Sexual Exploitation). CSE is trafficking.'

Colin was part of the reinvestigation into the Rochdale case.

'It was all over the press – also on TV.[1] I was in the Sexual Crime Unit at the time, dealing with human trafficking but part of this bigger team, and we were asked to re-investigate. We kept it then until the court case. We visited the victims and spoke to the witnesses again, getting the victims back on board. At the time, it wasn't seen as trafficking. Because we were used to dealing with trafficking we said, hang on, these kids *are* being moved – the distance doesn't matter. It's trafficking if they're being exploited. We had evidence of all the sexual offences, so we then pushed for trafficking offences – because it gives higher sentences. It would have been better now under the Modern Slavery Act, because it brought in more powers and higher sentences.'

But, I challenged him, one of the complaints about the Modern Slavery Act was that convictions were still very low. If it was so powerful, why was it not achieving convictions?

'One, lack of officers dealing with it. Two, victims not wishing to give evidence. So we look at evidence-led prosecutions. These used to be called "victimless prosecutions". That came from domestic violence cases, because they used to be termed "victimless", but there *is* a victim. It's the lack of funding that makes it difficult, the lack of

---

1   If you haven't seen the BAFTA-winning drama *Three Girls* then I urge you to find it. It's based on the account of Girl A, in a compelling book on one of the victims.

resources for those inquiries. I've been very vocal on this over the last few years. If you're looking at evidence-led policing on trafficking – don't forget the victim. Even if you're not using the victim in court, they're still in danger. Because when you've got that shitbag in that box, and he's done something to that victim, he doesn't care that she's not giving evidence. He knows she's told her story at some point. We're getting convictions now, but the sentencing is crap – if you have a look at the sentencing for evidence-led cases.

'If you've got a victim it's good – though not as good as it should be. But if you haven't, it's nowhere near as good. If you can get a victim on board, the trafficker nearly always pleads guilty, in my experience, and it's fantastic – you've got that victim there so the judge and the jury can see what's happened. The defendants either plea or are found guilty.'

Colin then spoke about the issue of victims who did not realise they'd been exploited.

'You get that mainly in labour exploitation. A little bit in sex work but not as much. Say it's someone in a car wash earning £5 a day. To us that's a victim. They're being exploited. They can't leave, they're earning £5 a day, and they've not got the right equipment and clothes for what they're doing. We've had people who, when we took their trainers and socks off, the skin of the foot has come off with them. And they're living on a shit mattress in the back of the car wash. But they don't see themselves as victims because that's £5 more than they were earning back in Romania.

'If we shut them down, where do these men go? And that little bit of money they were sending home is gone. So we try to work with them, educating them. Sometimes we've gone to the houses they're living in and they're actually dangerous, so we've gone out and bought fire alarms and put them up in the house. We've had nowhere to take the victims, so we've had to make their house liveable for the standards of the Fire Brigade and the Local Authority. Because if we told them they couldn't live there because it was dangerous, where were those eight men going to go?'

*

By this time, I had lost all sense of where we were in Greater Manchester. Which was probably just as well as our next stop was a safe house. It's unusual for the police to have this available to victims, and it had clearly taken work to get to this point. Colin gave me a guided tour, and while he was as understated as ever, I had the feeling he was proud to show me this place.

'It's got two bedrooms. Ideally, we only have one victim at a time, we'd never have victims from two different jobs and we'd be very wary of having two victims from the same job in case one is an "alpha". (Essentially a victim who has crossed over to work for the gang.)

'The idea is not to keep them here for long, just for that initial stage where we used to put them in hotels, or rooms in police training centres – when victims would be shit scared of police. This is somewhere neutral, it's away from everything. There has to be a cop here at all times, we'd never leave them on their own. But they can stay here as long as they need.'

We walked round the modest property, with Colin showing me each room. I found myself becoming quite emotional – the kindness behind every little detail was overwhelming. Gentle, sensitive touches awaiting people who have been shown no kindness for far too long.

'We've got beds, clothing in the wardrobes, rucksacks. We've got these rucksacks in stations now – pre-packed with toiletries, underwear, some clothes. We've got jigsaws, toys, knitting kits, mindfulness colouring books. We've got a cot here too. They can have a shower. We've got a new washing machine, a tumble drier, a vacuum cleaner. There's a TV. We've got a new suite and table.'

It was warm and welcoming, but I could only imagine what those walls had heard.

As we headed back into more familiar parts of the city, we drove through lightning and hail once more, weather befitting the grim topic. I asked Colin about the less well-known areas of trafficking he may have to deal with.

'Vietnamese cases are the ones we know least about, or have an understanding of why it happens. It's debt bondage, but is it on them, is it on their family, or is it on the village? Vietnamese victims go missing. If we raid a cannabis farm, and we take a victim away and then bail them for court (which is very rare) or put them in the NRM – they go missing every time. They *have* to. Their debt has gone up. If we've raided their cannabis farm, their debt has gone up because they've lost the cannabis.

'Because the "debt" is on them, or their parents or their village back home, they've *got* to keep earning that money. There'll be some connection to other Vietnamese communities, and this is where we don't know enough about it, because they'll find a way back to be able to pay it off. They'll go and find another cannabis farm, or they'll work in a nail bar, so they can pay off their debt back in their village. There are connections we're not aware of. It's the one area of trafficking we just don't know about.'

As Colin drove me back to Manchester Piccadilly, we talked again about what motivated him to stay in this role.

'I know it sounds corny but . . . you want to do your best for people. When you see the changes in victims when something good happens to them . . . I've had victims up here who end up getting a job, getting married, having children.

'It's about the families of victims too. There was a case I dealt with ten years ago, in Romania. The stepfather of the child came in to give a statement and he cried his eyes out for twenty minutes. He was telling us he'd been this girl's stepdad since she was one, and he'd not seen her for a year. He invited us into his home, gave us food and drink and he didn't have *anything*. He lived in a shack with some electricity and one room. He said he and his wife had agreed to eat one meal a day for ten years, so they could afford to put their daughter on a bus to school so she could get an education. It was at the school she met the trafficker – who raped her, beat her and forced her into prostitution.

'It just brings it home about other people's lives. It does sound corny but you're making a difference. You realise what a difference you do make to someone's life. That's why I've stuck with it for thirteen years.'

Though Colin has spent the majority of his time with GMP (Greater Manchester Police), recently he's been seconded to a specialist unit working across English and Welsh forces, based at Devon and Cornwall Police.

The Modern Slavery Police Transformation Unit (MSPTU) was set up after Chief Constables and Police & Crime Commissioners in England and Wales invested in a two-year programme to improve the police's response to modern slavery. Headed by Devon and Cornwall's Chief Constable Shaun Sawyer, MSPTU has been running since 2017, and while it doesn't investigate trafficking cases, its teams work across every policing region and has staff working within the NCA and in Europol.

They develop and share intelligence, look for best practice, train police officers and offer professional development to ensure all police officers and forces are as efficient and as highly trained as possible when it comes to spotting and fighting modern slavery. Indeed, the MSPTU Annual Report 2019 announced that the programme had 'supported police forces to deliver a greater than sevenfold increase in investigations against slavery, with the number of investigations rising steeply from 188 in November 2016 to 1,370 at the end of April 2019'.

MSPTU also worked with Border Force, GLAA, HMRC, Immigration Enforcement and the National Crime Agency to establish the Joint Slavery and Trafficking Analysis Centre (JSTAC) in April 2017. JSTAC was intended to integrate intelligence, uniting the key agencies most likely to first identify cases of trafficking and slavery, and enabling them to work together to share intelligence. Between 2017 and the MSPTU Annual Report of 2019, JSTAC issued more than seventy intelligence briefs, reports and assessments on a wide range of topics connected to modern slavery and human trafficking.

At the end of a city park in Vauxhall, London, rather unexpectedly, sits the National Crime Agency. Launched in 2013, the NCA is the UK's national law enforcement agency.

The head of the NCA's Modern Slavery Human Trafficking Unit (MSHTU), Adam Thompson, agreed to meet with me to talk through the national strategy and give me a steer on the scale of modern slavery in the UK. In a busy canteen, we found a quiet booth and I grilled him about the national response to these global crimes. He began by explaining the scale of the operation.

'I have a number of different teams, some that co-ordinate all the different law enforcement agencies, because with Modern Slavery – probably more than most of the serious organised crime threats – there are so many different law enforcement partners involved in tackling it. These include all forty-five police forces in England and Wales, Scotland and Northern Ireland; the Gangmaster Labour Abuse Authority on labour exploitation; the Border Force, Immigration Enforcement and NCA's own investigative teams – so many different partners involved. So I've got a big team which co-ordinates that effort, making sure all law enforcement is pulling in the same direction.

'Because it's such a global threat we need to work really closely with Interpol and Europol, but also bilaterally with each of our key priority countries, that is, those countries where most victims that end up in the UK come from. We want to make sure they're protected as much as possible, to try and help them avoid being exploited when they get to the UK in the first place. Working with their home countries helps us to do that, by putting that kind of prevention work in place.

'If we look at the statistics, we find that victims are often exploited by nationals from their own country. So we find Romanian victims in the UK being exploited by Romanian organised criminals or traffickers. It's the same for the Chinese and the Vietnamese.

'So other than where British offenders exploit people from numerous backgrounds, wherever they can find a vulnerability, quite often we find that the nationality of the offenders and the victims is the same so it's even more important for us to work with law enforcement agencies in those countries, to exchange information and intelligence.'

Adam went on to discuss his specialist and tactical advice teams, on call for the police or any partners involved in law enforcement, and his team focusing on prevention.

'Modern slavery and human trafficking have been designated as among the top serious organised crime threats affecting the UK, so we've got a role there. The NCA's statutory role is to make sure there is an efficient, effective response to each of those serious organised crime threats which are priorities. We have a role in co-ordinating two things mainly – the law enforcement response across the police, to make sure people are pulling in the right direction, but we also investigate cases ourselves, particularly those complex, sophisticated cases involving Organised Crime Groups.'

The global element of Adam's work fascinated me, so I asked him how much of the crime was generated in the UK, and how much came from overseas.

'It's an interesting one. What we're seeing more and more, if you look at the NRM referrals, is a huge increase in the number of UK nationals under eighteen who are being referred in as victims of trafficking. When people are about to give evidence for their referral into the NRM, we ask them where their exploitation has taken place. It does vary from year to year but in around 60% of cases there's been exploitation in the UK, and in about 30–40% of cases the exploitation has only taken place overseas. So they're victims but they may have been exploited en route to the UK. In Libya, for example, or if they've come through sub-Saharan Africa.

'There's a huge issue in the UK around things like County Lines. We know people who are exploited in forced prostitution, in forced labour, in Child Criminal Exploitation – usually drugs-related or cannabis cultivation. Domestic Servitude is another area which we

166

strongly believe is under-reported because people are very hard to find and rarely identify themselves.'

I was keen to get some sense of perspective from Adam around the scale of criminality in the nail bars we hear so much about.

'It's really difficult to say, in terms of likelihood. What we do know is people in Vietnam are recruited to work in nail bars, it's a recognised industry in which people will be trained. There are nail bar schools in Vietnam, so there will be a big proportion of people who have come willingly to the UK, and knew what they would be doing when they got here. They're working happily and send money back to their families in Vietnam.

'But we also know a number of people are being exploited. When you've got quite a big industry like this, and Vietnamese nationals have cornered the marketplace in nail bars, it also gives traffickers an opportunity to hide people in plain sight and exploit them. It's very difficult for members of the public to tell if workers are being exploited or if they're doing it willingly. If they don't speak any English it's even more difficult.

'At the moment in the UK there something like 1,500 investigations going on within law enforcement – that's police forces and all the other agencies that are involved. What we find, on the whole, is that the majority of these operations are reasonably low sophistication. They're people with familial links to crime groups who know somebody who may be able to supply a victim. It's often not what you think of as traditional or hierarchical Organised Crime Groups. In more sophisticated groups the human trafficking element is just one part of their criminal business model. Often they're involved in money laundering, drug trafficking or even firearms trafficking. There are lots of different things the more sophisticated groups would be involved in. Nail bars are just another way to make money.'

One name which has come up time and time again during my work investigating modern slavery has been Mark Burns-Williamson OBE. He's the Police and Crime Commissioner for

West Yorkshire and has been championing West Yorkshire Police in their efforts to fight slavery since 2012.

He agreed to meet me in his Westminster office before he returned to Yorkshire. Though Mark had never worked as a police officer, he had the reassuring stature and authority of someone who'd spent years working on the front line. In his warm West Yorkshire accent, he talked me through his strategy on fighting modern slavery.

'It was something that came to the fore soon after I'd been elected at the end of 2012. I was made aware of a major investigation West Yorkshire Police were undertaking at the time, rescuing a number of Slovakian nationals from addresses in the Leeds area. I was still relatively new in the role, though I'd been chair of the Police Authority previously, and I had to put together my Police and Crime Plan. So I met with the then Chief Officer team to talk about what they call their "strategic assessment model".

'It became fairly clear to me then that there was an OCG issue with modern slavery and trafficking that needed to be taken account of in the Police and Crime Plan. This was seven years ago, and the terms "modern slavery" and "human trafficking" – even though they were terms that had been around for a while – really started to hit home in terms of the reality of people being trafficked into parts of West Yorkshire. What then became apparent was the national scale of it.'

How did Mark perceive the scale of modern slavery within his patch, and the wider UK?

'West Yorkshire is predominantly a big urban area, with cities like Leeds, Bradford, Wakefield, Halifax and Huddersfield, and some of those areas are among the most deprived in terms of wards and local areas. There are factors there around cheap housing and environmental issues, so you can see why those areas have been used as a cover in some of the exploitation that's going on. But there is no doubt that there are locations in more remote and rural areas of West Yorkshire and other parts of the country where this is happening. And that becomes more apparent the more we know and investigate.

'Nationally, it's hard to say. What I do know is that the scale of this is definitely under-reported and under-played. I think to be fair, I have said [re the Home Office's disputed 13,000 figure] you can at least double that, if not more, in terms of what the true scale of this is.'

I asked Mark about criticisms that the UK just wasn't pursuing enough modern slavery prosecutions, despite the Modern Slavery Act in 2015.

'One of the key things is the amount of time it can actually take for these cases to end up at court. That's because of the sheer complexity of gathering evidence, protecting vulnerable victims and actually getting them to recognise they are victims. Then you've got all the issues around translation, disclosure, the volume of evidence, the fact that often officers need to travel abroad when it's a foreign national issue. So we shouldn't underestimate how difficult some of this stuff is, and the amount of work and time it takes. But it's absolutely the right thing to do in what are often horrific abuses of human rights.'

Considering Mark has spent almost a decade working in this area, I wondered how confident he felt that this was a fight the police were winning.

'I don't think we can ever be on top of it, given that we know it's under-reported. Despite the great commitment of law enforcement agencies, obviously including the police, that have carried out some great investigations and rescued and protected victims, we're up against that sheer volume, and how trends change.

'I am optimistic, because we know more, and we have learned, and there's an incremental increase in the number of investigations. But it's ever evolving. And there's always going to be more that needs to be done. And if people are being exploited, in whatever community, then that is not right. For me it's about trying to do the right thing. You have to bring it down to a human rights level. We're in a position to do something about that.'

13

BODY AND SOUL

*Modern Slavery is a cold, calculated and brutal business
model . . . It destroys the lives of its victims and is a shame to all of
us in a modern society.*

Patrick Ryan, CEO of Hestia

After listening to Elena's devastating account of being trafficked, after seeing the shadows that haunt her everywhere she goes, and after witnessing her journey as a vulnerable young woman alone in the UK, I wanted to explore the level of emotional support needed in order for survivors of such trauma to begin to put their lives back together. From dealing with physical scars to mental anguish, from pregnancy to PTSD, survivors of trafficking and modern slavery have a unique set of emotional needs which require specific care and attention.

As I've explored this issue over the last few years, I've encountered a number of charities dedicated to supporting survivors with emotional and psychological help. One particularly impressive charity working in this field is the Helen Bamber Foundation (HBF). Set up in 2005 by Helen Bamber, HBF has a tailor-made model of integrated care for people who have suffered as a result of trafficking, torture and other forms of human cruelty. It's their attention to the psychological element of care that has helped build their reputation. I'd heard of their work while getting to know Elena, as they offer a mother-and-baby community group which provides a wide range of support in the community to vulnerable women who are lone parents with traumatic histories of trafficking.

To help understand the psychological impact of trafficking and slavery upon survivors, I spoke to Rachel Witkin who is HBF's Head of Counter Trafficking & Publications:

'HBF has an evidence-based 3-Stage Therapy Model for Survivors of Trafficking and Slavery to help them sustain recovery and move forward towards reintegration and rebuilding their lives. It also has a specialist Counter-Trafficking Programme which has evolved from the particularly complex needs of survivors of modern slavery.

'People who have been enslaved experience specific problems in relation to trusting others, forming positive relationships and rebuilding agency and autonomy, so being able to establish a relationship of trust with a person who understands all aspects of their situation and can advocate for them builds a sense of safety and protection around them. This helps survivors to feel they have a welcoming space, and a dedicated team they can rely on to help keep them safe from re-trafficking and further harm. They become more able to talk about the traumatic things that have happened to them, which in turn helps professionals to gather evidence in support of their legal recognition and, in some cases, pursuit of justice.'

To better understand the impact of exploitation, abuse and the coercive controls employed by the traffickers on a victim, I turned to *Trauma-informed Code of Conduct for all Professionals working with Survivors of Trafficking & Modern Slavery* ('the TiCC'), written by Rachel Witkin and Dr Katy Robiant. This is aimed at all professionals of all disciplines who are working with victims of trafficking, provide them with a code of conduct that they can follow to apply trauma-informed techniques and methods to their work in order to establish and build trust with such a vulnerable group.

The TiCC explains how the brain deals with trauma, and how trauma can victim long term. It explains: 'When a person is

172

subjected to the threat of being killed or abused, or witnesses this threat in relation to other people, their body reacts in specific ways to enhance their chances of physical survival.' It goes on to explain how this reaction stops the hippocampus, the part of the brain responsible for our memories, from working normally. In contrast, the amygdala (which ensures our emotions, thoughts, feelings and sensory information are linked) continues to work extremely efficiently.

Therefore, 'Any future reminder of the traumatic event can trigger a survivor's memory to be vividly recalled as if it was happening again.' However, as the TiCC explains, due to the hippocampus not working at full capacity, some details of the event (the 'time and place information') are not linked to that reaction. 'As a result, the victim is often unable to access the information telling them the event happened in the past, in a different environment, and therefore they feel they are in the same, immediate danger that they were in when the original trauma occurred.'

It's hardly surprising that many survivors of trafficking and exploitation suffer from mental health problems such as PTSD, anxiety and depression as a result of their experiences. The TiCC states that often the extent of their suffering is not immediately obvious, as a consequence of their becoming used to hiding injuries (physical or mental) from others. In the course of being trafficked they have to become adept at minimising any suffering in an attempt to protect themselves.

It's this understanding of the survivors' vulnerability and mental health that is at the heart of how they are, or should be, treated when working with those responsible for their recovery. The TiCC gives very clear guidance on how to engage with those whom they're caring for as the journey to recovery begins, telling us that: 'Survivors may feel nervous, afraid and confused at a first meeting. Some may suffer signs and symptoms of distress, for example panic attacks or shaking, while others may be withdrawn or seem numbed. In some cases, survivors may appear to be detached, uninterested, or sometimes even hostile'.

The initial one-on-one meetings with survivors as they begin their journey are key, as trust begins to build. There are simple methods which can be employed to ensure this happens, making the client feel safe. It's also recommended that survivors should be offered 'minor choices and decisions' ranging from where they choose to sit in the room to being offered a choice of drinks, in order to establish a relationship which directly contrasts with their trafficking experiences.

As I continued to read through the TiCC, one thing jumped out – the importance of the use of language when working with a survivor. This ties in with what DC Colin Ward and the team at The Salvation Army told me about not all victims seeing themselves as such. It says:

> The concepts of *trafficking*, *exploitation* and *slavery* can be confusing or have little meaning for some survivors. However, the term *safety* is more widely understood, and translates well into other languages. While a person may not comprehend that they have been *trafficked*, they will be aware of having suffered violence or abuse or feeling afraid. Professionals, therefore, are encouraged to focus on the word 'safe', using examples such as 'Do you feel "safe"?' and 'Is [this or that person] a "safe" person for you?'

Keeping distress at bay is crucial during meetings – so if they feel overwhelmed, clients are encouraged to change their attention by focusing on the current moment, perhaps to chat about a nearby object, to move around or to discuss a practical issue to remind them they are in control.

It's also important to understand that 'not all clients will be able to make eye contact for some time, due to a 'history of subjugation to traffickers or the fear of any people who appear to be in authority'. It's advisable, therefore, that the survivor is reassured that their limitations are understood. Where possible, making 'gentle' eye contact can 'prevent feelings of loneliness and isolation . . .

feelings of shame will lessen and their confidence will improve . . . a powerful and corrective experience for those who are used to feeling diminished, humiliated, or mocked by others'.

It should hardly be a surprise that after being under the physical or psychological control of a trafficker and abuser, a survivor would still live in the shadows of that fear even once their liberty has been restored. There are risks of re-trafficking, and for some survivors perhaps of reprisals and/or attacks on family members. For others, the mental scars of being controlled are enough for them to live in fear that the trafficker has an ongoing hold on them.

In some cases, traffickers manipulate victims by tapping into their cultural or regional customs and beliefs, such as juju or forms of witchcraft. Ceremonies, often frightening, violent and including rape, are used by traffickers to frighten victims into obeying them. In many cases, the aim is to ensure that victims remain in debt bondage and don't tell anyone of their plight. Victims believe if they don't comply, evil spirits will cause them or their family members harm.

CHILDREN

In many cases, survivors of trafficking are parents (particularly the female survivors of sexual exploitation), and they bring their children to the meetings. Though the presence of a child, the report states, can provide a positive distraction during emotional conversations, it's also important that the well-being of the child is protected, as children can react to the distress of their parents. In addition, the subject of a survivor's child, or perhaps their pregnancy, can also be traumatic for the parent. Women who were sexually exploited may have had their child as a result of rape. Other reproductive traumas may also have occurred, and from a societal point of view, depending on their country of origin, some victims may feel shame for having a child outside of marriage, or for being a victim of rape. It is also possible that the survivor's child or children may have been killed, maimed or taken from them in the course of being trafficked.

PREGNANCY

Hestia is the main organisation in London supporting survivors of trafficking referred by The Salvation Army.

In March 2018, the charity published the results of research it had undertaken on the pregnant survivors it was supporting. The highlights were shocking:

- one in four female victims of modern slavery were pregnant when they entered Hestia's support service;
- two in three women received no antenatal care until their *third* trimester (before entering support services);
- one in three women were suicidal during their pregnancy;
- 16 per cent of women had slept rough while pregnant (before entering support services).

Overall, Hestia stated that pregnant women who have been victims of modern slavery 'continued to experience trauma and significant barriers to their recovery after they were freed' and 'experienced severe mental health traumas'.

The report found that pregnant women were unable to access the support they needed, with some waiting over a year to access perinatal mental healthcare. Considering the potentially complicated physical and emotional health issues victims of slavery face, the inability for pregnant victims to access the correct healthcare puts both mothers and babies at risk.

Poverty was also a concern, with the report stating that 'the subsidy women received from the Government was not enough to cover the additional basic needs associated with pregnancy, with all women relying on charity support and food banks for basic needs. This was compounded by a lack of suitable housing'.

And as I read through the rest of the study, one line jumped out at me, and brought Elena into my mind. Just as she was separated from her family during her pregnancy and the baby's birth, so were four in five women in Hestia's study. At a time when they needed as much support as possible, 'craving the support of their own mothers', the women reported feeling 'isolated, with feelings of shame and fear of honour-based violence preventing them from reconnecting with their families'.

On the release of the report, Hestia's CEO, Patrick Ryan, called for urgent action from the NHS and hoped that the report's findings would be considered by the Government's review of the NRM, which was at that time underway.

MALE VICTIMS OF MODERN SLAVERY

Seven months after the release of Hestia's study into the impact of modern slavery on pregnant survivors, they published an investigation[1] highlighting the experiences of male victims. They gathered data from 218 men, victims who had been forced to work in farms, construction sites or cannabis farms, sold for sex or used as slaves.

54% of male victims had slept rough (which as we have explored earlier, exposes them to a greater risk to being re-targeted). 47% of men had no living family, which of course added to their vulnerability, as did the fact that 92% of men showed signs of suffering from mental health issues, such as depression and post-traumatic stress disorder. As with many issues which affect the mental health of men, 'shame and embarrassment prevent men from asking for help'.

The report called for more accessible programmes and for more to be done to improve the availability of housing for victims, as well as protecting the homeless from exploitation. Following this report, Patrick stated:

> Modern slavery is a brutal and violent crime. The experiences of the men we are supporting are horrifying. Psychological

1 'Underground Lives: Male Victims of Modern Slavery', published by Hestia October 2018

manipulation, violence and rape were regularly used by their abusers to break their spirits and stop their escape. It is only recently that the true magnitude of the exploitation of men for modern slavery has begun to emerge. However, the availability of support has yet to catch up with the needs of these highly traumatised men. We need the public, private and third sector to better understand these needs and put in place the right support so they can recover from their trauma and go on and live the lives they dream of.

SUPPORT FOR SURVIVORS

Seeing the challenges that Elena has faced emotionally, as well as legally and practically, and after reading about the reality of survivors' recovery process, I wanted to speak to an expert about the mental state of those coming out of slavery, and how they begin to restore their lives. I arranged to speak to Ella Read, the Area Manager for Hestia's Modern Slavery Response Team. We met on a hot day in June 2019 in a trendy coffee shop in East London.

Ella is a warm, well-spoken, knowledgeable young woman who is clearly as passionate about helping survivors as she is well informed about their plight. She has an undergraduate degree in Psychology and a Master's in Psychology with a focus on modern slavery.

We sat down with iced coffees at a table under the air conditioning. Eager to share her knowledge, Ella began by explaining that when she started in her role three years ago the team consisted of only around thirty people, and has since grown to over a hundred.

'That's because of the number of people we're working with. We recently welcomed our thousandth client into the service, and over the last few years the statistics show the number of people we're working with has increased each year. We have 1,000 people in our care right now, which doesn't account for anyone this year who's exited the service already or who will come into the service after this point in time. That's a snapshot of where we are right now. It's completely terrifying that there's such a need for our service.

'In a way I wish my job didn't exist because I think the world would be a much better place if there wasn't a need for services like this. Unfortunately, the growth that we've seen over the last few years is only set to continue, and I think there are two main reasons for that. There's an increase in victim identification, with all the stuff we're seeing in the media, because there is increased public awareness that modern slavery exists and is real. Potentially as a result of this increased awareness, I think there is greater sophistication in how traffickers exert control over people. As a result of that there is an increase in the number of people who are being exploited.

'It's a low-risk, high-profit business. That's how traffickers see it, they see people as commodities, as people to be sold and to make money from. As much as I would love to not be here in a few years' time, I think there's just going to be more growth.'

I asked Ella if she was ever surprised by the extent of the cruelty she witnessed.

'Massively so. Coming face to face with survivors, I see they're people just like me, young women who wear clothes just like me, or put make-up on just like me, or want to have their nails painted just like me. It has been really confronting to come face to face with someone who just looked like a normal person, but who had had these utterly horrific experiences. When they start to tell me their stories and the abuse that they've suffered, often at the hands of their uncles, or their fathers, or their friends, or people that they really trusted – that's hard to process.'

Ella has supported an enormous number of survivors. Was there such a thing as a typical case?

'In terms of the most common types of exploitation the vast majority of our female clients have been trafficked into sexual exploitation. Lots of them are taken into commercial brothels, but also pop-up brothels, where they're essentially held in a house on what looks like a normal residential street. They are forced to engage in sexual acts against their will. The majority of the males we work with have experienced labour exploitation, so lots of them have been forced to work in the agricultural industry, or potentially in car washes, factories or construction sites.

'The vast majority of the people we work with are from Albania, and a typical profile of a survivor from Albania would be a young woman in her twenties who has been trafficked for sexual exploitation, who has probably been groomed by someone they think is their fiancé or boyfriend, but sometimes by their father or family member.'

I immediately thought of Elena, and realised that while meeting Marco was a seminal event and turning point in *her* life, to him, she was simply a 'mark' – and probably one of many. It was crushing to have it hammered home that while the bright, beautiful university student thought she was falling in love, she was being manipulated by a man who saw her as nothing more than a commodity.

It is this betrayal, this mental abuse which I would suspect does even more damage than the physical abuse. I asked Ella what kind of support Hestia offered those in their care.

'It varies depending on the individual. I think because we are the largest sub-contractor to The Salvation Army, the largest sub-contractor under the Victim Care Contract, we see the most cases. By extension we also see the most variety within those cases.

'Some people will come to us just after they have received their positive Reasonable Grounds decision, and they might be moved into one of our safe houses. Sometimes they arrive literally with the clothes on their back and the shoes on their feet. They may have just been identified in a police raid, and literally a day or a couple of days before have been in that situation of exploitation, and come to us in, essentially, a state of shell shock. They don't understand a) where they are or b) the system they've just entered. As much as they receive advice around what the National Referral Mechanism is, and what the process will look like, it is really, really difficult for them to understand and retain that knowledge.

So they'll come to us, into the safe houses, but be completely confused because of the extent of trauma they've sustained.'

After experiencing potentially years of physical and psychological abuse and control, victims find it horrifying to have to relive their experience. For some it can take years to disclose the extent of their ordeal, with some never sharing the extent of their experiences. Yet, the Home Office requires victims to recount their story and prove their victimhood through a series of interviews, as well as providing evidence to back up their experiences, thus demanding the victim takes part in a process that could further traumatise an already damaged person.

Supporting people through this is one of the roles of Ella's team.

'Once the individual is at a point where they're ready to engage with [psychological support] services, that's one of the things our advocates will do. Some people do come into the service immediately ready to engage with some sort of psychological professional.

'Some people come into the service so traumatised they have responded to what's happened to them by absolutely shutting down, and they don't want to engage with a therapist because they're not able to sit down and trust someone, and talk about what's happened to them. It's just too much. Then there is this horrible cycle where those individuals are severely traumatised and are unable to engage with any professionals, and because of that we can't get the relevant reports and documentation to submit to the Home Office which could impact their [Conclusive Grounds] decision.

'One of the positives for an individual of being in our service for a long time is that a lot of the people who are initially unable to engage with those professionals, over time as they build a trusting relationship with Hestia and with their advocate, they are eventually ready to open up.'

In addition to the traumatic effect the crime has had on victims, they are also subjected to lengthy waiting times as the Home Office decides their fate.

'In 2018 the average wait time was 615 days for a Conclusive Grounds decision,' Ella told me. 'The impact is really varied. Some people we work with actually say they'd rather wait for longer for the decision. They find the level of support they're receiving is so life-changing they'd rather the decision is further off, so they can continue to receive support and rebuild their lives.

'Then there are loads of other people we work with who are almost paralysed by the fear of this decision, and the fear of the impact the decision will have on their lives. They can't meaningfully recover because they're in a state of limbo. So it's really different with different clients. Some say they wake up every morning with this weight on their chest and all they can think is, "What if I get this decision today? What if I get it tomorrow? What if it's not in my favour? What if, what if, what if?" Which means things like counselling are pushed to one side because they're so consumed by this part of their journey they can't begin to process the rest of it.'

What is the impact when clients are told they have received a negative Conclusive Grounds and Ella's team have to exit them from the service?

'It's one of the more challenging parts of the job, for sure. I think that's where we as a team have to be mindful to manage expectations from the very first point of contact that we have. So from the first meeting with any client, we explain to them what the NRM is, what the potential outcomes could be, and what that means in terms of our support and their status in the UK. We put together an exit plan from the very first meeting. A big part of what we do is about empowering them when they're with us, so that essentially they don't need us when we're not there.'

After reading Hestia's studies on the impact of pregnancy on female victims, and the mental health of male victims, I asked Ella if she had noticed a gender difference in the recovery of clients.

'Obviously everyone is unique and everyone comes with a different set of experiences, but also hopes and dreams for the

182

future. As a general rule of thumb, I would say most of the women who come into the service are more likely to want to engage with someone around their mental health, so they tend to be ready earlier to be referred to a counsellor or specialist support around whatever their specific needs are. Generally speaking, it's much more difficult with the men. A lot of them come from very patriarchal countries, where they're told men must be strong and it's a sign of weakness if you sit down with a GP and tell them you're struggling with something. Men often, because of the countries and societies they come from, are more focused on wanting to be able to work. They're less concerned about the impact of their trauma in terms of their physical and mental health, and more consumed by the pressure of having to provide for themselves and their families, otherwise they feel they are failures. Their main cause of stress is often the fact they're not eligible to work.'

There is an added complexity in the care of some survivors – women who are pregnant or have children. Because most women recovered from slavery have been exploited sexually, many of the women in the NRM are pregnant or have children.

'Depending on where the individual is in their pregnancy, the first priority is antenatal care – so getting them registered with a GP, helping them to see a midwife, making sure they've had scans to check everything is ok with the baby, that there are no complications. We encourage them to have sexual health screenings. A lot of the women we work with have experienced Female Genital Mutilation, which has a huge impact on the ability to give birth safely, so an immediate priority would be the safety of the unborn baby and the safety of the mother going through the birth process.'

The mental health of the women, unsurprisingly, is also of great concern to Ella's team.

'We have women who come into the service who are pregnant, often – I'd say mostly – as a result of sexual exploitation they have experienced. They've got an added layer of trauma, as they've not only been exploited but they're now pregnant as a result. They don't know who the father is. They're in a new country where they don't speak the language, they don't know how the systems work, and they've got an unborn child they're going to have to look after. So a lot of them are at risk of self-harm when they come in. Some are suicidal.

'Immediate safety planning is put in place and safeguarding referrals are made to the Local Authority, so the women can get the support that they need. But actually the really beautiful and hopeful thing that comes from these cases is that these women are absolutely wonderful mothers. They're incredible.'

Considering that many of these children were born as a result of rape, it would be understandable for motherhood not to come naturally to these traumatised women. But after seeing Elena with her child, and how dedicated she was to its well-being, Ella's words didn't surprise me in the least.

'I think for a lot of the women, their baby is their lifeline. It gives them purpose outside of themselves. It gives them this amazing little bundle of joy to focus their energy and their attention and their time on. It gives them a real sense of hope and determination. A lot of the women have said they want to keep fighting and moving forward with their lives because they want to give their children the best shot.'

14

ELENA'S STORY: FIGHTING THE SYSTEM (2018)

I don't have any more hope. I don't know what can I do more. My life is more hard now.

A text from 'Elena' on 14th May 2018

It was 18 months since I had first met Elena and over a year since I had last seen her.

When we had our initial conversations, in the grim coffee shop in London, I knew she had been given a positive Reasonable Grounds decision (stage one in the NRM assessment process of deciding if someone is a victim of trafficking or not), but was still waiting to hear if she was to be granted a positive Conclusive Grounds decision.

Since she had arrived in the UK in the summer of 2016, I was sure that by now her fate must have been decided, and as I'd not heard anything to the contrary, I assumed her future in the UK had been secured.

I was wrong.

After leaving Elena the previous winter, I'd asked to be kept informed of her story. Then, in May 2018, while on my way back from a holiday I got an email telling me the bad news. She had not been granted a positive Conclusive Grounds decision. She had received a letter from the Home Office, so she had 48 hours to be removed from the NRM and the formal support networks around her.

My heart sank as I thought about the exhausted and almost broken young woman I had met last year, how pale and quiet she was, and how desperate to move on from her trauma. She told me later, 'Getting a negative Conclusive Grounds was very, very bad for me. In all this time I was in counselling therapy but then I needed more after they bring me negative decision. I was very scared for my baby's life, for my life. And for our futures. Maybe for them it's just one conclusion. But for our lives it's big dangers. On that day the solicitor tell me the news of negative decision, my caseworker came to my house to say sorry they have this news, but I have to be strong and to look to the future.'

As Elena was still awaiting her asylum application decision (many victims of trafficking and modern slavery have both applications running alongside each other) she was still to be housed in NASS (National Asylum Support Service) accommodation, but for how long was debatable. An asylum application with a negative Conclusive Grounds, I was told anecdotally weeks later, was pretty much a non-starter. One source told me, 'She's from Albania? No chance. She's from the wrong country'.

At that time, I didn't know I would be telling Elena's story, and I didn't know what a journey we were about to embark upon. If I had, I'd have kept better notes than the frantic scribbles I found in my notebooks, as I tried desperately to get to grips with a complicated and impenetrable system of legalities, processes and systems, which as a British-born woman I had never had to think about before.

Seriously, if you've never had to face what asylum seekers face, take this moment to be utterly, fundamentally, bloody grateful.

As I made my way home through the Welsh countryside, my first desperate call was to Bernie. I explained the situation to him, and he told me Elena could appeal the decision. He recommended a law firm with whom he works regularly as an expert witness – Wilsons in north London. A friend who works for a

186

charity helping migrants also promised to email me long lists of local resources to make sure Elena had some sort of practical support in the meantime. A ring round of my friends with kids made sure Elena and her child would have a new influx of clothes and toys. Small gesture of kindness from strangers, after such a crushing blow.

The next couple of weeks I recall as a blur of familiarising myself with the legal channels open to Elena, while calling and emailing the potential new solicitor Bernie recommended, in whom I'd placed so much hope (without quite getting to the point that they blocked my number). I'd even contacted Elena's MP.

Then I had a call from the law firm. As long as we could provide the relevant paperwork (and there was a lot of it) and prove Elena was eligible for Legal Aid, we could have a meeting with one of their team. Relief soared through me. While Elena and I were in constant contact, not being able to give her any firm news, as we both tried to understand the best next steps for her, was frustrating. But finally it felt as if we might be getting somewhere.

In order to secure the meeting with the new lawyer, they had asked me for a copy of the CG decision. Elena sent photos of each page and, while whizzing through the document on my phone, I was struck by two things. The length and language of the text, outlining definition after definition of trafficking and exploitation, and how hard it must be for a nervous victim reading it not in their native tongue. Also, how the relevant part of the document – the decision – is buried deep inside. I could imagine all those desperate men and women pouring through pages and pages of impenetrable legalese, desperately trying to find the simple sentences that would change their lives.

Then something else struck me: the language used to tell a victim they are not believed. It's shocking:

For the reasons set out below, it is considered you are not a credible witness and therefore, no weight is attached to your evidence.

Her inability to answer questions about the route she and Marco took, and the hotel they stayed in once in Belgium was seized on, as was, incredibly, the fact that Elena had managed to escape the traffickers altogether:

> Your claim that you managed to escape your traffickers is considered to be inconsistent with your claim to have been forced into prostitution by Marco and kept in a house for approximately ten months.

Her fear of returning to Albania, of being traced by Marco, was dismissed out of hand.

Doctors' reports were also dismissed:

> Due to the internal inconsistencies in your account, your credibility has been damaged to the extent your claim to be exploited cannot be believed.

The document went on to conclude that Elena was not a victim of either human trafficking or modern slavery:

> Your account is rejected in its entirety.

The wording was so final, so sure of its rightness, that for one awful moment I even questioned Elena's story myself.

The summer of 2018 was scorching, and as I met Elena for the first time in eighteen months we were both clearly nervous about the legal meeting, and uncomfortable in the blazing heat. Elena had her baby with her, now a toddler in a pushchair, and they had already endured a hot, claustrophobic train journey before she reached me.

We met at the local mainline station, before braving the tube to travel for another hour across London. Once we had battled count-less stairs with the buggy, dealt with a screaming baby who understandably had no wish to be on the London Underground in stifling heat, *and* come out the other side – we still had a walk and a bus ride to get us to the solicitors.

The reason I'm explaining the detail of this journey is to highlight that fact that appointments with doctors, dentists or lawyers, and even visits to friends, are not necessarily at locations on the doorstep of the survivor. They cost money. Most Londoners and visitors probably wouldn't think twice about the price of a cross-zone trip, but when you're living on less than £70 a week, spending over £10 on travel is prohibitive.

In the end, while I secretly topped up her Oyster card, Elena eventually chose to travel a different way from me, in order to save money. We then met on the Underground line further on in the journey, becoming experts in tube logistics.

On that first visit, just getting to the lawyer's office felt like a huge win, as we basked in the air con and ate the bag of snacks I'd brought to keep us going. We were waiting for Siobhan, the lawyer who could be about to take Elena's case.

When she arrived in reception to greet us, I was instantly reassured. Young, warm, yet calm and impressive, she had a soothing Scottish lilt and a deeply reassuring presence. We were soon joined by an interpreter, Ana. She was equally kind, and I felt, if this was going to go somewhere, we'd struck gold.

With the copy of the Home Office decision, and the piles of personal papers she'd amassed while she'd been in the UK, Elena sat down to hear from Siobhan.

Much of that day's appointment appeared to be admin-related. Siobhan clarified that everything discussed with her was confidential and that nothing went to the Home Office without Elena's consent. Then she explained the next steps, outlined her case and set her up on the system. After that, some key matters were addressed.

Siobhan explained that the decision by the Home Office was one of the worst she had seen. It appeared there were fundamental errors in the Home Office's interpretation and consideration of

Elena's account. They accused her of being inconsistent, when, according to Siobhan, she was simply lacking detail – hardly surprising when she was being interviewed while heavily pregnant, and traumatised.

The Home Office said Elena was 'too vague' in her accounts. Siobhan objected to this as a statement saying it went against trafficking guidance and they should have asked her for more information. She explained that if there was a lack of information in a statement, or any inconsistencies, it did not mean a victim was making it up. As I had heard from several people I'd interviewed, many survivors who have been through traumas such as trafficking and exploitation are emotionally scarred, unable to recall events, subconsciously unwilling to recall events, or didn't realise the importance of details at the time.

We were also told that Elena's negative Conclusive Grounds decision was intrinsically linked to her asylum case, and while it could be possible to still get a positive asylum decision, it was hugely unlikely. If the asylum case was refused, this could lead to an appeal in court in front of a judge. But trafficking decisions don't allow for appeals. The best hope was for her case to go to 'Judicial Review', where a judge would look at faults in the decision-making process, as opposed to the decision itself.

However, before we got to that point, Siobhan told us there was an immediate option: simply writing to the Home Office to ask them to reconsider their decision. We could submit stronger, clearer evidence, putting right the mistakes in the original paperwork, and, crucially, including evidence to prove the negative impact the delays and the ultimate decision had had on Elena's mental health.

It's possible to twin-track both options so if necessary, we were ready to go to court, but Siobhan was hopeful it wouldn't come to that, and that the Home Office would simply look at the new evidence and reverse their decision. We were against the clock though, as there was a three-month time deadline for all this to happen.

Siobhan seemed positive, I was overwhelmed and Elena was despondent. She had already waited two years, and didn't want it to take so long, time and time again. Siobhan was reassuring, telling her that while there was no timescale on how long reconsideration would take, there were arguments for them to make a quick decision, including the length of time Elena had already waited, the fact she had a child, and that they were living in limbo. Though she realised this was hard, Siobhan asked us to wait longer, but wait for the right ending.

All at once, we were in a flurry of admin, with paperwork being photocopied, questions being asked about NASS and Legal Aid, and the next appointments being made for us to return so that Elena could give a new statement.

By the end of that first appointment, Elena was exhausted, the baby was awake and full of beans, thankfully oblivious to its mum's challenges, and the sun was still beating down on us as we made our way home.

The rest of the summer was taken up with legal appointments. I managed to get to most visits with Elena. I was surplus to requirements from a legal point of view, but my being able to act as a babysitter was crucial. Her baby was growing into a lively toddler, and she needed peace and quiet to take in the legal ramifications of every visit. Plus, strong as Elena was being, she was reliving some deeply distressing moments in her life, which she (and all victims) need to do away from distractions. Not only that, it was upsetting for the child to see its mother in such an emotional state.

Appointment after appointment was taken up with Elena recounting her story in great detail. Her English had improved since I first met her, and Ana, the interpreter, was excellent, so during the hours we were in the small meeting rooms, more and more of what Elena went through became apparent. As did the mistakes in translation that had clearly occurred in her initial asylum interviews. Some were so basic, like the names of her traffickers, it was infuriating. Fortunately, sitting down with Siobhan and writing a more comprehensive account, she could correct everything that had been misunderstood in initial asylum interviews.

'In my Home Office interview it was very difficult. I felt that I could not open up and fully talk about it to the interpreter and interviewing officer. I tried to answer the questions as well as I could but by giving the minimum information required because it was so hard to talk about. I don't know if it is something I will ever be able to talk about in detail.'

Siobhan advised us it was also a good idea to send the Home Office a psychological report, so one Saturday morning I went with Elena to a central London office for her to have a three-hour appointment with a psychologist. She finally emerged desperate to see her baby (she found being separated for too long made her anxious), exhausted and pale. I tried to lighten the mood by joking that my morning had been harder than hers as the nearly-two-year-old had me running around in circles. Luckily that made her laugh, but it was clear, once again, what reliving her experiences in Belgium had done to her.

In August, something came up that had nothing to do with Elena's appeal but it did show the level of bureaucracy those attempting to stay in the UK face. The card Elena used to access her weekly subsistence, her ASPEN card, stopped working. She couldn't get any money out of her account.

Call after call to countless helplines saw us at 'number 34 in the queue', 'number 55 in the queue', with no one being able to give us an answer as to why the card had stopped working, or where a replacement had been sent. When Elena went to one of the regional Home Office centres (with her baby in the pram) and told them she had no card and no money, they just said another one was in the post and would be there in days, seemingly oblivious to the fact she could not feed herself or her child – the child in front of their eyes.

Still the card didn't appear, and we were lost in a loop of calling the Home Office, Migrant Help or her Housing Support Officer. The latter was rude and unhelpful and couldn't seem to grasp the fact that Elena had no money or access to food; she claimed she was unable to act on anything without some mystical 'code' which no one seemed able to generate.

Ironically the only people who made any sense or offered any help were the physical *makers* of the card, who told us they had been given the wrong address for her. Replacement cards were repeatedly being sent to the accommodation Elena was put in when she first arrived in London. They told me another would be made immediately and sent to the correct address. In the meantime they called her housing provider and told them to get cash to her as soon as feasibly possible. (They turned up the next day with a Tesco voucher, but by this point Elena had had no money for three weeks, so why the rush?)

During this three-week period, no one offered her alternative forms of access to money or food. She was relying on the kindness of the other women in her house, the local church, and bits of cash from me which I had to force her to take. Looking back over the messages between us, almost a year later, I find it just as infuriating.

One call left me sobbing with frustration and rage. Someone had told me about the Home Office's Destitution Line. Genius, I thought, these will be the people to get her access to cash so she can eat. I couldn't have been more wrong.

I can't begin to tell you how horrendous that call was. A rude, uninterested and frankly obnoxious woman told me, after going round in circles, that Elena was not eligible for the destitution payment because she had money in her bank account. The fact she had no card to access it was irrelevant. If she had no money at all, they would help her. But she had the money. Therefore 'the computer says no'.

I couldn't believe what I was hearing. For the first time in my life, I was mortified to be British.

*

Then something changed.

On a rainy morning in November, I was sitting on the 38 bus heading to a long newsroom shift. My phone pinged at 8.38.

Morning, my dear Louise. I just want to say I am so happy and crying for my happiness. Siobhan call me today and say they accept the decision.

The Home Office had reversed their decision. Elena had been given a positive Conclusive Grounds. There was still a long way to go, but suddenly the day didn't look so gloomy.

15

THE CHILDREN

One of the most distressing areas of trafficking and modern slavery which, despite the horror, can't be overlooked, is the subject of child trafficking. It's a murky and evil world, but one that is all around us.

When I began researching this, I realised how little I really knew about child trafficking and slavery, as is evident from my preliminary notes:

- child slaves in mines and factories – abroad (laptops, diamonds, clothes?)
- sex trafficking – Thailand?
- internet/online sexual exploitation – everywhere
- children begging and working with gangs in London – trafficked?
- UK – child sexual exploitation (Rochdale and Rotherham was trafficking)
- UK – 'County Lines' (vulnerable young people being groomed/threatened to deal drugs)

That was it. The sum total of my knowledge around child exploitation and trafficking, vague stereotypes from reading newspaper headlines which were too distressing to delve into. But I had to start somewhere, and the following definitions enlightened me.

Child *trafficking* is defined as 'transporting, recruiting or har-bouring people for the purpose of exploitation, using violence, threats or coercion'. As the charity Anti-Slavery International explains: 'When children are trafficked, no violence, deception or coercion needs to be involved, trafficking is merely the act of transporting or harbouring them for exploitative work. When away from their families, they are at the mercy of their employers'.

Child *slavery* is the enforced exploitation of a child for their labour for someone else's gain. The ILO states that on 'any given day in 2016':

- 152 million children were trapped in child labour
- 73 million were in hazardous work
- 19.6% of child labour takes place in Africa, the highest prevalence
- 48% of victims are between five and eleven years old
- 58% of victims are boys
- 70.9% of victims are working in some form of agricultural exploitation

By now, I had become confused by definitions surrounding what constitutes 'child labour' and 'child slavery'. Both sound appall-ing, and the need to categorise them at all seems redundant when the outcome for the child is equally toxic.

The charity Anti-Slavery International offers a helpful break-down of the difference, and why the nuances are important. These are the six main categories. *Child Work* is defined by Anti-Slavery International like this: 'Some types of work make useful, positive contributions to a child's development, helping them learn useful skills. Often, work is a vital source of income for their families'. They go on to explain that *Child Labour* is not slavery, 'but never-theless hinders children's education and development. Child labour tends to be undertaken when the child is in the care of their parents'. *Hazardous Work* is defined as the worst form of child labour. This is described as 'irreversibly damaging children's health and development through, for example, exposure to dangerous machinery or toxic substances, and may even endanger their lives'. Then there is *Child Slavery*, 'the enforced exploitation of a child for their labour for someone else's gain'.

There were two other areas which I'm embarrassed to have overlooked in my notes: *Child Marriage* and *Children in Armed Conflicts*. In relation to Child Marriage, the organisation states that: 'Many marriages involving children will not amount to slavery, particularly between couples aged sixteen to eighteen years. But when a child didn't give their consent to a marriage, is exploited within it or is not able to leave, that child is in slavery'.

The information on Children in Armed Conflicts is equally clear: 'Children forced to take part in armed conflicts don't only include child soldiers but also porters or girls taken as "wives" for soldiers and militia members. Children involved in conflict are severely affected by their experiences and can suffer from long-term trauma'.

Within these definitions, it makes sense that the statistics around child slavery versus child labour could vary wildly.

Anti-Slavery International, quoting the ILO, say of child slavery that worldwide 10 million children are in some form of 'slavery, trafficking, debt bondage and other forms of forced labour, forced recruitment for armed conflict, prostitution, pornography and other illicit activities'. They also go on to state:

- More than 700 million women alive today were married before their 18th birthday
- More than one in three (about 250 million) entered into a union before age 15 (UNICEF)
- 300,000 children are estimated to serve as child soldiers, some even younger than ten years old (UNICEF)
- 15.5 million children are in domestic work worldwide – the overwhelming majority of them girls (ILO)

It was clear I needed to speak to those working on the front line in this area, so my first port of call was the International Justice Mission (IJM). I'd met a couple of the team when they were in previous roles elsewhere, and luckily Euan Fraser and Molly Hodson were happy to share their knowledge with me once more. Due to work commitments for all of us, we had to swap thoughts via email. Considering the subject matter, I was often grateful for the emotional barrier this provided.

We began with an explanation of the work IJM does.

IJM has a global team of lawyers, social workers and investigators who work in partnership with local police, prosecutors and authorities in twelve countries to find and rescue people trapped in slavery and violent oppression, to walk with survivors as they journey to freedom, and to hold slaveowners and traffickers to account. We've helped rescue over 50,000 people from slavery and oppression.

We seek to bring about justice system transformation, so that the law works to protect those who are vulnerable to modern slavery and other forms of violence.

By working alongside law enforcement as a case progresses from initial investigation to arrest, charge and prosecution, we are able to identify problems and gaps within the system. IJM then works with our partners in the justice system to develop high-impact interventions that address the most critical issues and secure sustainable change, for example through providing specialist training or advocating for additional resources.

Our team has spent more than 20 years on the front lines fighting some of the worst forms of violence, including human trafficking and modern slavery. We have seen that where the law enforcement response to slavery and other forms of violence measurably improves, prevalence of the crime dramatically declines. In the areas in which we have worked we have seen reductions in the prevalence of modern slavery; most notably in the Philippines where we have seen reductions of 79%, 75% and 86% in the number of children in commercial sexual exploitation in Cebu, Manila and Pampanga respectively.

The first thing I wanted to establish was the kind of exploitation facing children around the world. Was I right in thinking it was mainly to do with sexual exploitation online and mines and factories abroad, or was that lazy thinking?

Children are known to be exploited in a vast range of ways. From forced labour exploitation, to trafficking for sexual exploitation. For example, IJM works to tackle child trafficking in Ghana, where children are trafficked into the fishing industry on Lake Volta, the world's largest man-made lake. Thousands of children work in its massive fishing industry – and many of these children are held in slavery. Children as young as three years old are abused and malnourished. They are forced to rise before dawn to go out on the lake, diving down into the dark water to untangle fishing nets. The work is dangerous, and drowning is a constant threat. Violence is extremely common on the boats: often children will be beaten with paddles, or thrown into the lake, caned, slapped or beaten with ropes.

Examining the global reach of IJM's work shows me that there is no end to the way children are abused. In brothels, traffickers are using 'harsh and extremely violent conditions' to exploit boys and girls for sex. The number of girls being sold in bars and brothels eventually rescued by IJM runs into the hundreds. In sweet factories – a place associated with children, of course, but not for the reasons you would now expect –victims are often lured into slavery by the promise of a good job. IJM have seen children 'enslaved in sweet factories for years'. Rice mills, quarries and mines, according to the site, appear to be areas where entire families are targeted. Parents take jobs, and the children are forced to work there too.

Much of IJM's global work seems far removed from the streets of Britain, so I asked Euan and Molly how common it would be for children who were trafficked from abroad to end up in the UK:

In 2018, 3,137 children were referred to the National Referral Mechanism . . . These children came from eighty-five countries. The high number of children identified of different nationalities – most often Vietnamese, Sudanese and Albanian – tells us that the international element cannot be ignored and there is an urgent need to look at the systemic causes of vulnerability to exploitation in order to bring about sustainable prevention.

1,421 of those children were British nationals – the majority exploited for their labour (which includes criminal exploitation).

This particularly high number of British children being identified and referred for support is in part due to increased understanding of child criminal exploitation, primarily in the form of children being forced to transfer money and drugs across the country along so-called 'County Lines'. Previously such children have been criminalised as gang members for committing drug and other offences. However, increasingly these children are understood as being exploited by gangs and in need [of] protection and support (although there is still considerable work to be done in this regard).

The reference to eighty-five source countries led me to think about logistics. How would a child be brought to the UK? Sold by its parents? Stolen? Coerced?

This would depend very much on where they are coming from and the nature of the exploitation. Some will enter the UK on legitimate visas, others will be smuggled into the UK only to find that they are then indebted to their trafficker and forced to work for them. A significant number of Nigerian children

200

are exploited in domestic servitude. Parents may well have been involved, believing that relatives in the UK would provide the child with access to education.

The au pair visa is known to be open to abuse by traffickers.

Children who have been forcibly displaced from their home country, and are perhaps in refugee camps, are known to be susceptible to exploitation, as traffickers prey on their vulnerability.[1] Others are brought to the UK and exploited by organised criminal gangs which have established networks and routes – for example Vietnamese children trafficked to work in cannabis farms.

Terrifyingly, many children don't need to be moved in order to be exploited.

Online sexual exploitation of children (OSEC), also referred to as cybersex trafficking, is a growing form of modern slavery, involving the live sexual abuse of children streamed via the internet.

Children as young as two have been rescued from the Philippines when they are discovered to have been sexually abused in their own homes, sometimes by their own families.

In the Philippines, IJM tackles the online sexual exploitation of children, a form of sex trafficking which was unimaginable before the digital age. It involves the live-streaming of child sexual abuse over the internet, paid for and directed by paedophiles – often from Western countries. Paedophiles and predators anywhere in the world can now search online

---

1 The Dubs Amendment to the 2016 Immigration Act sought to ensure that unaccompanied child refugees would be given safe passage to the UK to be reunited with relatives. However, despite campaigning by Lord Dubs, a child of the Kindertransport, the amendment failed to be enshrined in UK law in the EU Withdrawal Bill. MPs voted against the amendment in January 2020, meaning the UK does not now have to provide shelter and care for unaccompanied child refugees.

and wire a secure payment to an adult who sets up the live 'show'. The more abusive the show, the more the customer pays. The Philippines is a global hotspot for online sexual exploitation of children, but the online consumers of this vile abuse are often from the UK and other Western countries.

IJM has formed a new partnership with the UK National Crime Agency, Philippine and Australian law enforcement – The Philippine Internet Crimes Against Children Centre (PICACC) – to promote best practice, share resources and facilitate intelligence sharing to more effectively tackle this form of abuse. IJM has supported over 150 cases and assisted Local Authorities and law enforcement to rescue more than 500 survivors.

Over 50% of IJM's clients have been twelve years old or younger, the youngest just three months old. A global response – including governments, law enforcement, NGOs and tech companies – is urgently needed to tackle this disturbing global crime. Molly and Euan elaborated on this:

In 2017, the Philippines Department of Justice received on average 3,800 reports of online child abuse per month (an increase from an average of 1,000 per month in 2014). IJM has seen first-hand that when local justice systems are properly equipped to proactively identify survivors and hold traffickers to account then the prevalence of slavery and violence falls dramatically.

Prior to tackling online sexual exploitation of children, IJM partnered with Philippine authorities and law enforcement to assist them to address in-person commercial sexual exploitation. In 2010 after working with local police, prosecutors, courts and aftercare providers for four years to develop a specialist response to the problem in Cebu, an independent study found there had been a 75% reduction in the availability of children for exploitation.

Following this success, IJM conducted similar projects in Manila and Pampanga, seeing reductions of 75% and 86% respectively.

According to Molly and Euan, OSEC is known to be particularly prevalent in the Philippines for several reasons including:

- the widespread use of the English language
- increased availability of internet connectivity
- availability and common use of money-transfer services
- the high number of unregistered internet connections through pre-paid services, such as mobile devices and data plans

This made for such distressing reading it was hard to imagine this crime can ever be stopped. I asked the team about how the future of anti-slavery work would play out. What could we be hopeful about?

Slavery, and other forms of violence, thrives where the justice system does not work to protect the most vulnerable. IJM has seen that when the laws are enforced, survivors protected and perpetrators held to account, the prevalence of slavery falls dramatically. Each year, IJM sees hundreds of violent traffickers convicted for their crimes, thousands of individuals rescued from slavery and tens of thousands of justice system officials trained in the fight against human trafficking.

In the early 2000s, Cambodia had an out-of-control epidemic of commercial sexual exploitation of children: the Cambodian government and NGOs estimated that between 15 and 30% of those in prostitution were children.

IJM has partnered with the Cambodian justice system, and as a result we have witnessed a dramatic reduction in child sex trafficking in the three largest commercial sex markets in Cambodia: a 2015 study found that less than 0.1% of people in the sex trade are children aged 15 and under.

It is essential to address slavery at source. We see this in relation to exploitation in supply chains. Business[es] ought to take action to avoid forced labour in their supply chains. However, slavery – like all other crimes – cannot be solved by the international private sector. It also requires an effective response from local governments and law enforcement to enforce existing anti-slavery laws. Only these local agencies in-country have the mandated responsibility and authority to respond to and prevent slave labour.

I wondered how Molly and Euan stayed motivated, considering our simple email exchange had left me deflated, and simultaneously raging and tearful. Their calm response was an example of why they do their job and I don't.

At IJM we are encouraged by the signs of breakthrough that we regularly see – children being taken from situations of exploitation and into support, and children who then go on to become advocates for change. We see perpetrators being held to account, justice systems changing to respond to the problem and the number of people – adults and children – in slavery falling. We've seen slavery decrease by up to 86% in places where we've worked.

Despite these successes, ending child exploitation still seemed an overwhelmingly gargantuan task, and I wondered if it was something the public could help with at a micro level.

Child trafficking and slavery is not a distant problem, it's connected to each of us in our everyday lives because of the products we consume – from clothing to coffee, and mobile phones to make-up. Also, slavery happens in our communities too. But rather than being overwhelmed by the dark realities of slavery and its scale, we would encourage people to be hopeful, to take action with us and be optimistic that this vile abuse can end – we're already seeing major breakthroughs and reductions in slavery where IJM works. We believe it is possible to end slavery in our lifetime and we'd love more people to join us in the fight.

There is no doubt the plight of children around the world who are trapped in any form of exploitation is horrific. But surely it's the kind of thing that happens in other countries? We don't send children down the mines here (any more), plus the fact that children have to stay in school until they're 16, and we are a wealthy nation means kids in the UK are not at risk of such exploitation? Wrong.

According to the NRM figures in 2019, nearly half of all victims of modern slavery found in the UK in 2018 were children. We also must bear in mind that while 3,137 under 18s entered the NRM, these are the children who were identified. It's impossible to know how many other young people are in the UK and not known to the authorities. Of these 3,137 victims, the majority were British and had been trafficked *within* the UK. It appears that this isn't a problem that will go away any time soon, as the number of child victims found is growing every year.

The exploitation of children in the UK tends to be defined in two main ways – Child Sexual Exploitation (CSE) and Child Criminal Exploitation (CCE). However, once targeted, it's not unusual for the victim to be exploited in a combination of both. Both crimes involve the perpetrator targeting a vulnerable child, 'grooming' them with gifts, offers of friendship and support in situations where perhaps the child previously felt alone and misunderstood, and eventually coercing them into sexual or criminal activities by wielding power over them.

In 2012, the Rochdale grooming scandal (followed by Rotherham, and a host of other cases around the UK) brought the issue of CSE to the public's consciousness. Teenage girls had been groomed by gangs of men, then abused, raped and transported to other towns and other abusers. In 2019, it's CCE which is making more headlines, specifically in the form of County Lines drug running, where (mainly) young people are used to move and sell drugs from cities into smaller towns and more rural areas to enable dealers to put distance between themselves and the supply chain.

It's only over the last few years that abuse such as this has become categorised as trafficking, due to the fact victims are transported for the purpose of exploitation. It's also only recently that CCE has been included under the umbrella of modern slavery, because the victim is exploited, and forced to commit a crime via coercion. The change in this thinking has also led to those who were once identified as criminals being recognised as victims.

Anyone watching the UK news over the last couple of years or so won't have missed the seeming surge in County Lines cases – a form of modern slavery which, according to the National Crime Agency, has become a £500 million industry in the UK alone. Young people are transporting drugs around the UK at the behest of older, manipulative crime gangs. The children and teenagers recruited are vulnerable, groomed and at some point straddle that fine line between being victims of a gang and co-conspirators in drug dealing.

The National Crime Agency defines County Lines as:

The term used when drug gangs from big cities expand their operations to smaller towns, often using violence to drive out local dealers, and exploiting children and vulnerable people to sell drugs. These dealers will use dedicated mobile phone lines, known as 'deal lines' to take orders from users. In most instances, customers will live in a different area to where the dealers and networks are based, so drug runners are needed to transport the drugs and collect payment.

In the NCA's data from 2018, the agency states that potential victims were aged between eleven and fifty-six, but with the majority of NRM referrals related to those aged between fifteen and seventeen. This is thought to be because 'they provide the level of criminal capability required by the offending model, but remain easier to control, exploit and reward than adults'.

While the report reiterates that vulnerable children (those in poverty, experiencing family breakdowns, with behavioural or developmental disorders, or those excluded from mainstream schools) remain key targets, kids from stable backgrounds are also on the radar of the drug gangs. This is thought to be because they don't have a criminal footprint and therefore are less likely to attract attention from the police.

In July 2019, The Children's Society released a report into the criminal exploitation of children in the UK by drugs gangs intending to groom them for violence and exploitation. The main age group for exploitation was deemed to be fourteen to seventeen but the charity warned the grooming age was getting younger, as there was evidence that primary school age children as young as seven were being targeted.

Following that report, The Children's Society recommended changes in the law and called for an increase in resources to tackle the issue. They also stated that 'the vast majority of police forces and Local Authorities across England and Wales were not able to share figures of the number of children affected by criminal exploitation in their area'. They also stated that children caught up in criminality should be treated as victims not criminals, with the number of children affected running into tens of thousands.

In July 2019, sixteen gang members were jailed for more than 61 years for running Class A drugs through County Lines across the South East, after a joint operation by the Met and Kent Police's Operation Raptor.

Between August and November 2018 officers identified the gang were running the following 'County Lines': Si Line was run from London into Bognor Regis, Sussex; AJ Line was infrequently operated in towns and villages on the borders of Berkshire, Hampshire and Surrey. This was the only identified drugs line where the line owner would spend extended periods of time in the dealing location. Pepsi Line and Jeezt Line ran between London and Medway, Kent. The gang were also responsible for the sale of crack cocaine and heroin in several parts of South London.

In Birmingham, a shocking report hit the headlines in 2019, when Birmingham Children's Trust revealed 236 youngsters had been identified as being 'at risk of, or were being, criminally exploited'. The National Crime Agency estimates that there are currently ninety lines running out of the West Midlands, sixty of them from Birmingham.

May 2019 saw the first conviction of a County Lines-related child trafficking case for Dyfed-Powys Police, in Wales. The victim was also thought to be the youngest in Wales. The perpetrator was a teenager from Sutton Coldfield, who trafficked the victim to Llanelli to sell drugs. He was sentenced to four and a half years. He pleaded guilty to trafficking a fourteen-year-old to sell drugs, and six counts of supplying and possessing heroin, crack cocaine and cannabis. The child was found and reunited with its family.

Despite the consistent rise in attention that the crime of child exploitation has been receiving, it appears there are ongoing issues within the system designed to protect them.

The UK Anti-Trafficking Monitoring Group stated last year that the UK Government is failing to protect thousands of children from exploitation due to its lack of strategy preventing the trafficking of children. Their 'Before the Harm is Done' report stated that while there were numerous strategies to tackle exploitation, they were not unified, and received different levels of attention and resourcing, resulting in many children only receiving help once the harm was done and a criminal offence had taken place.

It also went on to criticise the lack of comprehensive awareness-raising programmes for doctors, nurses, teachers or social workers, who could help identify children at risk early and prevent further abuse.

The charity ECPAT (Every Child Protected Against Trafficking) has voiced concerns about how 'fit for purpose' the NRM is when working with child victims – questioning the quality of the data collated and how it can be used to build an analysis of child victims. This in turn, according to the charity, affects how practitioners can best assess the needs of child victims.

In its 2018 report 'Child Trafficking in the UK 2018: A Snapshot', ECPAT also states that as of 2016 the data on the children referred into the NRM who got a positive Conclusive Grounds decision was no longer publicly available, and notes that 'a trend is apparent where child victims from the UK and the EU are more likely to receive victim status than some of those from countries outside the EU. This raises concerns about a potential institutional bias against non-EU nationals'.

A 2018 study by ECPAT, along with charity Missing People, found that a quarter of trafficked children who were in the care of Local Authorities in 2017 disappeared, raising concerns they were back under the control of their exploiters. The UN Convention on the Rights of the Child defines an unaccompanied child as a 'child who has been separated from both parents and other relatives and is not being cared for by an adult who, by law or custom, is responsible for doing so'. The report warned that trafficked and unaccompanied children are thirty times more likely to go missing than other children their age.

It also stated that one in four trafficked children were reported as missing from care, as were 15% of unaccompanied children. Almost 20% of the missing children had not been found. The report stated:

> This highlights the failure of Local Authorities to adequately safeguard these children, who are already extremely vulnerable . . . What's more, there is still no systematic recording and reporting of these issues at the Local Authority level and no central Government data collection or reporting to assess trends and ensure effective interventions.

Vietnamese children comprised the highest number of those missing, followed by British.

ECPAT's analysis reported that among the reasons the children go missing are 'a lack of trust in authorities and carers, the continuing control of a trafficker or exploiter, a lack of appropriate accommodation, uncertain immigration status and fear of immigration control'. One victim who had disappeared from care told ECPAT, 'I can see why young people run away to their trafficker. Better the devil you know'.

In May of 2019, a victim of child trafficking known has 'H' won £85,000 in compensation form the Home Office and Ministry of Justice, after he was detained at Morton Hall immigration centre – and sexually assaulted. The Vietnamese victim was trafficked into the UK in 2013 to work on a cannabis farm. He was abused sexually and physically, and once the house in which he was being kept was raided, he was charged with cannabis cultivation and sentenced to eight months in a Young Offenders' institution. From there he was sent to Morton Hall, a detention centre in Lincolnshire.

Not only did it emerge H was being illegally detained within Morton Hall, while he was there a fellow inmate attempted to rape him. He was assessed by clinical psychologists, who reported he was left traumatised by the attack, which also triggered memories of the abuse he had suffered at the hands of his traffickers.

The Home Office went on to accept it had gone against its own policies by not only continuing to detain H illegally for another six months after the attack (despite deeming him a victim of modern slavery) but also by attempting to deport him back to Vietnam. The Court of Appeal overturned H's conviction for cannabis cultivation and the CPS admitted the case should never had been prosecuted.

The Government said:

The welfare of vulnerable detainees is of the utmost importance and we are carefully considering the implications of this case. We have made significant improvements in recent years...

but the Home Secretary has made clear we are committed to going further and faster in exploring alternatives to detention, increasing transparency . . . and improving the support available for vulnerable detainees.

Over the course of investigating trafficking in the UK, I'd come across the work of Stephen Chapman, the Anti-Slavery Co-ordinator in Wales. After connecting online, speaking on the phone and exchanging emails, we were finally able to meet face to face.

In an old pub in the heart of Westminster, former police officer Stephen talked me through the Welsh response to trafficking and slavery – which he oversees.

'In 2010 the Welsh Government recognised people were being exploited and that's when they created this job. In 2011 the first Co-ordinator was employed, and I came into the job late in 2012. I've never entered a job with so many unknowns. No one could tell me what the level of slavery was. People were in denial. It was Operation Imperial that was the wake-up call for Wales and the UK.'

Stephen was referring to the Darrell Simester case – a British man held for thirteen years by a traveller family, after they picked him up on the side of a dual carriageway. Stephen was clearly still appalled by the case.

'Why was it a wake-up call? Well, until then, if you asked people about slavery or exploitation, they would just shrug it off and say it's about women being brought over from Africa or Eastern Europe into the sex trade. What we had with Darrell Simester was one of our own. A UK national being exploited by a UK national. So when that was in the media, people noticed. Before, they were probably not interested.

'Operation Imperial is still very much alive, and they're still [investigating] victims who've been kept for up to 30 years. Once this was going on, the public were interested. We launched campaigns, we launched training, we launched a leadership group. We realised this was the time to strike, and something needed to be done. What we needed were the tools. I know a lot of people will complain that the Modern Slavery Act doesn't go far enough, but it was a great start and let's hope with the review it will get stronger. Until then, officers were having to scratch their heads to think what to prosecute people with. The CPS is a great organisation, but they can only prosecute what's brought before them.

'The Welsh Government sees this as one of our national priorities. First of all we got the Local Authorities on board, then health, then the fire service and the ambulance service, and we've got great partners with law enforcement. We fund a lot of NGOs, we've got our own children's commissioner. When I invited people to join me in setting up a leadership group, why would they *not* do the right thing?

'We've got the will. We've got dedicated people in the police, the PCC, our own Children's Commissioner and a Head of Safeguarding. We've got the good and the great, people who can go out there looking for offences of slavery, but also what they're good at is getting together and giving us a strategy and making organisations deal with it.

'In Wales we've got a cohort of trained investigators and prosecutors. Slavery is complex, investigating and prosecuting is complex, so you need to train people. We got together with police and CPS colleagues, and developed our three-day course. We take great pride in Wales in our national training programme. We trained a cohort of eighty investigators and prosecutors last year, but across Wales we've trained over 10,000 people. This is all within the Welsh Government National Training Framework.'

Independent Child Trafficking Guardians (ICTGs) (previously known as Advocates, or ICTAs) are an outcome of Section 48 of the Modern Slavery Act. Their role is to provide specialist, and crucially, *independent* support for trafficked children and to advocate on their behalf, helping them navigate the complex system in which they find themselves. The scheme was trialled by the charity Barnardo's in 2014, and since 2017 the Home Office has commissioned the service in several early adopter sites – Wales,

Greater Manchester, East Midlands, West Midlands, Hampshire and Isle of Wight, and Croydon.

ICTGs essentially act as guardians for a trafficked child, dealing with legal, immigration and welfare needs, making sure they are in the NRM and ensuring all steps are taken to keep them safe and prevent re-trafficking. As yet, ICTGs are not a resource that can be offered to every potential victim around the UK, as the scheme has yet to be rolled out nationwide. This has prompted concerns that the level of care on offer around the UK isn't consistent, with many vulnerable victims unable to access the same support as those in a different area.

Stephen explained it's a scheme that has worked very well in Wales.

'We thought we could do something different, and I think we have done. When the Independent Child Trafficking Advocates were first brought in, I asked if Wales could be included. I was offered them for a few Local Authorities, and I said it's either all twenty-two Local Authorities or we don't want to be in, because in Wales we don't play postcode lottery. We're a country not a region, so it's got to be the same whether you're in Conway or Cardiff. There's got to be consistency.

'We work with our partners Barnardo's Cymru (Wales). We trained our ICTAs and also trained everybody involved in dealing with children. We started the project on 30th January 2017 and by 28th February 2018 we had identified ninety-four children in Wales.

'What was disturbing was we were the only area to have children under ten years of age. The youngest were children as young as two, three, five. We had young girls being brought here for sexual exploitation from across the world. Straight away we got further funding for other ICTAs to be employed across Wales. We've dealt with over 300 children who thankfully are now being safeguarded. And the Barnardo's team? If anyone deserves a medal they do. Can you imagine? Two-year-olds?'

I spoke to Stephen a few months later. Their youngest victim was now a ten-month-old Vietnamese baby girl.

'What is also disturbing is virtually 50% are UK children. They're not all involved in County Lines, there are other forms of exploitation, of criminality. We dealt with a case last year where a sixteen-year-old Chilean boy was found in Monmouthshire, working with three men. They'd all been charged with burglary. The QC in the case had just completed his three-day training course with us. Back in his office, he saw he'd got a burglary case involving four people. When he looked closer, he saw there were three Welshmen and a sixteen-year-old boy from Chile. Well, straight away the lights came on.

'The sixteen-year-old was a victim, because he was a young boy. He was being pushed through the windows to open the doors. Like Oliver Twist. So this is another good thing about the Modern Slavery Act, Section 45, defence. The QC was able to stop the case, get the young boy acquitted, bring in an ICTA, and the ICTA worked with him. The boy is now back home in Chile and the men are doing ten years each.

'When we say slavery is all around us, it's not just about the metals in our phones. We've got to be aware. Are we going to beat this? Yes, we are. Are we going to beat it in a generation? I think it may take a little bit longer.'

16

SURVIVOR'S STORY: J

J is in her mid-twenties and from the North West of England. She agreed to be in touch with me via email about her experiences as a survivor of Child Sexual Exploitation (CSE). Her story is powerful but deeply distressing and what follows is an account of physical, sexual and emotional abuse.

From the age of thirteen, she was exploited by groups of older men. Her first exploiter was a neighbour in his seventies, who was known to the family. What J's family didn't realise was that he was on the Sex Offender Register.

'My experiences at the age of thirteen were the start of my ordeal, and I can now see what made me a lost thirteen-year-old. I was befriended by an elderly neighbour who was in his seventies and well known for dealing drugs, as his home was used to store, deal and hide drugs, as well as weapons and metal.'

Like so many other survivors of sexual abuse she was groomed with kindness, presents and attention. J's home life was challenging and, with an absent father, she appreciated this man's kindness, but then felt obliged to reciprocate with sexual favours when he demanded them. As his control intensified, so did the scale of the abuse.

'He passed me to gangs of Asian and Afghan men. To this day I could not say how many. I was forced to have sex. The numbers grew, and the men worked from takeaways and taxi firms and were the owners of derelict houses, where they would take me and force me to have sex. I was locked in, and I remember being scared and reported missing.

'The older man facilitated this and received payments, and then he passed this on to another ringleader, who then started the cycle again. It started with me thinking the elderly man was an escape from a chaotic home life. He offered me a place to bunk off school, hide, and also have simple things such as cigarettes, new school shoes or a lift to school.

'The other men drove me to different places, locked me up and on some occasions gave me substances before they made videos. Men would come in one by one. If I refused, they would beat me, hurt me and insert objects, such as glass, lighters or batteries inside me.

'This was their kind of ownership. They said the battery would make me work harder so they left it in for a day. They said they would grass me up if I grassed, and burn some of my hair off as punishment. One time they smashed a glass bottle and forced it in there. The glass tore my insides and my periods stopped.

'They would watch, wait and keep giving me different phones or SIM cards so they were in control of all that, threaten my family and throw fireworks, semen and condoms through the door to signal their presence. One had a drill and he threatened to use it on me. He drilled his own arm to show what he could do. They forced me into cold showers and slapped me, gave me a broken face and ribs. Being doused in petrol was the worst.

'They asked me to lie about my age, to be older or younger depending on the customer, and give me fake IDs, and try to use me for sham marriages so they could get a visa. Sometimes it could be as many as eight or twelve men, and if I was out of it they would carry on one by one and until I woke up.

'Because I was from an Asian background, there were issues of shame, dishonour and of a female being a "slut". I felt the ordeal would bring shame and dishonour. My family life was at risk.'

During this period, J was living at home then eventually, on and off, in a series of refuges. In 2014, she finally escaped. This

216

followed an incident where the gang doused her in petrol and attempted to set her alight.

Despite the horrors J experienced at the hands of the gang, her route to safety and recovery was deeply complex. J had no idea that what was happening to her was trafficking. She was often refused help from agencies supporting women from domestic violence and homelessness because she 'didn't really fit the criteria', plus being associated with the gangs meant she was considered to be putting the other women in refuges at risk.

I asked if she contacted the police, or if anyone encouraged her to speak to law enforcement.

'My experiences with the police were varied. I first came to their attention when the gang got one man to follow me who raped me on my way home, in a public place. I was found by a dog walker who heard my screams and dialled 999. As I thought he was going to kill me, but they managed to detain him and he went to prison for sexual assault.

'But then the gang both threatened and compensated him, so he would kill for them because he had nothing to lose now. If you had asked me at the time I'd say I just knew I was born to lie on my back.

'The police would always find me and initially they tried to get me to talk. Sometimes I would call them but in all honesty, I was at times inconsistent and misleading because I was scared. I even called them pretending to be someone else because I needed help or didn't want to go through the process of making a statement, or could not give descriptions. One police lady and sergeant were nice and believed me and knew something was wrong and they tried to help. But later the case was taken over and the police treated me as a suspect for making wrong lifestyle choices.

'They took my diaries and everything for evidence. I became more and more dishonest to avoid them. They told me that I never fitted the criteria of a victim, i.e. I was clever, I went to a good school, I was Asian and not white, so the men would not prey on their own kind, the older man was too old to get aroused or harm me.

'The kind police lady bought me make-up once to help hide my bruises and was there when they took the glass out of me. The police found me completely naked and hiding when the men threw me out of the car, and then they said I was a "known prostitute" even though I was in [the] middle of town hiding behind a bin because I had no clothes on. I don't know why they did that, I really don't. It felt like I was watching myself and I thought I'd die.

'The men had often drugged me. I fled a refuge because I was the youngest there and I wanted the drugs they'd got me hooked on and I was scared. I never thought I'd live and the police told my family to expect my body in a police bag and the next time they knocked on my mum's door it might be to say I was dead.

'Apart from the two nice ones, I hated the police. If only they had looked harder they could have done more. An off-duty officer found me when I had been doused in petrol. They said there was no DNA and my recollection was inconsistent. They said maybe I had thrown the petrol on myself. My behaviour became challenging and I said whatever I could to mislead them because I could not grass up the gang because they had hidden a phone in my bra.

'The injuries have left me with tears and cuts, inside. And an anal fistula. They used words for me they should have used for the traffickers. This hurts more than what happened. I still keep in contact with the lady officer informally and the DS. They believed me and that kept me alive. What is comforting to know is that changes have been made and are still being made. This will give survivors hope.'

J eventually finally contacted Victim Support who advised her to get in touch with The Salvation Army. This was the first time she had heard the phrase 'human trafficking' or that she was entitled to support.

'I accepted it as a way of life. The police and social services used many words to describe me – "pest, liar, chaotic lifestyle, complex, prostitute, inconsistent, cunning, wanting it". Social workers called it "non-compliance, non-engagement"; school called it "naughty, truanting, troubled"; hospital called it "accidental" or at times didn't call it anything.

'I went through services such as social services, refuges and the police. No services were able to offer support as I never quite fitted the criteria. I was too young, too old, too vulnerable, too complex, and carried increased risks. The police notes said I had a "history of being lured and trafficked", but I didn't know what that meant. I came home from hospital and knew that the gang knew I had been talking to the police.

'I refused to engage with the police, and a lady from Victim Support told me I needed to leave now, and to call my officer to secure a refuge space, but this was declined because the abuse wasn't coming from a family member so it was not domestic abuse. She then gave me the number for The Salvation Army. I remember thinking, "This is it, they have all given up, and it won't be long until I'm back". But when I called The Salvation Army they came within two hours.

'Straight away there were gentle voices and they *got* it. They got that I needed help, they got I needed it now and they offered me a safe place. At first I thought "What's the catch?" but soon I learnt there was no catch. They cared enough about me, even though I was not the "perfect victim". It was only The Salvation Army who saw it for what it is was and helped me understand what it was and that it can happen in the UK. They helped me make sense of my experiences.'

The Salvation Army took J to a safe house hundreds of miles away from where her abuse took place, though she admits she was so traumatised by her experiences that initially she was very mistrusting and not really able to engage with the support she was offered.

'The safe house was scary at first. All girls want to mark their territory and I was scared in case there was a fight or my stuff got stolen. But this place was different. They gave me a clean bed, a box of deodorants and a clean mattress. It was so nice to be away. I was still scared and thought I'd be thrown out. I tested the boundaries thinking it would not be for long. The other girls turned out to be amazing. Some didn't speak English but we got on so well. Then once when I kicked off someone senior from The Salvation Army came to help me. Because I was on strong meds and treatment, they helped me move to aftercare.

'It was the start of my recovery and freedom. I had time to rest and believe I was safe. I was always a determined person, and The Salvation Army helped me so much by believing in me, and seeing me as a human.'

J's recovery was, in my view, nothing short of miraculous, deeply impressive and an example of the human will to survive.

As her confidence grew, and she was secure in the fact she was free from the grasp of her traffickers, J decided she wanted to work with vulnerable people herself. This was no easy feat considering the barriers she faced, in particular the ongoing medical attention she needed following her own abuse – both physical and emotional. However, she has managed to secure a position training in social care and is working miles away from where her traffickers *are still at large*.

J still, of course, has dark days when she struggles to come to terms with what has happened to her, and the injuries sustained during her exploitation often affect her ability to work and live a normal life. But there is no doubt she is determined to continue on her path to recovery.

'I would say to begin to move on, you have to create your own sense of justice and fight back, fight for those who are in similar situations, there's so much more to do. I have achieved things I thought I never would. You have to move away from the typical narrative of what a victim is, and understand they have to fight. I have only managed to move on because of The Salvation Army and their help. If not I truly believe I would be back and dead.

'The rescue was only the beginning of the recovery, it goes on and on and some days are worse. Some say I am too numb but I am learning that given the opportunity you can begin to heal and believe in your worth and never allow yourself to be silenced. My traffickers destroyed my body, my spirit, but not me. The Salvation Army helped me to celebrate the scars, the pain and see it as [a] triumph.'

17

SUPPLY AND DEMAND

This is a subject I really didn't want to tackle.

The concept of supply chains is one which, as a consumer, has always made me uncomfortable. It is one thing to be aware of slavery on your doorstep – looking for signs in nail bars and car washes, recycling centres or hotels. But trying to navigate the commercial world in order to avoid buying goods touched by slavery seems a mammoth task. One which, to my shame, I've turned a blind eye to. Not because I don't care, but because I don't know where to start.

The technology we use is made up of countless components from all over the globe. Clothes are made in anonymous factories on the other side of world. Even a supermarket trip can be confusing – knowing you should avoid buying certain foods from certain countries but not knowing *exactly* which ones they are. My general awareness, but ignorance on the specifics, has made trying to Do The Right Thing a confusing and overwhelming experience.

Though this book is about trafficking and slavery in the UK (and I could have dodged the complex and frustrating issue of supply chains altogether) there's no getting away from the fact that even in the security of our homes, we are touched by slavery.

What can we do about it? As consumers, buying goods in shops or online, how are we to know the provenance of what we buy? And what could we possibly change?

I wanted to tackle my understanding of this global issue head on, and a friend who works in retail introduced me to the work of the charity Hope for Justice, and specifically their initiative the Slave-Free Alliance. The case against the Polish crime gang (see Chapter 8) was uncovered by outreach workers from this Manchester-based charity – though I was unaware of this huge operation when I went to meet them.

My first contact with Susan Banister was over the phone in 2017. She'd agreed to give me an overview of slavery in supply chains, and how the problem was tackled by corporations and the consumer. Her insights were incredibly helpful as I began to navigate this complex area. Later, we arranged to meet at Hope for Justice's HQ in Manchester so we could speak more in depth.

The thing that struck me immediately when I entered their city centre office was a huge wall covered with padlocks. Susan, an engaging and dynamic woman, explained that each lock represented a victim whom the charity had rescued. Working across four continents, Hope for Justice has specialist teams working with law enforcement to identify victims of modern slavery and move them into safety, before assisting them to repair their lives. They also have dedicated hubs in the UK with specialist investigators building intelligence on potential cases.

Susan is the Head of Business Development of Hope for Justice's social enterprise initiative, the Slave-Free Alliance, which works with businesses in order to help them examine their supply chains and work towards being slavery-free. In the boardroom, Susan and I sat down with coffee as she began to talk me through this.

'Slave-Free Alliance is a membership organisation so people pay to be members. We are there to support those members. They carry out a self-assessment to see where they are on their journey, and that's private to them. There are no league tables, we're not about naming and shaming, but it gives them a really good starting point when they can say, "Ok, we don't know much but we can do something about it".

'We then do a gap analysis on their business. We look at their policies and procedures with a very focused eye on modern slavery, and we then give them an action plan for the year, indicating where we think their highest risks are.

'What I say to businesses is, with the Slave-Free Alliance we are here to help you. I always describe it as putting our arm around you and saying, "We've got this together. If we find something, we can deal with it together".'

I described my feeling of being overwhelmed about trying to buy goods as ethically as possible. I referred to my mobile phone and laptop. There are so many physical elements to the devices, what would a supply chain even look like?

'The minerals that are involved in making it. The electronics in China that are being made could involve exploited labour. The distribution getting it to whichever country. The distribution when it's *in* whichever country. All those elements can touch exploited labour and slave labour. We talk about a supply chain, but it's actually a supply net. It's very complicated.'

As I was already aware, one of the key elements of the Modern Slavery Act is Section 54 – demanding transparency in supply chains.

'Section 54 says any business with a turnover of £36 million or over has to issue a Modern Slavery statement indicating what they're doing in relation to eradicating modern slavery either from their own organisation or their supply chain. They *could* turn around and say, "We're not doing anything". It must be signed by somebody on the Executive Board. The number of statements I see that are actually quite good, but they've not signed it . . . All the time. I'm always going into businesses saying, "You do know your statement's not compliant?"

'In the Modern Slavery Review, one of the things that was recommended was that it should be mandatory for businesses to put their statements in a central repository for all businesses. For me the sensible thing is, you do your accounts, you send them to Companies House, you send in your statement, and they check you've got the turnover they need and the statement, and this should be managed by the Government. Nobody at the moment is checking the validity of statements. We want these statements to be really helpful, saying, "You know what, we *did* find something and this is what we did about it".'

In 2013, the collapse of the Rana Plaza factory building in Bangladesh killing over 1,000 workers made headlines globally, highlighting working conditions many people around the world are forced to comply with. Susan stressed that it was not just the international element of supply chains we needed to be aware of: businesses in the UK could be culpable also.

'A lot of the places we're finding victims are the distribution centres of the big retailers. Most of the victims we find in these kinds of places have been trafficked from Eastern Europe. So Lithuania, Hungary, Romania, Poland ... So you've got your worker, who has the right to work in the UK. The trafficker has brought them over and put them in a UK address. They very often take them to open a bank account. Then what generally happens is they take them to a recruitment agency, because it may not be as scrupulous as other businesses would be. An HR department would do more. The workers are then legitimate on paper, with national insurance numbers. So how does the business employing them know they've been trafficked? They only know they've come through an agency.

'It's making people understand what the signs are, and it's through the casual conversations we have when we do site investigations that we find victims. Because we're asking the right questions. If I brought you in, and you were trafficked, the trafficker will have told you what you must say. And you will say it because you don't want to lose your job. You still believe the trafficker is helping you out.

'The more people who are trained in business to spot this, the better. But if people are not aware how prevalent it is, and that it's hidden in plain sight, then they're not going to do the training because they're not going to see the value in it. Is there an element of, "We don't want to look because we don't want to find it"? There's a little bit of that, and that could be because they don't want to deal with it at all, or because if they find something, then they have to do something about it.'

One high-profile case of worker exploitation in the UK was at the Kozee Sleep bed-making firm, where the boss, Mohammed Rafiq, was found guilty of human trafficking. His workforce of mainly Hungarian men were paid £10 a day, with forty-two men living in a two-bedroom house. The company supplied beds to companies including Next and John Lewis, and the ethical audits carried out by retailers had failed to identify the exploitation in the factory.

Susan told me that audits are not a failsafe for identifying modern slavery.

'Audits are not, in my opinion, the tool to find victims of modern slavery. They have a purpose such as identifying issues relating to health and safety and general labour standards but are frequently being used as a tick-box exercise. Modern slavery is complex so to address it properly you have to look specifically and purposefully. If you don't, you will miss it. Franchises, for instance, can slip through the net because they haven't got a supplier relationship, they're business owner to business owner. Hotel chains can slip through the net as well.'

There are also potential dangers in outsourcing.

'Cleaning, catering – that kind of thing, that's where they could find something. Let's face it – if you find a victim in Company X's head office in London, it won't be the company that's *supplying* Company X, it will be Company X *itself* that ends up in the papers. Another example – some companies use garages, and the garages use car valeting companies. We investigated car valeting companies, and from being on site and talking to the owners of valeting companies, we identified a potential victim.'

As I began to get some understanding of the complicated world of supply chains, the idea of ever being able to end slavery seemed less and less likely. There were so many moving parts of the problem, and so many conflicting agendas and priorities at play that, as a layman, I now believed a more coherent approach was needed.

Susan agreed.

'We need everybody to come together. That's what the Slave-Free Alliance is about. We need businesses to join because then we'll have an impact. One of our members – a huge company as far as the UK market is concerned – sources from China, and in some of the places they source from they comprise a tiny, tiny fraction of that business. So they have no leverage there at all. We need everybody to come together so we can turn around and say to businesses in China, "You can't run overtime the way you're doing it", or "You need to put heating in the accommodation you're providing to your workers", and that kind of thing.'

There was still one thing I wanted to know more about. How could we as consumers leverage the power of our pound, and identify where slavery is as we shop?

Susan sighed.

'It's really difficult. The best thing we can do is make people aware that it's here. Making people aware of what could be happening on their street. Pop-up brothels happen all the time. Once you know about it, you see it everywhere. I would love for car washes and nail bars to be licensed by the council. There are legitimate ones and non-legitimate ones, and we need to be able to tell the difference. Why should it be down to you or me to work that out?

'Raising awareness is the best thing we can do. Getting businesses to take responsibility is the next thing. We as consumers can put pressure on businesses to do more. That's what we can do. Say, this is important to us. It's better if we are willing to pay a little bit more [for goods] then we're not in a race to the bottom.'

It was fitting that I was in Manchester to find out more about the global slave trade in the twenty-first century, because in 1862 the people of the city made their own stand, led by the founders of the high street supermarket the Co-op. Believe it or not, the

Co-op's fight against exploitation continues today – with not only a celebrated approach to dealing with slavery in supply chains, but also by running a scheme where survivors of slavery can get into paid work.

Paul Gerrard is the Campaigns & Public Affairs Director for the Co-op and he agreed to assist me in my quest to be a better consumer. In his warm and commanding Manchester accent, he spoke with passion about the business he's clearly proud to work for.

'We're an £11 billion a year business. Because we are a co-operative business, we're not listed, we're not a PLC, and we're not on the FTSE 100. We're predominantly a food business and have suppliers from sixty-eight countries and four continents, employing half a million workers. We are a big business with global supply chains, from Thailand to Brazil, Italy to Africa.'

After Paul and I had swapped stories about our northern heritage and shared memories of Manchester, he gave me more background on the city's, and the Co-op's, commitment to fighting slavery.

'We have history on slavery that nobody else has got. If you go down Deansgate in Manchester, where the John Rylands library is, on the opposite side of the road there's Lincoln Square. And on Lincoln Square there's a statue of Abraham Lincoln, which is a bit unusual for a city in the north of England. In 1862, Lincoln was fighting the American Civil War. One of his tactics to starve the confederacy of money was to put in place a naval blockade to stop them exporting their goods and products. If they can't export, they can't make money. If they can't make money, they can't buy guns and boots, and they can't win the war. What was the biggest export the confederacy had? Cotton.

'Manchester was called Cottonopolis. Lincoln put in his blockade in 1862 and what happened? The Lancashire Cotton Famine. 80% of the cotton used in the cotton mills of Lancashire and Manchester came from the deep south of America. It was the first humanitarian disaster of the industrial age. So as a result of the fight against slavery people were dying on the streets.

'What do the working men and women of Manchester do? They get together on 31st December 1862 and they say, "You know what? Slavery is evil. Slavery is beyond comprehension. So we will write to Lincoln and will tell him to carry on what he's doing, even though we're starving". He wrote back, and the letter is in the archive. It says what they've done is an act of chivalry and courage unknown in any age or country. That's why there's a statue of Lincoln in Manchester.

'The organisers who got people together for that meeting at the Free Trade Hall in Manchester, who drafted the letter that 5,000 people approved, were the founders of the Co-operative Wholesale Society. The CWS. Which is now the Co-op Group. Our Founders led the emancipation movement in England.'

Fast forward from 1862 to 2019, and the Co-op, in a fight led by Paul, is still working for a slavery-free world. He told me that one of the fundamental steps in making a change is honesty.

'If any business, of any size, particularly if they have international supply chains, but even if they only have domestic ones – if they say they haven't got slavery in their supply chains, they are either lying, stupid, or just not looking.

'Honestly, any business of any size who has anything like normal global supply chains carries the risk of slavery. If you look at our slavery statement for 2019, or 2018, you will see examples of where *we* found slavery in our supply chains. Even a business like ours, and I would suggest that we, and probably people like Marks & Spencer, Waitrose, Marshalls PLC who do granite and stone for gardens, who are some of the most sophisticated companies in terms of tackling supply chains, will have slavery in their supply chains.'

While I was impressed by his blunt candour, I wasn't sure how the average Joe could make wise purchasing choices if the retailers themselves couldn't be sure of their slavery footprint.

Paul was characteristically honest.

'If a consumer says to me, "Well, how can I guarantee it [a slave-free supply chain]?", the answer is you can't. You can't. What you can do though, is see if the people you are spending your money with are doing two things.

'One. Go onto their website and find their slavery statement – which they must provide by law. If you can't find it on the front page, they're immediately breaking the law. The Modern Slavery Act Section 54 says if you have a presence in the UK and a turnover of more than £36 million then you've got to produce a statement. That statement can actually just say they don't care, but it's got to be approved by the board, signed by a director and have a link to it on the front page of the website. If you can't find it straight away, I'd be worried as they're clearly ignoring the law, and what does that tell you about how much they care, and what they're doing about it?

'If you find it, read it. If there are vague statements like, "We have a zero tolerance policy for slavery", it's worthless. If you look at what we do, or Marshalls PLC, or Marks & Spencer, you'll see numbers there! We'll be working with suppliers overseas, we'll be going down the supply chain, we'll be doing the right things. You only have to read a couple to pick up what kind of business it is.

'For a consumer supply chains are really complicated. So what do you do? Don't look for a guarantee because they're lying and can't give a guarantee. Have a look at the slavery statement. Does it tell you anything? If it just says, "It's terrible" and it's a load of fluff without any numbers in, doesn't tell you where they operate or where their suppliers are, if it hasn't got any depth to it, that tells me they don't really give a shit, so there's a much greater likelihood of something happening in their supply chains than there is in, for example, Marks & Spencer.

'Number two, I would suggest, is ask them what they do to support survivors of slavery. The businesses which really do care will do things. Some could be in Bright Future [the Co-op's scheme to get survivors back into paid work] but you don't have to be. BT aren't a member of Bright Future but BT spend a shedload of money on Unseen, on the Modern Slavery Helpline. What do companies do from a CSR (Corporate and Social Responsibility), from a philanthropic point of view to support survivors? That will give you an indicator as a consumer whether they take this seriously. Have they got a statement and what are they doing for survivors? And if the answer to either is you don't really know or you can't find out, that would immediately start to ring alarm bells for me.'

I asked Paul if companies had to take their Modern Slavery statement seriously, or if it was just seen as a box-ticking exercise.

'The Act set the parameters. The problem is, they haven't enforced it. Government have never used any powers whatsoever to enforce the Act. The last figure I saw was that 50% of businesses who should have produced a statement haven't. Haven't bothered. 35% of the Government's *own* suppliers haven't produced a statement.

'So unless there is a moral, value-driven imperative, then I think businesses are doing this on a risk/reward basis. What's the risk of something going wrong? And is that penalty painful enough to withstand it? Because at the moment the only risk they have is that it's found somewhere in their supply chain by a journalist. Because there is no risk in terms of the Government saying "these 3,000 companies are shysters". That's not going to happen.

'At present, unless there's a value-driven imperative within that business, all businesses have to achieve is a pretty standard low-level compliance to produce something. But even if they don't do that, there are no consequences. None whatsoever. Unless it is a value-driven imperative in a business, most businesses will do the bare minimum and some won't even do that. Because there's no risk.'

I asked what happened when slavery was identified in a supply chain, and what steps were taken. It turned out that was more complicated than simply cutting off the guilty party.

'Our response is first, let's make sure the people who are being exploited are safe. Next, let's see if we can help that supplier do the right thing, and if they want to – great, we will work with them and then that's another supplier doing the right thing. If they don't want to be helped then you cut them off. But most suppliers will want to be helped. We visit suppliers. We train those suppliers. We train *their* suppliers. That's how we try and protect victims.

'There are 136,000 people in the UK in slavery, 40 million worldwide. There is no way that you will not have something in your house that somewhere in a supply chain has got slavery. For example, your washing machine. When did you last get a new one? What happened to the old one? One of the most prevalent areas for slavery in the UK is in recycling and scrap dealer yards. Waste and recycling.

'No matter what you do, you can't satisfy yourself that you're not engaged with the slavery trade. What you should do though, I suggest, is hold businesses to account. What do they to protect their supply chains? We have 4.6 million members who all own one share, and I tell them I can't guarantee there is no slavery in Co-op supply chains. But what I can guarantee is that we do *everything* we can to make sure it doesn't happen, but if it does happen, to learn the lessons, and finally, to take care of the survivors.'

18

ELENA'S STORY: FIGHTING FOR HER FUTURE (2019)

The time will kill me. Now is more months to wait and to stay like this.
A text from 'Elena', February 2019

After the joy of getting the Conclusive Grounds decision reversed, both Elena and I felt there was real hope for her. However, while the CG decision confirmed her as a victim of trafficking and slavery, it was the asylum status that would affect the next five years of her life. When the CG decision was received back in November, the hope was that the asylum decision would come quickly. We finally heard in February 2019 in an email from Elena's solicitor, Siobhan.

Hi Louise. Elena has asked that I email you to update you. Unfortunately, her asylum claim has been refused. This is disappointing but unfortunately very common. We will be appealing the decision.

Siobhan reassured me that it wasn't as bad as it sounded, and she had the next steps prepared. In the meantime she said I should try not to worry.

Elena was devastated.

Hello dear Louise. I am very worried. I don't have power for nothing. I don't know why they bring me that answer.

I sent her back some platitudes about staying strong but her reply was simple.

Yes, but the time will kill me. Now is more months to wait and to stay like this.

The day of the meeting arrived, and Siobhan was really upbeat. She confirmed we would appeal the decision and that we had a strong case. Apparently the Home Office accepted two out of the three aspects of Elena's case: 1) that she is a trafficking victim and 2) that she is Albanian (which seems an odd and undisputable thing to question but apparently it happens).

The element of her case they *were* refuting was the fact that it was not safe for her to go back to Albania. Elena's position on this was clear.

'I claimed asylum because I am terrified about going back to Albania. Marco always made it clear to me . . . that he would find me . . . that it would be possible to find me anywhere in Albania if I got away from him. I know the Home Office have asked why I cannot move [to a different Albanian area] but as someone who has lived in Albania I know that it is very easy and just a matter of time for someone who is looking for you to be able to find you. Albania is a very small country . . . If you are able to pay it is very easy to find someone.'

Elena gave us information on the power she believes Marco has, which I can't substantiate, but it was clear just how terrified of him she truly was.

She also said she could not go back to her family.

'If you have been with more than one man, or multiple men like me, then that is dishonourable and brings shame on your family. It is even worse for me because I have a baby. No one will marry someone who is not a virgin . . . Divorcees can't remarry . . . Society considers you to be a whore, the word in Albanian is *kurva*. I feel extremely uncomfortable using this word. It has such a serious meaning in Albania. People who are considered to be like this are discriminated against. No one would want to associate with someone like this . . . I would not be accepted anywhere. I struggle because of the way that I was brought up not to see *myself* in the same way. I think this is because I have still not got over what happened to me. I think, and hope, because I have seen another way of thinking in the UK . . . that I will be able to stop focusing so much on my past and seeing myself like this.'

The next step in Elena's appeal was to go to a tribunal to give evidence to a judge, in front of a representative from the Home Office, who would also get to question Elena, and any witnesses called. Siobhan explained she would submit a document from a Country Expert Witness in order to outline for the judge the reality of life for Elena should she be removed back to Albania.

All *we* could do was wait for a court date. And as Elena said later, 'For the court I have one more hope. Maybe the court will bring me good news.'

In the run-up to Elena's appeal, an article by May Bulman, the Social Affairs Correspondent for *The Independent*, caught my eye. Government figures had been released showing that more than half of Home Office immigration decisions are overturned when challenged in court. Bulman wrote, '52% of immigration and asylum appeals were allowed in the year to March 2019, with 23,514 people seeing their refusals overturned'.

The article went on to quote Chai Patel from Joint Council for the Welfare of Immigrants:

In the background of every case you see in the media of someone whose life was destroyed by the Home Office, there are thousands more whose cases never get any attention. These figures bring home the reality of that. When the Home Office chooses to resist an appeal, it gets it wrong more often than it gets right, and yet all of the consequences fall upon the people who wait years in limbo, separated from their families, or in detention, or who are deported.

The report also quotes the response from the Home Office:

Every asylum and immigration application is considered on its individual merits in line with the immigration rules.

Caseworkers are given extensive training and mentoring to ensure they are able to deal with the complex issues they may encounter, and there are managers and senior caseworkers on hand should they need further advice or guidance. Appeals are allowed for a variety of reasons, often because of new evidence presented before the tribunal which was not available to the decision maker at the time. We are committed to continually improving the quality and accuracy of decision-making to ensure we get decisions right the first time, and all allowed appeals are review[ed] to ensure we capture relevant lessons.

It was a damning insight into the current immigration system.

On the day of the appeal hearing, the first thing that struck me as I searched for Elena in the courthouse were the many notices announcing each case being heard that morning – a staggering number. So many hopeful and desperate people with their names publicly on display, with each case announcement beginning 'Secretary of State versus . . .'.

Talk about David and Goliath.

Walking down the corridor to the waiting room, for the first time in this entire experience the enormity of what we were about to face hit me, and I began to feel very emotional.

Walking through the double doors into the waiting room, I found Elena, accompanied by two other women – a representative from her local Salvation Army church, and a representative of a charity based in Elena's area which offers support to trafficking victims. Elena was pale and nervous, but clearly comforted by the support around her. The two women were kind, caring and certainly made me feel better with their presence, never mind Elena.

Elena's barrister, dressed smartly in a black suit but with a warm smile, greeted us, introduced herself and took us through to a meeting room. Essentially, while we were there for moral support, there was also a chance the barrister would call upon us to give evidence before the judge. That meant we were not allowed to stay in the room with Elena, to hold her hand or offer moral support. The only people with her would be the barrister, whom Elena had met only once before and who would be sitting near the judge and not with her, the legal representative's interpreter and a court-appointed interpreter.

Eventually it was time for the tribunal hearing to start and for us to walk with Elena down to the court. We all headed out of the small waiting room with its too few chairs, down a drab corridor, and waited again outside one of many rooms which are set out like a typical courtroom, albeit on a smaller scale. It had a raised platform at the top where the judge would sit, two opposing desks below him (in this case for Elena's barrister on one side and the Home Office representative on the other) and a third desk facing the judge, where whoever is giving evidence would sit. Against the back wall was a row of chairs for any observers.

As we were about to wish Elena luck and then go back to the waiting area, we were given some news which shocked me. The Home Office representative, a scruffy, unimpressive-looking man (contrary to the image one builds in one's mind of such an intimidating opposition) had not brought Elena's case notes.

This was a staggering piece of information to process. It was the Home Office who deemed her not fit for asylum, yet when given the opportunity to prove their point, to argue their case, when they had the lives of a young woman and her child in their hands, they hadn't even turned up to court with the right paperwork. After listening to other barristers talking outside their courtrooms, I realised this was not uncommon.

Elena's barrister told us that the judge had given the Home Office representative the opportunity to simply not fight the appeal, considering they weren't prepared, and for one brief moment we thought perhaps we wouldn't need to fight any more, that it would all be over. However, despite the lack of case files and the offer from the judge not to contest the appeal, the Home Office representative declined, and simply got copies of the files from the court in order for the tribunal to continue.

This delayed Elena's hearing even further.

Eventually, just before lunch, it began. The three of us who were there to support her sat in the waiting room and waited to see if we would be needed. Eventually I was called, and sat between Elena's barrister and the Home Office representative to answer questions from both of them, and the judge.

If I ever had expectations that I would be an articulate, passionate and Sorkin-esque orator in such a situation, they were dashed dramatically in the fifteen minutes I was before the judge. It's a deeply intimidating situation when the stakes are so high, and when one badly phrased sentence or thought could potentially affect the future of two vulnerable people.

I was asked about the support I'd offered Elena, what her life would be like if she was forced to leave the support system she'd built up around her in London, and how she would cope if she was returned to Albania as an ex-sex worker (no matter what the circumstances) and an unmarried mother.

The experience was a blur for me so I can't imagine how Elena felt, and I was bloody glad when I could leave. As I turned to leave the room, I saw Elena had tears rolling down her face.

When the hearing was finally over, Elena came out looking pale and tired, and struggling to keep her eyes focused. We offered to take her for lunch, to unwind and get some fresh air. But she declined, desperate to get home and see her child.

And that was that. The hearing was over, but we would have to wait up to six weeks for a decision.

In the last week of June, nearly six weeks since the tribunal, Elena sent me a text message.

I was terrified to open it, and my heart was pounding as I did so.

We win in court. We win in court but I'm confused. Something else is happening I can't explain to you, but Siobhan will call you.

240

Just then my phone buzzed. It was Siobhan. I asked cautiously if I had understood Elena correctly, and that the judge *did* rule in her favour. Siobhan said, 'Yes, but it's a funny one.'

I groaned inwardly wondering why *nothing* was ever straightforward for this poor girl.

Siobhan explained yet another complex legal situation. We had won in court. The judge ruled in her favour so Elena and her child could stay in the UK for the next five years. It sounded like fantastic news to me, so I was confused as to why Siobhan sounded deflated.

It soon became clear why. The judge did not grant her asylum. He granted her Humanitarian Protection. Siobhan was quick to reassure me that for Elena the outcomes were the same and she wouldn't be affected by the terminology of the case.

But morally, she was frustrated. Siobhan said the judge hadn't agreed that it was not safe from a refugee perspective for Elena to return to Albania. Siobhan strongly disagreed, adding that morally Elena deserved asylum. I was trying to focus on the fact the outcomes were the same, but a sense of injustice seemed to undermine the good news.

There was one more kick in the teeth. The Home Office had two weeks to appeal the decision.

That meant Elena had yet *another* wait before she could allow herself to fully accept that she had some security for the first time in years. It felt like a hollow victory. There was no big moment of celebration. Even being told she had been granted Humanitarian Protection didn't allow her to breathe a sigh of relief.

It meant more waiting. More hoping.

Two weeks later, there had been nothing from the Home Office. Siobhan said that as the deadline had passed we were home and dry.

At last. But I felt robbed of this moment for Elena. What should have been a hugely joyous event was an anticlimax. Simply a case of waiting for the other shoe to drop and hoping it didn't. I should have known by now there are no real winners. Crossing the finishing line, after all she had been through in her young life wasn't a huge moment of symbolic celebration. It was simply hoping another battle didn't need to be fought.

She deserves better than that. All victims of this crime who find themselves in the care of this country deserve better than that.[1]

---

1 I put Elena's experiences to the Home Office, to give them a Right to Reply. They said they didn't comment on individual cases.

19

WHAT'S NEXT?

After spending six months immersed in the world of anti-trafficking and slavery, speaking to those on the front line in the fight against this abhorrent crime and witnessing policy and political changes throughout that period, I felt I was better able to reflect on where we are now, and where we're going.

One thing I was aware of as I began to do so, was that the political landscape continues to shift around us. There seems little doubt though that the prime focus for the foreseeable future will still be Brexit. Depressingly, one person I spoke to on this journey, before Theresa May resigned, told me, 'When the Prime Minister steps down, do you think Boris Johnson's going to care about this?'

As the outgoing PM, Theresa May, the woman credited with bringing modern slavery to the statute books and the political agenda, faced her final PMQs on Tuesday, 23rd July 2019, she was applauded by Labour MP Vernon Coaker for her efforts. However, he went on to add, 'We still face many issues and challenges. Last year, as part of Government policy, we locked up 507 potential victims of modern slavery as immigration offenders. That cannot be right, and surely we need a change of public policy to treat them as victims, not criminals.'

In her response, Mrs May said, 'We have been looking at how we deal with victims and the referral mechanism. It is important that we have had an independent review of the 2015 Act, which proposed a number of recommendations for improving how victims are treated, and we will be taking most of those recommendations on board.'

The Modern Slavery Act Review was commissioned to examine four areas: the Independent Anti-Slavery Commissioner; Transparency in Supply Chains; Independent Child Trafficking Advocates and the more general 'legal application' which covered the definition of exploitation in the Act; Slavery and Trafficking Reparation Orders and the statutory defence.

In March 2019, the final review was submitted to Sajid Javid, the then Home Secretary, and it was put to Parliament in May 2019. The Government accepted many of the recommendations, saying:

> The Independent Review of the Modern Slavery Act 2015 has provided an opportunity to reflect on how the UK can enhance its legislation on modern slavery, and ensure it is implemented effectively. The Government has accepted the majority of recommendations made by the Independent Review and has already begun work to implement these.
>
> There are several recommendations that the Government has committed to consult on or consider in more detail, in order to understand the impact on affected groups and to inform practical implementation. To support this, the Government has launched a consultation on transparency in supply chains. The Government has also committed to publish a further update to Parliament on the Independent Child Trafficking Guardians recommendations, ahead of national rollout of the service.

By June, I was crouched over a laptop watching Westminster Hall on Parliament TV. Frank Field MP opened the session on his review and began by saying, 'I find it impossible to describe the horrors that people try to convey to us about the experience of being enslaved in this country, in this year and at this time. That is partly because one does not want to break down speaking in this debate.'

He went on to explain that his team had picked up four themes that we would look at: the Anti-Slavery Commissioner; giving greater importance to supply chains; the role of advocates for children involved in trafficking; and the legal working of the Act.

There were eighty recommendations made in the review, and in the Westminster Hall session Mr Field chose to emphasise one or two in particular. One focused on the lack of data collected on victims once their 'period of safety' ended. It was a concern that had been echoed time and again as I interviewed people working in this area, and as Frank Field said, 'Most of our forebears would have been scandalised if they had allowed an Act to continue with that lack of data collection.'

He also stated, 'We had views about the Independent Slavery Commissioner, which the Government, for their own reasons, disregarded.' The inaction of thousands of companies to comply with Section 54 also came under scrutiny, as did the apathy of the Government to punish them.

Finally, there was one observation which, many would argue, struck at the heart of the disconnect between the Government's rhetoric regarding modern slavery and its treatment of victims. The much-alluded-to conflict between the Home Office tasked with dealing with victims of this crime and its workings within the Hostile Environment.

Mr Field said of this, 'We thought it was important to realise that, all the time, there is this great conflict in the Department between its wish to bear down as effectively as possible on those merchants of evil – the slave owners – and its responsibility for immigration.'

He went on to recommend that the Home Office's Modern Slavery Unit should be moved under the remit of the Cabinet Office.

After the review was released, I contacted Mr Field to be interviewed for this book and he agreed to answer my questions.

How did you come across the subject of modern slavery? Your opening remarks for the review debate last month were incredibly moving, and it's clearly something you feel hugely connected to.

I became involved with the subject of modern slavery when Patrick White, who then headed my office in Parliament, recommended that I accept an invitation to speak at the Centre for Social Justice's launch event for their report, 'It Happens Here', which really put the issue on the political agenda. The room was full of organisations trying to rescue and support victims of modern slavery. The press conference went on for far, far too long. I decided to get up and beg for thirty more seconds of the audience's time. I said that we needed to call slavery what it was, not simply trafficking, and, I said, we needed an Act to change the world as Wilberforce had done.

I spent that summer with a member of staff, Tim Weedon, lobbying Fiona Hill, the political advisor to Theresa May, then Home Secretary, for an Act. Meeting after meeting took place. Then, all of a sudden, we were told that the lobbying had been successful and Theresa May was interested in a bill.

I chaired the scoping inquiry on that bill and the joint Select Committee considering the draft bill the Government brought forward. During our scoping exercise, the members of the commission, Baroness Elizabeth Butler-Sloss, Sir John Randall and myself, listened to the testimony of slaves. I have never recovered from hearing and witnessing those sessions.

You were involved in the Modern Slavery Act creation, plus were central to the Modern Slavery Act Review – how important has it been to you to impact this issue from the opposition benches?

I have been involved with virtually every aspect of the Modern Slavery Act as the issue strikes me as so urgent that I wanted to make sure first that we had an Act and then that the Act was properly implemented and improved upon. There were some parts of the bill, for example, that we knew were not as strong as they could be, but had to meet as wide approval as possible in order for the bill to pass. Our Review then looked at beefing those sections up – specifically the section on transparency in supply chains, where we wanted to improve the quality of modern slavery statements and the level of compliance with that requirement.

The Conservative Government has presented us with impressive rhetoric on Britain's fight against Modern Slavery since 2013. However, those working on the front line, and the experiences of victims, show the reality of tackling this issue within the policy of the hostile environment. How can they claim to tackle the crime while at the same time persecuting the victims?

The Home Office 'brain' is divided. One half is focused on reducing immigration and another is interested in tackling modern slavery. The first gets political priority. In their nervousness about creating a loophole for illegal immigration by giving right to remain automatically to victims of modern slavery, proven victims are getting a raw deal when it comes to support.

One of the recommendations is for the Modern Slavery Unit to be taken out of the hands of the Home Office and into the Cabinet Office. Why did you come to this conclusion, and will it make a difference while we are under a Government with an obsession over immigration?

It is the Home Office specifically that deals with immigration. So putting the Modern Slavery Unit in the Cabinet Office would give it some degree of separation from the urgency to reduce immigration. Most importantly, we need an Independent Anti-Slavery Commissioner who is genuinely independent rather than a Home

Office employee so that he or she can hold the Government properly to account and scrutinise its workings.

Which of the recommendations are you most hopeful will happen?

The appointment of the International Envoy on modern slavery,[1] which Theresa May announced in her speech at the ILO Conference in June, is already underway. So that is one recommendation which I can be most confident will come to pass.

How hard was it to work within the remit of the Review, and what would you have loved to have investigated if you'd had the freedom to? Were the restrictions placed upon you frustrating and could you have challenged the parameters?

The Prime Minister asked us to undertake the Review so set our lines of inquiry and provided us with a secretariat from the Home Office. We were initially concerned about their level of independence, so we also employed a former House of Commons clerk. As it transpired, there were no issues on this front. I had wanted to look at the NRM and victim support, but we were told that because that was already being reviewed and reformed we could not do so. I hope to do so at some point in the future. Towards the end of the Review, we then decided that we would also like to look at trafficking for prostitution but the Home Secretary, Sajid Javid, did not

---

1 The Modern Slavery Act Review recommended that the Government create the role of an International Envoy to tackle modern slavery, which the Government accepted. Theresa May announced the introduction of the role, which was described as 'an Ambassador based in the Foreign and Commonwealth Office who will represent HMG interests on modern slavery and migration in key international fora and with key partner countries' (The UK Government Response to the Independent Review of the Modern Slavery Act 2015).

approve of this and declined our request for the support of the Home Office secretariat. We were not dissuaded, however, and put together our own secretariat from two NGOs familiar with the area. We hope the results of that inquiry will be published in October.

Ultimately, how do you feel about the Government's response to the Review, and what are your hopes for the UK's response to Modern Slavery?

I am pleased that the Government has said they will accept or partially accept the majority of our recommendations. But agreeing to something in principle is very different from implementing it – and doing so with a sense of urgency. Much depends on whether our next Prime Minister adopts modern slavery as a priority and ensures action is taken quickly. The consultation of businesses will also be crucial as to how much the Government toughens up its stance on supply chain reporting. If they shy away from attaching penalties to those companies who do not comply, then this part of the legislation will continue to lack teeth and a central means of preventing modern slavery will be lost.

When we look at the future of the anti-slavery fight, there are two other factors we should briefly consider. The impact that climate change and environmental changes have, and the importance of technology, by using data and AI to improve the response.

Last year I saw a tweet which referred to a correlation between modern slavery and climate change, and I was intrigued. It made sense – we are seeing a rise in climate and weather-related disasters, on a scale which displaces communities, leading to poverty and migration and therefore making greatly increased numbers of people vulnerable to traffickers.

The change in our climate also impacts the environment in which many people work, with certain industries in decline, once again creating poverty and making entire groups vulnerable to exploitation. Looking into this further, I found that a report on this very subject was released last year from the University of Nottingham's Rights Lab, Royal Holloway University of London and the UK's Independent Anti-Slavery Commissioner, which concluded this is an area which needs deeper investigation and understanding in order to tackle the issue. Essentially the report focused on links between modern slavery, environmental destruction and climate change, identifying key sectors – fisheries, agriculture, forests, and factories – and highlighting how interlinked the crises are.

Fishing in Thailand was used as a specific example of the vicious circle – demand for cheap food leads to exploitative conditions, which leads to 'over-fishing' and then an 'eco-system decline'. The report also highlights similar issues around deforestation.

There's no doubt that technology has already impacted the crimes of trafficking and slavery, sadly to the advantage of the traffickers, in the main. Firstly, social media is a prime hunting ground for gang members looking to lure the vulnerable, and secondly, as technology advances, so do ways the criminal can abuse the victim. ECPAT said in their 2018 report, 'Child Trafficking in the UK 2018: A Snapshot', that in 2017, the National Crime Agency warned that cyber sexual abuse was on the increase, as was 'the use of live-streaming platforms by online sex offenders'.

The anonymity of the digital world and the development of the dark web means the criminal can contact, manipulate and abuse thousands of young people in the UK and around the world.

It's not just children who are at risk. An investigation by the Scottish *Sunday Mail* in 2019 exposed how traffickers were using the website Vivastreet to sell women in Glasgow. In echoes of the Stan case in Blackburn (Chapter 2), the paper began looking into the ads on the site after Scottish anti-trafficking body TARA reported a 42% increase in sexually exploited women using their services.

However, the digital world in which we now live has also brought positive developments, with global connectivity meaning grass roots operations in remote areas are able to forge relations with bigger organisations, so it's getting ever easier, when possible, to reunite families separated by traffickers.

Plus, with the vast majority of us owning smartphones, apps from the Modern Slavery Helpline, Stop The Traffik and The Clewer Initiative means that it's never been easier for members of the public to report suspected cases of slavery. Bristol-based TISCreport (Transparency in Supply Chains) is an open data register which joins up TISC reporting around the world, identifying organisations with no modern slavery statements. It has harnessed Artificial Intelligence to automatically assess compliance globally. An investigation by Oceana, an American conservation group, found that the Global Fishing Watch mapping platform, which tracks fishing boats wherever they are in the world in order to identify suspicious behaviour, could also be used to spot trafficking and slavery at sea.

To explore tech developments in the fight against slavery further, I met Sarah Brown, Head of Research and Intelligence at Stop The Traffik. Founded in 2005, the NGO focuses on prevention and works with multi-sector partners around the globe to gather intelligence on the crime.

Sarah and I met for coffee in Lambeth, and I warned her she would have to explain this area to me as if to a child, considering all I knew about 'data' was that my phone used it. She laughed, and gave me a brilliant explanation.

'We basically mean stories and information. It's best not to use the word data. What we are collecting are people's stories and information about their journeys and what's happened to them. How they started, how they were recruited, how they were moved, what type of exploitation they suffered, how they were controlled and coerced and where they ended up. We're looking at all that information so we can then share what we've learned with people on the ground, so they can take action.

251

'A few years ago we took a step towards an intelligence-led approach, an evidence-based approach. We've run focused campaigns because we know there's trafficking everywhere, but we must be even more targeted to be most effective. To do that you must be more intelligent about where and how you run prevention activities and who you target, and you're only going to be able to do that if you have the information. So that's where gathering global data started.

'We are all about collaboration and partnerships. We believe the people who've got the best information are the people who are there working with it. We will ask them to share information with us in any way they can, so that we can analyse it, and produce insight around the hotspots and note trends, patterns and correlations, and what appears to be making people vulnerable, and share that with the people on the ground so they can be targeted in their responses.

'We've always worked around awareness raising, prevention and campaigning. Working with the public, working with partners. The best way to prevent is to raise awareness and then deliver initiatives based on the information you've gathered. We sometimes advertise. We will share information with people, and if we've got evidence we'll have a schedule of locations we want to target, based on the analysis we've done. We then use Facebook ad credits, create videos in collaboration with our local partners so that we get the content right, and deliver a campaigns in the local language. We can geolocate it and we can demographically target these.'

It's explained to me that Stop The Traffik's ads can target vulnerable people in a specific community or language. Once they've seen the ad, they can be redirected to a local specialist organisation if they need help or advice.

Now I was confident that I understood how STT used data, I braved the subject of Artificial Intelligence, or AI.

'Robots, right?' I asked Sarah.

She humoured me with grace, and explained the concept of 'machine learning', in particular in relation to the Stop The Traffik app. The app must be simple so a consumer can report suspected exploitation with ease. But the STT analysts need to devour all the information given in order to paint as full a picture as possible of any potential patterns.

'For us to do any analysis on that text, we need to pull out the key information in a structured format. That's what AI and machine learning can do. They will identify patterns of activity relating to people, locations, gender, recruitment methods and so on.'

There's no doubt great strides are being made in harnessing the digital world to help combat slavery, and quite rightly, Sarah is proud of what's already been achieved.

'We have reached over six million people through our social media campaigns, and with some campaigns 45% of people who saw them said they would now do something differently. We are achieving change and, most importantly, behaviour change.'

20

ELENA'S STORY: HER FUTURE

It's been three days since we could breathe a sigh of relief and accept that Elena can indeed stay in the UK. That there would be no challenge from the Home Office. That she has a future ahead of her (for the next five years at least).

As Elena's child is in nursery in the mornings now, she has two hours a day to herself, so we arrange to meet in the coffee shop that has become so familiar to us both.

When I walk in and see her waiting for me, it's no exaggeration to say that it's like meeting a different person. The shadows under her eyes have gone. Her skin is bright and she's made an extra effort with her appearance. The weight of uncertainty hanging around her young shoulders for the last three years has been lifted, and she has a sparkle I've never seen before. Elena is naturally beautiful, but for the entire time that I've known her, understandably, just getting through the day has been her main objective and that took its toll. Now though, she's smiling as a twenty-five-year-old should be able to smile – with genuine happiness and hope.

The entire purpose of writing this book was to shine a light on what survivors of trafficking and slavery go through, and to help give them their voices back. So it seems only right that I hand over this chapter to the person who finally has the power to speak of her own experiences.

ELENA'S STORY

It is extremely difficult to live in a new place where you have never been and you have never imagined going to. And simply saying 'it is extremely difficult' is nothing compared to experiencing every single pain, every single tear, every pain which feels endless. If I were to make a comparison, I was like an infant who needs their mother after they are born. I was like a baby without a mother who has to grow alone because this had been my fate. I did not know how to speak, where to go, and how to use a map because in my country I had never used it. It is so difficult wanting to be able to say what you feel but not being able to do that as not everyone is interested in hearing your pain. Every day was painful but I was getting strength from thinking about my baby coming to my life. I didn't want my child to feel different from the others or to miss out on anything. At the end of the day, my child was totally innocent. Something that gave me strength was the fight that I had in my past in my country to turn my dreams in reality. How could I blame my dreams for things that happened to me? Blaming my dreams is out of the question. In life you should not punish someone when what happened to them is not their fault, as sometimes things can happen by accident.

To be honest, I do not want to talk at all about Marco, and I pray that I will never see him again in my life. Because of what he did to me, I suffered depression for four years. I do not want to think one second about him.

For me the most difficult things were not knowing English and also being in a big place, having to adapt to it and learning things on my own. It was difficult knowing that you were alone and without any support and also not being able to express the pain you have inside to people you do not know. At the end of the day, they have their families whereas I was alone. There was also the fear that I was going to be judged about my past.

Waiting such a long time, without a doubt, was psychological torture because every day you keep wondering what will happen with your life and the life of your child. For the Home Office it may have only been a decision but on the other hand there were two people waiting to find out what would happen to them. I was in a terrible state. It was impossible to sleep. Sometimes I was eating too much, and sometimes I did not want to eat. I was not able to start trusting my female friends as I kept thinking they would not be able to understand me. Living for three years in this kind of state is a very long time. Only someone who has gone through something like this is able to understand. I needed therapy, without a doubt, as otherwise I would not be where I am, especially raising a child on my own.

When I received a positive NRM decision, of course I felt relieved, but not many things changed within me, possibly because of the amount of suffering I had experienced to get to this point. This was a plus and an extra step for me, but things had not yet ended. I suppose I could say that I was happy for a few minutes. This decision did not take away the pain I had gone through and it did not give me any reassurance as to what was going to happen to me in England, but I suppose I can say that I was happy.

The day of the court hearing, I was very anxious as that day my fate was going to be decided. But in this world, just as there are bad people there are also good people. I had the emotional support from three people who have been by my side and helped me so many times. They were very good friends at such difficult moments in my life. I hope one day in the future I will be able to pay them back for everything that they have done for me. For them maybe it was not a big deal what they did for me, but for me it was an enormous support in all sort[s] of ways. It was the first time in my life that I was in a court hearing, and I was focused on the questions that I was being asked so that I could answer them. It was finally the moment for me to say what I had been waiting to say for three years. A few weeks later I received the very good news that I would be able to initially live here for five years and restart a new life with my child here. Thank you for giving me a second chance to live my life.

I felt very happy because I had waited a very long time for that day. I had sacrificed a lot to get there. I was happier for my child who will now be equal to other children. And both our lives are safe now. When this decision, allowing us to live in the UK was made by the Home Office, it was as if my child and I were reborn. I wish that with the passing of time, there will be a day that I will be able to leave the past in the past and be strong for the future. And little by little I will follow my dreams which were cut short.

I am waiting to receive the card from the Home Office, but currently I have to find new accommodation and a new nursery for my child which will hopefully be close by. I have many dreams which I want to accomplish in the future. My first one is to learn English as well as I can and then I would like to work in the same area that I studied in Albania. This is my dream.

I will work hard to look after my child so that I have a little one who is polite and respects others, and works hard in school. I hope to make all my child's wishes come true, within my means, as I am a single mum. I hope I can make it. I am very emotional about my future here within the next five years. I hope I am able to do the best I can for both of us.

21

CONCLUSIONS

As I came to the end of my investigation into trafficking and slavery in twenty-first-century Britain, I felt as if much has changed since I began the journey, but also that nothing has changed at all.

For Elena, thankfully, her life has changed considerably. She is still dealing with the scars of her experiences. But for the first time in years she has the security she needs in order to begin to put her experiences behind her and build a future in the UK. She now has a flat, and when her child starts school, she hopes to return to work. Her life may be modest, with every penny accounted for, and every friend initially kept at arm's length – but it is a life she has reclaimed.

As a nation, we seem to be on shifting sands. We have a different Prime Minister and Government than when I began working on this, and we are in the process of leaving the EU. However, some things, sadly, have not changed. Around the world 40.3 million people remain in slavery. One in four victims are children. The estimated number of slaves in this country is still 136,000.

Nail bars, car washes, brothels, restaurants, takeaways, factories, farms, recycling centres, hotels and office buildings, and even private homes are all places where those slaves could be hidden in plain sight – looking like the average worker to you and me, but living in unimaginable horror away from customers and clients. The perpetrators of this $150 billion crime care nothing for the degradation and trauma they inflict on their victims – after all, they are a multi-use asset, unlike drugs or guns which can only be profited from once. Humans can turn a profit time after time after time.

The majority of those I've spoken to fear that we will never see a slavery-free world, for as long as there are human beings, there will be cruelty and crime. That said, these dedicated and impressive campaigners and welfare professionals are determined to heal the victims and fight to end slavery for good. As the Government continues to wrestle with the country's response to modern slavery and trafficking, those working in the anti-slavery sector continue to 'hold their feet to the fire'.[1]

The Government needs a consistent and compassionate approach to supporting victims, with the decisions being made on their Conclusive Grounds status entirely separate from their immigration status and nothing to do with their country of origin. Tailored, individual support should be the norm, with no time restriction placed on how long a survivor's recovery should take. If the UK really wants to be a global leader in the fight against slavery, our Government must put the needs of the survivor at the heart of its strategy – and mean it.

Though no one from the Home Office was available to be interviewed for this book, I outlined the criticisms and concerns addressed in these pages and they sent me the following response:

> The Government introduced the first dedicated modern slavery legislation in the world, with the Modern Slavery Act 2015, and implemented an ambitious Modern Slavery Strategy which has been in place since 2014.
>
> In addition, in July 2018, the Government commissioned an Independent Review of the Modern Slavery Act 2015. The Review considered where the Act is working well and where implementation can be strengthened. The Government responded

---

1   A comment made by SNP MP Stuart C McDonald at the Westminster Hall debate on the Modern Slavery Act Review.

formally to this Review in July 2019 and the Home Office is implementing many of the recommendations made in the report.

In October this year [the] Government published the 2019 Annual Modern Slavery Report which sets out action taken over the last year in tackling this crime. This includes the launch of a Single Competent Authority and an investment of £10 million to establish the Policy and Evidence Centre on Modern Slavery and Human rights.

The National Referral Mechanism (NRM) is the process by which the UK identifies and supports potential victims of modern slavery by connecting them with appropriate support, which may be delivered through the specialist Victim Care Contract, Local Authorities and asylum services. In 2017, [the] Government announced a package of reforms to the NRM, which included the creation of the Single Competent Authority in April 2019, which enables decisions to be made in a more efficient and streamlined way. The Home Office has also established Multi-Agency Assurance Panels to provide additional independent scrutiny to negative decisions, ensuring quality decision-making. Whilst in the NRM, adults can receive accommodation, financial support, assistance in accessing mental and physical healthcare including counselling, and access to legal support. Pregnant victims of modern slavery also receive tailored support during this time, including support accessing doulas, and are provided with the equipment necessary for caring for a young child within their safe house.

Home Office staff in Immigration Removal Centres undertake training on making referrals to the NRM. As a result, potential victims of modern slavery are regularly identified in detention. When confirmed victims of modern slavery with a positive Conclusive Grounds decision from the NRM do not qualify for leave to remain in the UK, they will be detained only if it is necessary for the purposes of their removal and, in line with the adults at risk policy, only when the immigration considerations in their case outweigh the vulnerability considerations.

The Home Office has also rolled out Independent Child Trafficking Guardians (ICTGs – renamed from Independent Child Trafficking Advocates in line with the recommendations of the Independent Review of the Modern Slavery Act) in one-third of Local Authorities across England and Wales. ICTGs provide an independent source of advice for trafficked children and somebody who can speak up on their behalf.

The UK is the first country in the world to require businesses to report on the steps they have taken to tackle modern slavery through the 'Transparency in Supply Chains' provision in the Modern Slavery Act. To ensure businesses are complying with Section 54 of the Act, the Home Office has developed more user-friendly business guidance on effective reporting under the Modern Slavery Act. Over 3,000 businesses have registered on our Modern Slavery Contacts Database to receive regular guidance and resources to support effective reporting. Thousands of transparency statements have been published and businesses are now more focused on this issue than ever before. While the majority of companies have published statements, we are concerned about those that publish poor-quality statements or that fail to fulfil the basic legal requirements. The Home Office has written twice to the CEOs of businesses identified as being in scope of the legislation, with clear information about how to meet their obligations. Those who persist in flouting their obligations can expect to face tougher consequences. The Home Office is now undertaking an audit of compliance and may publish a list of non-compliant companies or seek injunctions against non-compliant companies.

Following the final report of the Independent Review of the Modern Slavery Act, the UK Government launched a public consultation on potential legislative changes. These include setting a single reporting deadline on which statements must be published, mandating the topics organisations must cover in their statement, introducing civil penalties for non-compliance and extending the scope of transparency provisions to cover certain public sector organisations. The consultation closed on 17 September 2019 and the Government will respond in due course.

Finally, the Modern Slavery Act also established the role of the Independent Anti-Slavery Commissioner (IASC). The Government is supporting the recently appointed IASC, Dame Sara Thornton, in fulfilling this important role. For information, the IASC published her strategic plan in October setting out her priorities for 2019–2021. The Independent Review of the Modern Slavery Act considered the independence of the IASC role and the Government agreed to take forward a series of recommendations relating to the IASC.

In the meantime, there are many committed and remarkable people making *real* change day in day out. The charities I've encountered do life-changing work for their clients. They give those in their care the chance of a new life and a hopeful future. Concepts like the Safer Car Wash app from The Clewer Initiative (the church's response to modern slavery) and the Modern Slavery Helpline are helping empower the public to spot exploitation and to report it.

Some businesses and institutions are beginning to show awareness of the complex needs of survivors, and taking action to help, for example HSBC's move to allow them to open bank accounts. This may not seem particularly ground-breaking – it's just a bank account after all. But when survivors begin their journey back to freedom, there is a very good chance they will be without basic forms of identification. For a survivor, being without this is what prevents them from being able to accomplish basic tasks like open a bank account. HSBC's scheme will work around this by having dedicated staff members who will work with the client and their charity through the process. The applicant will attend an appointment with their representative (who has to provide their own passport) and bring a letter on headed notepaper from the charity in order to show proof of address. A simple system, but to a survivor, having the autonomy to look after their own finances is hugely symbolic after the exploitation they have endured. It also goes some way to ensure financial independence, therefore protecting them from poverty and the risk of re-trafficking. It's a major step on the road to building a new life.

A chance meeting at Doncaster train station has led to slavery survivors living in the Sheffield area being able to return to education. Northern College has been delivering adult education for fifty years, specialising in social justice education. It runs the Free Thinking programme – a course for survivors of modern slavery.

Jane Williamson and Paul Gibson developed and run the course, the syllabus of which is focused on subjects which don't rely on the student's standard of reading or writing, ensuring students can enrol regardless of their level of education before becoming enslaved. Survivors study subjects such as living in the UK, which includes geography, history and public services, plus creative subjects like photography. Workplace skills are also taught, and the course is open to anyone who is in the NRM, or who has been exited, regardless of the decision.

This unique programme was born when Northern College senior manager Chris Lamb bumped into the former Chief Exec of the GLAA and former South Yorkshire police officer Paul Broadbent. During their conversation about the crime of modern slavery, Paul told Chris how survivors of slavery have difficulty accessing education, and suggested Northern College, with its specialism in social justice education, could be the institution to help.

A year later, the course was launched, advised by a steering group including charities Snowdrop, Ashiana and City Hearts. They've now run the course three times, and when they complete it, students graduate in a formal ceremony (hats and gowns included!).

In a phone call with the two educators, I suggested the first graduation must have been an emotional event. Paul was modest about their contribution.

'That day was so busy and we were running around, organising everything, so we didn't have time to be emotional. Afterwards I took stock and looked at the pictures and thought . . . yeah! But it's the students who've put the work in and we've played a small part in that.'

Jane shared with me just how life-changing the course had been for a typically isolated group of people.

'With courses like this the students become much more part of the community. They've got friends outside the safe house, friends they've made at college. We have one student who went on to have an art exhibition in Sheffield. He's now got the support of the local artistic community, he's been given a free workshop to work in, and some really established artists have asked about doing collaborations with him. It's fantastic. It makes a difference. We are in a hostile environment and the chances are they will get a negative decision before they get a positive one. But having the support of the community makes a big difference.'

Returning to paid employment is also a key factor in a survivor building a future. The Co-op's Bright Future initiative, which takes survivors of slavery and gives them a paid work placement and then a job, has won many plaudits.

The Co-op's Paul Gerrard (Chapter 17), explained how such a ground-breaking scheme came to pass.

'We thought what we'd do is partner with City Hearts to see if we could develop a model that takes a slavery survivor who is ready and legally able to work, and put them in a four-week paid work placement. The two key things were 1) it's paid and 2) there's a guarantee of a job. If you can do the job, we will give you a job. We started in January 2017 with two people – a lady in Manchester and a gentleman in Merseyside. Both did the four weeks. Both had been trafficked and in recovery for three or four years. Both came in, both did it, both came in for an interview (a non-competitive process) and both were offered the job. The woman now works in the care sector, and the man is still in the Co-op. He's been Colleague of the Year, he's got his own place, he's got his own friends and he's got his own life.'

The scheme has made quite an impact, with one of its beneficiaries meeting his fiancée through it, and another being able to have his first holiday abroad. Now Bright Future has forty-eight partners and has opened up to other businesses who would like to offer opportunities to survivors.

Paul was passionate about the importance of the initiative.

'Slavery's not about manacles these days. Sometimes it is, but not often. It's about control. Of your safety, your family's safety, your money, your movement, your choices. Paid employment gives slavery survivors control. It gives them dignity, for a start. If you've not been paid to work and now you are, there's dignity involved. It gives them hope, because when you've got dignity and you're working, you can see a future.'

Throughout the writing of this book, and my wider work in this field, one thing has struck me more than anything. I have never met a more diverse group of people united by such passion for a common goal: to end the crime of modern slavery. They are a remarkable cohort for whom their work is a passion, a vocation and a cause. From police officers to lawyers, volunteers to policy makers – this work, this mission, is under their skin. You can sense it within them.

I asked Paul what he thought his emancipation supporting forefathers in the Co-op would think about the fact he was still fighting slavery in 2019.

'I think they would be horrified there is slavery left in the world, and in the United Kingdom. They stood in solidarity with those enslaved in the United States, and those fighting it like Lincoln. I can say, as a Co-operator, I stand in solidarity with those in slavery in the United Kingdom, and those fighting it.'

Wales's Anti-Slavery Co-ordinator Stephen Chapman reiterated to me, 'We are the voices of the victims.'

266

The victims need as many voices speaking for them as possible. Politicians, Local Authorities, NGOs, charities, businesses, health professionals, religious leaders, educators and us, the public – it is all of society that must stand up to slavery.

Echoing Andrew Wallis's desire to see a 'Blue Planet' moment – where the world gets a wake-up call strong enough to make us take a stand – Joanna Ewart-James, the Executive Director of Freedom United, told me we needed a societal shift in understanding.

'I think that as much as everyone can work really hard in their space, doing research, writing policy guidance, changing laws, I really strongly believe that unless we have an active society that is engaged, and a community of people big enough that it starts to shift cultural norms, you're not going to get progress because society is not being held to account for behaviour that allows modern slavery to survive. If we don't get the public mobilised on this issue, taking action . . . We need to create a will. That will isn't going to be generated unless we're all calling for it.'

Call for it we must.

Once you have witnessed first-hand the devastation that this crime leaves in its wake, it's impossible to unknow, to forget, or to move on. It's impossible not to be moved by the bravery of the survivors. Not to be horrified by their experiences.

It's impossible not to take our simple freedoms for granted.

And it's impossible to gain an understanding of this crime and then not do anything about it.

I hope Caroline Haughey won't mind my quoting the end of her 2017 speech to RUSI – because she sums this up perfectly.

'Robert F Kennedy said this in South Africa in 1966 –

"*Each time a man stands up for an ideal, or acts to improve the lot of others, or strikes out against injustice, he sends forth a tiny ripple of hope, and crossing each other from a million different centres of energy and daring those ripples build a current which can sweep down the mightiest walls of oppression and resistance*".

'Human trafficking and modern slavery is oppression of the meek, the vulnerable, the needy. We, who are empowered with freedom, and liberty, and choice, and opportunity, bear the moral responsibility to be those ripples.

'We can make a change. We are making a change. The landscape will continue to evolve, and we must all be part of it.'

ACKNOWLEDGEMENTS

Many incredible people contributed their knowledge, time and faith for this book, and for that I am incredibly grateful.

The first thanks must go to Daisy Buchanan, who recognised the potential in this idea, and introduced me to her literary agent.

Diana Beaumont believed in the importance of giving a voice back to survivors as soon as I outlined my idea, and she has been a crucial and gently guiding hand ever since.

Bob, Moira and the team at Sandstone Press will have my thanks and gratitude forever, for understanding how imperative it is to bring the issue of modern slavery to the public. And, of course, for looking after a novice writer so well.

A personal thank you to Dick Hobbs, my University of Durham Sociology of Crime tutor who inspired me to pursue a career in crime journalism. Bernie Gravett was the man who drew my attention to the abhorrent crime of trafficking almost a decade ago. Since then he has patiently shared his knowledge and time, as I have endlessly attempted to bring his experience to the public. Both have changed the course of my life.

I would also like to thank Katherine Lawson from the Office of the Independent Anti-Slavery Commissioner and Kate Roberts, formerly of the Human Trafficking Foundation and now at Anti-Slavery International, for being endlessly patient with their time, and for being voices of sanity during my investigations.

Thanks to Guy Head for his constant sharing of hot off the press information in the sector. Saima and the team at Croydon Community Against Trafficking kindly contributed to my understanding of the issues, as did Victoria Marks of ATLEU, and the peerless Lara Bundock of Snowdrop. Also the brilliant Phil Brewer, who, despite his workload kept my spirits up when the subject matter got too dark, deserves a special thank you.

Finally, of course, thank you to all those who gave their time for this book – Isobel McFarlane and the team at The Salvation Army, Stephen Chapman, Andrew Wallis OBE, Justine Currell, Rachel Harper and the team at the Modern Slavery Helpline, DC Colin Ward, Adam Thompson, Mark Burns-Williamson, Kevin Hyland OBE, Caroline Haughey QC, Paul Gerrard, Susan Banister and the Hope for Justice team, Josh McLean, Ella Read and all at Hestia, Rachel Witkin, Molly Hodson and Euan Fraser from IJM, and Joanna Ewart-James. Plus of course Sarah Brown, Paul Gibson and Jane Williamson. A special thanks to Florence Gildea and Frank Field MP for their kind (and speedy!) contributions.

There will never be enough words to convey the gratitude I feel towards Siobhan at Wilson Solicitors LLP, the legal team at Garden Court Chambers and our translator Ana from 'Team Elena'.

Thank you from the bottom of my heart to Mr M and J for sharing their stories.

Finally, Elena. I will never be able to comprehend what she has been through, and yet she stands with such dignity and strength. To relive her experiences in order to protect others is the ultimate bravery. I wish her lifelong happiness and peace.

LIST OF ABBREVIATIONS

ATLEU – Anti-Trafficking and Labour Exploitation Unit
ATMG – Anti-Trafficking Monitoring Group
CCE – Child Criminal Exploitation
CSE – Child Sexual Exploitation
CSJ – Centre for Social Justice
CSR – Corporate and Social Responsibility
ECAT – European Convention Against Trafficking
ECPAT –Every Child Protected Against Trafficking
FLEX – Focus on Labour Exploitation
GLA/GLAA – Gangmasters Licensing Authority (now Gang-
    masters and Labour Abuse Authority)
GMP – Greater Manchester Police
GSI – Global Slavery Index
HBF – The Helen Bamber Foundation
HTF – Human Trafficking Foundation
IASC – Independent Anti-Slavery Commissioner
ICTA/ICTG – Independent Child Trafficking Advocates (now
    Independent Child Trafficking Guardians)
IJM – International Justice Mission
ILO – Independent Labour Organisation
JSTAC – Joint Slavery and Trafficking Analysis Centre
LEAG – Labour Exploitation Advisory Group
MSA – Modern Slavery Act
MSHTU – Modern Slavery Human Trafficking Unit

271

MSPTU – The Modern Slavery Police Transformation Unit
NAO – National Audit Office
NASS – National Asylum Support Service
NCA – National Crime Agency
NGO – Non Government Organisation
NRM – National Referral Mechanism
NSPCC – National Society for the Prevention of Cruelty to Children
OCG – Organised Crime Group
OSEC – Online Sexual Exploitation of Children
PICACC – The Philippine Internet Crimes Against Children Centre
PSNI – Police Service Northern Ireland
SOCA – Serious Organised Crime Authority (now NCA)
STT – Stop The Traffik
TARA – Trafficking Awareness Raising Alliance
TISC – Transparency in Supply Chains

www.sandstonepress.com

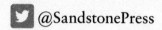 facebook.com/SandstonePress/

@SandstonePress